Pardon My French

Anne-Marie Smith first obtained a Licence ès Lettres at Bordeaux University in 1968. After teaching in Zambia, she gained a Diploma in TESL and a Doctorate in Linguistics with the University of Papua New Guinea, where she lived and worked. In Western Australia, she taught English in a multicultural context. She worked with migrants and with Indigenous communities near the Western Desert and in Roebourne and the West Pilbara. After working in Perth for Amnesty International WA, she moved to Adelaide. With the Multicultural Writers Association of Australia, she edited an anthology which was shortlisted by the Human Rights Commission for the Literature Non-Fiction Award in 2009. Volunteering with the Writers Centre library, she became active with PEN. She enjoys learning languages and now writes from home for herself and her grandchildren.

To Piteur

Anne-Marie Smith

Pardon My French

Acknowledgements

My husband Peter, my children and grandchildren gave me the strength to write this memoir. Thank you. I hope others enjoy it too. My friends Heather Nimmo and Lindy Warrell helped me produce a memoir with a professional finish and gave it a fully South Australian context. I thank you both for your patience and support! *Merci aussi à Nanou et Dominique pour leur encouragement et leur franchise très Française!*

I acknowledge the support of Peter Bishop of Varuna and of the Sydney Life Stories team in the eastern states of Australia. But it was Western Australia that opened my eyes to the world I now belong to. Thank you, Barbara, Carol, Digna, Mary, Allery, Caroline, Declan, Angela and Zulfah and my many wise West Australian friends – you helped determine my Aussie spirit. And to Eileen and Andy, my African and Papua New Guinean friends respectively, you were the catalysts of my early cultural changes; I keep the memories.

A few names have been changed. I regret that sadly some of the people in this story have passed away.

To all the friends I made in so many countries, I thank you for helping to shape me; I had a magnificent time getting to know you.

Pardon My French
ISBN 978 1 76041 519 8
Copyright © Anne-Marie Smith 2018

First published 2018 by
GINNINDERRA PRESS
PO Box 3461 Port Adelaide 5015
www.ginninderrapress.com.au

Contents

Europe — 7
Fille de gendarme – Gendarme's daughter — 9
Y'a pas d'eau! – What? No water! — 18
En solex – Riding a Solex — 37
Echanges culturels – Cultural exchanges — 43
Un Anglais! – An Englishman! — 61

Zambia — 73
En brousse – Life in the bush — 75
A travers l'Afrique – Across Africa — 88
Mama-Patrick – Mama-Patrick — 95

Papua New Guinea — 113
Arrivée chalereuse en PNG – Warm arrival in PNG — 115
Culture moderne en PNG – Modern PNG culture — 131
Les langues et la politique – Language and politics — 143

Australia — 159
Chocs culturels – Cultural shocks — 161
Le claquement du portail – The clang of the gate — 183
Au Nord du Tropique – North of the Tropic — 199
Résistance – Resistance — 218
Le cycle de vie – The cycle of life — 227

'*La vie est un cercle qui s'élargit jusqu'à joindre le circulaire de l'infini*' – Anaïs Nin

Europe

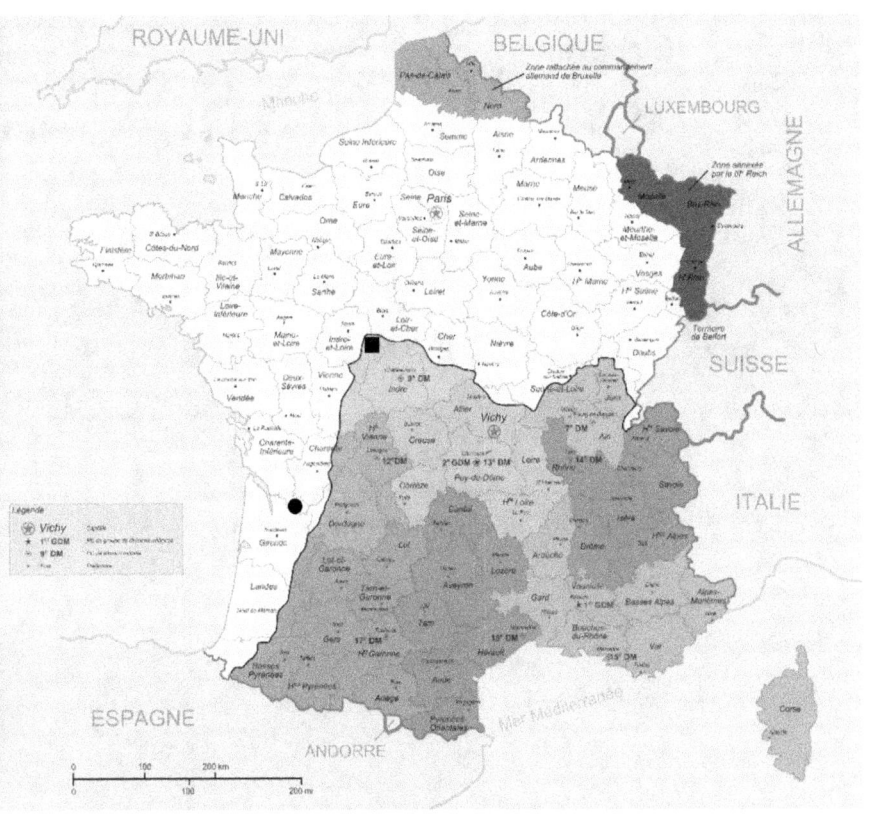

Line of demarcation dividing France south-west to north-east, 1941–1943.
The line was between my grandparents' villages, Bertric-Burée and Verteillac.
● Libourne (occupied zone).
■ Loches, where two siblings were born in the free zone (Vichy government).
(Carte_Armée_d'armistice.jpg: https://creativecommons.org/publicdomain/zero/1.0/deed.fr)

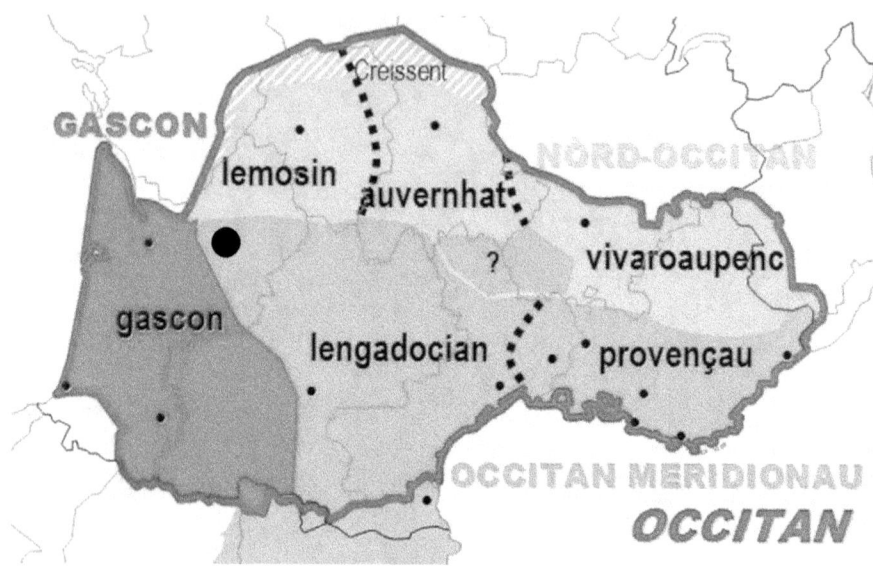

Languages of southern France or Occitanie.
● My grandparents' Périgourdin Languedoc.
(https://en.wikipedia.org/wiki/Occitan_language)

Fille de gendarme
Gendarme's daughter

'Yours, Yayi, was a dramatic entry into the world,' my mother said of my birth.

On that day, the sound of a bridge blowing up resounded in our small town near Bordeaux. She told me the doctor and nurse discussed strategies over her bed. Was the German army covering its retreat north or was the Resistance cutting off its path? The Second World War wasn't over yet, but within a month of my birth, the traumatic occupation of southern France was at an end. Dark-eyed and petite like my sister, I was born into a family that had probably not had much excitement until the advent of the war.

Both my parents came from the Dordogne, a rural part of southern France. Their families were farm workers in adjacent villages in the Périgord region. My grandparents on both sides were peasant farmers and their names show that. My father's name, Bordier, meant 'farmer tenant', while on my mother's side the name Granger meant 'barn people'. My parents married at the start of the war. Called up to the army, my father suffered a knee wound, which invalided him out. As soon as he recovered, he took up a career as a gendarme. It was the closest to being in the army. In France, the gendarmes' role was to supervise the country regions, while the *agents de ville* dealt with law and order in the cities. Most gendarmes lived in small gendarmeries based in regional towns. For my father, signing on as a gendarme meant attending the gendarmerie training school for two years in the town of Loches, just south of the Loire valley, in the unoccupied zone of Vichy France.

At the June 1940 armistice with Germany, the French agreed to a line of demarcation that divided the whole of France from the south-west to the north-east. Any part of France north of an artificial line, based on the army positions at the time, became part of the occupied zone, while sections south of the line became the free zone. The government of France run by Maréchal Philippe Pétain relocated to the spa resort of Vichy.

Loches was in the free zone while Tours, just across the river, was in the occupied zone. My mother had joined my father in Loches and they had their first two children there. My eldest brother Philipe was born in 1941. The name Philippe, after the initially popular head of the Vichy-based government, was a popular one for many boys born in that year. Pétain's popularity soon faded because of his collaboration with Nazi Germany. Philipe, whose name had an administrative spelling error in it, was always happy that his first name was different to that of the maréchal's. My sister Marie-Jeanne, soon to be nicknamed Nanou, was born a year later. Then my father obtained his first posting in a small southern provincial town of the unoccupied zone, close to his native Dordogne. It was near Bordeaux, where the Isle and the Dordogne rivers meet to later flow into the Garonne. Its name was Libourne. I called it home. I was to live there for the first twenty years of my life.

The demarcation line affected my parents' access to their families over three years. The line travelled north from Libourne to the Dordogne. It followed the shortest route to my grandparents' farm, separating my father's village Bertric-Burée in the west from my mother's, Verteillac, in the east. My mother needed to get a pass when she took her two children and her bicycle off the bus to visit her parents. Monitoring of permits and crossings became so difficult that the line was repositioned at times. Some homes had their front garden in one zone, with their backyard and chooks in the other.

The shameful three years of a divided France ended in a worse outcome in 1943. France had to wait till July 1944, my birth month, for the dismantling of the line of demarcation. I don't know whether I brought some light into my parents' life.

Home for me was in the barracks of the Libourne gendarmerie with my parents. Life there was monotonous. As a gendarme, my father spent most of his time in an office as secretary to the captain. The Libourne gendarmerie was a compound, securely positioned behind massive and sturdy double gates that were big enough to take in the width of two Citroën *traction-avants*. The gateway hid a very wide and long open space with houses on either side. To enter the premises, the residents had to wait until a smaller metal gate opened. Although accessing it was awkward on one side because of large steps, it was wide enough for a pedestrian and their bicycle. When the gate opened, the whole compound heard its hinges creak. Receiving guests was rare. None of my friends wanted to visit someone whose house was behind locked gates.

The pedestrians' gate was strategically located, just below the office windows that allowed for direct surveillance onto both the yard and the main street. The duty officer saw anyone arrive, leave or loiter. The gendarmes' children (and I resented this) weren't allowed to have a key for this gate. We had to ring a bell which was too high for a small child to reach. Amazing how wrought-iron structures facilitated scaling to it. We waited until the gendarme on duty, if he wasn't too busy on the phone or talking to someone, could leave the office to unlock the heavy gate with his long, rusty key.

Past the office, lining up either side of the central driveway and neatly laid out with flowerbeds and canna lily edgings, were some maisonettes. These homes, all of the same design, housed about ten families of resident gendarmes. If you walked in downstairs directly through the corridor and kitchen, you emerged into a back veranda. On one side there was a built-in shed door, at the back of which my parents hung a frightening-looking gas mask my father had kept from the Second World War. 'Just in case,' my mother said, when I asked why they kept it. I developed a terrible fear of it, as our parents threatened to put us in the shed if we told lies. With my siblings, we tested the potential ordeal, pushing each other into it.

Opposite, there was a partly covered laundry tub. In the middle was a paved area, used for outdoor eating. It further opened onto a garden plot that ran parallel to the neighbours' gardens, ending with a row of corrugated-iron sheds. Some families used theirs as chicken pens. We added a rabbit hutch to ours. Although my siblings all talked of their fond memories of feeding the pet rabbits, I was scared of them. There was a story that someone, I never found out who it was, had threatened to put me in the hutch if I was naughty.

My parents spent a lot of time in the vegetable garden and grew enough food for our basic needs. My mother preserved green beans, peas, and tomatoes and never considered buying lettuces or tins of peas from shops. Of course, these backyard vegetable plots were a source of neighbourly interaction, be it friendly or competitive. Parents talked of their children but boasted of their vegetables. I suspect the height of the beanstalks served to promote a modicum of privacy as well as producing valuable crops of beans. Most of my parents' close friends were families of gendarmes who had retired or transferred to another town. Apart from relatives, rarely did anyone visit us at home. My mother didn't socialise or like us to mix with outsiders, whom she called *les autres*. Of 'the others' there were only very few families we might on occasions rub shoulders with. We had picnics with some or attended family functions with others.

The front courtyard was common to all. Situated on the other side of a row of official garages was an open space we were happy to play in so long as there were no manoeuvres in progress. In the afternoon, all the gendarmes' children returned home from school. After eating their snacks, usually a slice of bread with some chocolate or cheese, they rushed out to play. There was a lot of racing around, screeches of joy, arguments and fights. I didn't like the way boys and girls fell into separate groups. Nanou and I always made sure we joined in with the boys for games. Hide and Seek was a regular activity for us. Given that we all lived in a barracks, it was logical for us to play a favourite French game called *au Gendarme et au Voleur*, which is a bit like Chasey or

Cops and Robbers. We all dreaded the moment when our mothers' voices put a sudden end to our fun. 'Time to come in for homework,' echoed their voices.

Facing our front door, there was a metal grate made of two flat panels either of which lifted up from the middle vertically towards the sides. The grilles covered a makeshift staircase that led directly into the cellar. I'll always remember the night my father left to go to the office in a hurry. As he walked back to the house, he fell into the cellar. In the rush, he'd left one side of the grate open. He managed to avoid injury by grabbing onto a ladder rung. My mother switched on the porch light to see his head poking out above the grate. We laughed lots but not one of us thought to help him up.

Near the main office, the yard included a set of lock-up cells. I nearly went into jail there once, for stealing. It happened when I was about four and before the stages of formal school and homework, I started going to *l'école maternelle*, the nursery school. It was like preschool nowadays where children receive stickers or stamps from their teachers as rewards for good work or effort. In France, they gave a reward card they called *bon point*. When you got ten *bon points*, you got a certificate. One afternoon, I pinched a *bon point* from one of my schoolmates, Bernard, to bring my own lot up to a complete ten. But Bernard was the son of one of our neighbours, so my mother heard of my snatching the card, and my father chewed my head off about it. 'A gendarme's daughter never steals,' he said.

I thought that Bernard only had a few *bon points* and would receive his own certificate for his lot of ten cards the next day. With my nine *bon points*, I wanted my award before him, so I'd taken the card from him. I didn't like to come second to anyone, especially a boy. I still don't. Not so long ago, I was second in line at a job interview, and that annoyed me greatly. I made it my business to check whether it was a boy that got 'my' position. This preschool episode, however, has haunted me all my life.

When my father started to reprimand me, I raged back. 'The boys always win. That's unfair,' I said, 'and anyway Bernard lives in our gendarmerie too, so what's the problem?'

That didn't help at all. My father took me by the hand and started to drag me towards the yard to the lock-up, 'where people who steal get taken for the night'. I was petrified, instantly screaming profuse apologies. I was then made to return the reward card and say sorry to Bernard.

Despite a fairly strict upbringing, I have fond memories of my father and of my home life. The children were allowed to leave the table towards the end of a family meal. Because I was the youngest, and this lasted about eight years, I was the one to sit on my father's lap and dunk a sugar lump into his coffee. The fun was experiencing the melting sensation and disintegration of the coffee-soaked sugar lump. It was the closest I came to the Proust experience with a *petite madeleine*. Tasting his coffee made me feel like an adult and my father's favourite.

There is another memory I relish. I must have been slightly older when the latest-model vehicle arrived as part of the gendarmerie supplies. It was a motorbike with an attached sidecar, pronounced *sidcar* in French. I fought my siblings to make sure I went for a spin in the seat of my father's sidecar. We only went around the car yard, but it was thrilling.

My parents both left school at the age of fourteen. In the 1930s, the award issued then was the *Certificat d'Etudes*, a statement of school completion before secondary schooling, which only a few children continued to. At that time, there were major hurdles to further education. Usually the level of education depended on social status, where someone lived, and the expenses involved. Children either went to earn a living or supplied their parents with labour at home. My mother was proud to have signed for a hairdressing apprenticeship. She had to leave home for the week to stay in Ribérac, about fifteen kilometres away, riding her bicycle there and back and relying for earnings on her hairdresser's tips. Later in life, she only practised her skills on her own children, although we all tried to encourage her to go to work.

My father was eligible for high school because he had taken and passed the secondary entry test but his family made him take up an apprenticeship. He became a clerk with a local notary. Though he admitted that office work gave some status to his farming family, he felt throughout his life, and all of us knew it, that he had missed out on further education. Yet he managed to enjoy the challenges of life and obtained career promotions. In his first years of service, his role was to patrol outside the town. In the 1940s, the only means of transport available to the gendarmes were bicycles. My father's roster included the local winegrowers. At the start of the grape-picking season, he sometimes brought back some wine in the half-litre fur-insulated flask we used in summer for keeping water cool. Most winegrowers discarded, donated or drank their very first brew. This rough wine or *vin bourru* was still in fermentation. We used to drink it with fresh walnuts or chestnuts as they were just in season in October – a cheap and popular occasion.

I heard stories of how my father made sure he rang his bicycle bell when he approached some estates. 'Well, the small *vignerons* only wanted to keep on the right side of the law,' he once said.

When I heard this, I was shocked. My father was always such a stickler for the rules. I gathered enough courage to ask him whether that meant he was bribed. He was adamant that he hadn't been and never would be. I trusted his response. Later, I came to reflect how little I had known him or spoken to him as an adult about his life in the 1940s. After he passed away, I liked to romanticise him as a hero who had helped the people of lower status.

For many years, I was the third of three children but then I was usurped. My father had planned a holiday by the seaside in the sheltered basin resort of Andernos, off the south Atlantic coast, and he gathered his children to tell us that our mother was to give birth in September. He told us she needed some rest because of albumin complications in late pregnancy. She'd been instructed to put her feet up as they swelled dramatically if she stood for a time. He didn't have to tell us how she wouldn't have rested if she stayed home. My mother was rigorous with her children and tireless in her duties. The three of us were glad to see her reclining in an outdoor chaise longue. It gave her an unaccustomed restriction and us a refreshing sense of autonomy.

We loved our free coming and going and running around while she was lying down. I revelled in my newly found independence and, at age eight, even earned my first pocket money. Instead of learning to swim at the beach with my siblings, I chose to help the ticket lady at the permanent sideshow roundabout. I liked mixing with people. Soon after, my mother gave birth to a healthy son, called Jean-Marie, her fourth and penultimate child (although, at the time, she was sure he would be her last). And I never really learnt to swim.

It was a surprise when, ten years later, she was to have another last-born. I was really excited. My eldest brother was then twenty-one. I still lived at home.

One Easter Monday, my mother woke me in the night. She had gone into labour and was off to the hospital. Standing at the top of the landing, I called out, '*Bonne nuit*,' as she left.

'Not goodnight!' she said shuffling down the steps. 'I've never fallen asleep yet when giving birth.'

Our youngest brother, François, became a favourite with my parents. He became their eternal youngest and was a great anchor for them when the other children had left home. I got to know him well in his early years as I was commuting home from the university campus every week. I caught the Saturday afternoon bus, which stopped opposite the gendarmerie. In his first year, my mother used to hold him up at the kitchen window so he could watch me get off the bus. I can still see him waving and jumping for joy.

After I left home, and whenever I returned, my parents greeted me with a steak *frites à la bordelaise*, chargrilled on vine stock and further perfumed by home-grown shallots. That went well with a glass of

Haut-Segottes, from the chateau in the St Emilion area where I used to go grape picking. I also loved any of the heavy dark-red Pomerol wines that my father stockpiled from the small chateaux scattered at the entrance of my home town.

Another flavour I missed after leaving home was the lingering taste of *saucisson*, a hard salami which was popular with some of the passengers on the Bordeaux to Paris train. In the 1950s, they sliced it off, peeled it with their Opinel knife to eat with their baguettes. Because the journey lasted all day, my mother packed a snack in my very first suitcase, a small hard-top chequered black-and-white valise, and the smell of *saucisson* seemed to follow me everywhere. For me, *saucisson* became the scent of homesickness.

Y'a pas d'eau!
What? No water!

I have found that the Anglo-speaking world loves to romanticise France. Seeing Paris as the city of light, they believe picturesque provincial France to be full of wine, sunshine and quaint characters. Not the country I knew!

To me, the Dordogne was nothing but a land of dreary cellars and bleak toilets, and I felt that I'd had more than ample exposure to them. Dunnies aside, life in southern France probably wasn't very different to that in some remote parts of the Australian outback.

My grandparents' farm was an hour's walk from Verteillac, a tiny village of about a thousand people, which never had any claim to fame. In summer, I used to spend holidays as a child in villages whose names ended in -ac. Signalling a locality with a water point, -ac derives from *aiga*, the word for water in the Occitan language spoken widely in Southern France.

'*Y a pas d'eau!* There's no water.'

I'd just sat on the outdoor toilet and my cry of disgust at not finding water was lost in the wilderness. A bad start to my summer holidays! At my grandparents' farm, the outdoor toilet was not altogether hygienic either. It was built around a dark hole with a wider than life wooden base. The centre of this makeshift seat was covered with an ill-fitting zinc lid. It was a remnant of a *lessiveuse*, an earlier day washer. This old-style boiler turned out the sort of white-laundered sheets and towels that'd make television advertisers envious. When sitting on the toilet, a rickety structure covered with a slanting tin roof sheltered you from wind and rain. There was, however, no sign of water that I recall. Sitting there, whenever I heard any noise, even the chickens pecking at the ground, I'd scream a tentative '*Qui va là*? Who goes there?' – a phrase I had learnt from the heroes of my swashbuckling comics. Having privacy in my grandparents' outdoor toilet wasn't an option. Surrounded by a structure of planks that didn't quite join, I felt the need to hum a tune if I was in there, just in case somebody suddenly wanted to use the toilet who hadn't first peered in to know if the toilet was free.

Le Petit Clos, whose name meant small and enclosed premises, was a small farm that belonged to my grandparents. Situated near the small town of Ribérac on a hillock, off the village of Verteillac it was minuscule by Australian farming standards. As a child, I used to fear danger.

'*Attention aux grottes*. Watch for grottos,' my grandfather said. 'You'll easily fall in around here.'

'Small dogs have disappeared, you know,' my cousin whispered in cryptic tones.

Although located in the Dordogne Département, the region around the farm didn't compare with the nearby tourist attractions of Sarlat. There lay Les Eyzies or the world-renowned grottos, Les Caves de Lascaux, which as one rumour has it, were discovered after a small dog fell in to a hole.

Nanou and I spent hours looking out for the arrival of the few local delivery vehicles that turned off the main road and chugged their way up the hill and into *l'allée*, the pebbled driveway. We'd fight about whose turn it was to stand on the shaky bench under the small boxwood tree to be the first to spot the odd rickety blue-green Renault delivery van. It always parked by the gate in the shade of the huge pine tree about once or twice a week, depending on whether the butcher had run out of meat before he got to us. In the end, we agreed to take turns collecting the bread delivery, twice a week.

When my rostered turn came, I made sure to look out for the baker's yellow Volkswagen. As I heard its distinctive effort to come up the drive, I ran indoors to find a coupon on the mantelpiece, under the wooden box of *gros sel*, rock salt. Next I raced to reach the baker's van to hand it over, then proudly walking back into the house with a country loaf that would last for a half-week. My parents had impressed on me that coupons meant the bread came in part from my grandparents' crop. The village baker issued my grandparents with bread vouchers in exchange for the wheat they took to the mill once a year and from which flour was made. In early farming days, coins and cash were a rare currency.

Once a day, however, the juddering sound of the *facteur*'s moped was a signal for another test of my survival in what I considered treacherous country. Letters and bills were rare but if you wanted to access the only reading matter worth having at the farm, *La République (Périgord)* you had to grab it fast. With luck, and advanced scanning skills, you might read it before it was cut up for use in the toilet.

My family spoke a variant of old French, a version of the Occitan spoken in the Dordogne which people then dismissed as a backward patois. Occitan was the language of the Languedoc region (which literally means 'the language of oc', where *oc* was the word for 'yes'). Although I never used it much myself with my grandparents, I understood it enough to follow instructions. My parents spoke it fluently. Later, going back to France, I noticed that Occitan had been revived through schools. I can purchase recordings of songs and stories I used to hear and repeat as a child. I can still sing a well-known song whose words vary slightly in most variants of regional Occitan. '*Se Canto*' tells of a youth sitting under a branch while a bird sings:

Se canto, Que Canto	If it sings, let it sing
Canto pas per ieu	It sings not for me
Canto per ma mio	But sings for my love
Qu'es al luènh de ieu	Who is far away

Soon after the stay in Andernos that we had all enjoyed with my mother, a further treat awaited me. Our paternal grandmother had come to help in the house when my mother was to give birth. Because I was still the youngest child, I received Mémée Mélina's full attention.

Possibly because she was my father's mother, the family only saw her for a half-day when we visited her sons or daughters, usually at Ribérac or in Bertric-Burée. I hadn't yet become close to her, but I really liked her. She gave me her full attention, and I relished her sojourn with us. Sadly, she never stayed with us again.

I found several things interesting about her. First, she'd only wear long black dresses. Secondly, she had a very pointy chin that appeared to lift up towards her mouth. French calls it *un menton en sabot*, a chin that juts forward, shaped like the pointy end of a clog. She also used the longest hair clip I'd ever seen to hold her hair so tightly pinned back that it appeared to me to be black and white, striped all the way to her chignon on top of her head. It is obvious now that she must have been greying. What I liked most about Mémée Mélina was her soft singing voice. She'd tell me all about bird songs and imitate the sounds they made. Some of them, like the *merle* or blackbird, are similar in Australia. She'd teach me how to make the sound of the *coucou* or cuckoo in early spring – great, but not as entertaining as the kookaburra laughter my Australian grandchildren love to imitate!

Life in rural southern France was regulated around harvesting times. Villagers came together for their annual ritual chores and took turns within each village helping one another to reap the wheat or whatever grain they had planted. In June, every day was harvesting day in Verteillac. Although my grandparents managed the farm by themselves all year round, they needed extra hands one weekend. My parents, uncles and aunts drove over to help out. The last day of the arduous efforts culminated in a large and happy event. Everyone came together for a feast: food, drink, songs and multiple shouting matches. On that evening, benches and trestles materialised from nowhere and we set them up in the front courtyard. There was always a separate table for children and we loved being allowed to stay up late. We ran around the house and the bushes screeching happily until someone got hurt.

These occasions were the times friendships were forged with friends and cousins. These were happy times for me. I liked mixing with new batches of people. It brought relief from the oppressive closeness of my immediate family.

The harvest feast, *moisson*, went late into the night. Marking the start of summer, it was very soon to be followed by another festive event, the local 14 July celebrations. Held in the village square, which actually was more of a rectangle, with plenty of shade and space to set up stalls for *le jour de fête*, the event was just as comic as in Jacques Tati's film of the same name. The day was full of excitement with displays, roundabouts and an evening of music in the dance hall at night, with all the old people watching that their granddaughters didn't touch a boy's hand, unless of course they were ballroom-dancing.

One year, I must have been fifteen, at the end of a dance, I dared leave the floor holding hands with my dancing partner. Just as we stepped outside the hall, Nanou appeared to tell me that our maternal grandmother, Mémée, wasn't happy. She explained that if I wanted to 'talk to boys', *parler aux garçons*, it would always have to be out of sight from parents, aunties, grandparents or of anyone who knew our family. She said that getting caught out would ruin it for us, the girls, and our parents would use it as an excuse for us not to go out.

Over the years, Nanou and I often debated this, and she argued it in vain with our parents. We saw it was accepted for boys to go out with girls or even hold hands with them. Philipe was blasé about his flirtatious habits. One neighbour reported him for walking home across the fields with someone's daughter! Other girls, Nanou explained, could talk to boys, but we couldn't! She complained that although she was only one year younger than Philipe, she was made to stay back home with a sister (that was me) who was two years younger. I'd try and appease her by agreeing with her about the disadvantage girls suffered but didn't feel bad for being at the centre of this deprivation of her liberty.

At the Petit Clos, my maternal grandparents also cultivated a small area of about fifty rows of vines, and at the start of autumn, the whole extended family returned for another weekend at the farm. The September gathering for grape-picking was usually an exciting time, and one of my favourites. Usually at the end of the school holidays, this was significant because it was just before the children were to start their next year of academic education. They all felt as if they had become older already. My uncle from Angoulême, Tata Alice's husband, was our hero then. He'd managed to set up a press in my grandfather's barn and appointed himself chief trampler for the day. For us kids, it was a treat to join in with him as his helper for a few minutes.

In the early years, because I was still young, I was free to walk to the end of a row and watch my father. He wore a wooden contraption on his back called a *hotte*. Everyone emptied their basket into it as he walked along the rows. He then climbed a small ladder onto the trailer parked nearby, tossed the full load into the barrel and set off again to repeat the same trek. Later, someone drove the trailer and the large barrel to the barn. A new one was loaded and the process started again. It was a hard slog.

One year, there was an episode that my family didn't let me forget. At one stage of my wanderings in the late morning, I felt thirsty and went to the end of the shadiest row, where we kept the drinks. I found a bottle and took a swill or two. It was wine that had been warming up in the sun throughout the morning. The story goes that I couldn't walk straight on the way back to lunch. Apparently, Mémée kept me at the farm and I slept through the afternoon. I don't recall this, or even being told off for it. In retrospect, I figured either I'd gone through a rite of passage that no longer made me an outsider, or someone felt guilty that they hadn't kept an eye on me. Yet nothing stopped any of my relatives later in life from recounting and embellishing this embarrassing event.

The others, adults and children, worked hard, squatting at the base of vine stocks. All you could hear was the regular snip of their secateurs and the occasional swear word followed by hearty laughter. We'd move along the row, usually by sideways squatting at ground level. Few stood up, as it wasted time and someone might tease them for looking around, dreaming and not concentrating on the job. Besides backache at the end of the day, you could get nasty blisters not so much from using a pair of efficiently whetted secateurs but from regularly seizing the flat wooden basket you had to trail on the ground as you went. Riling and cruel comments were targeted without delay at anyone who ate grapes or who dropped too many of the riper ones on the ground. Those who ever dared to complain about the workload wouldn't last till the next day. Being labelled an outsider was the ultimate put-down. The last thing you wanted was to suffer the sneers reserved for those from the city: 'Is that how you guys behave over there in Bordeaux, then?'

As a teenager, I went on to do grape-picking as holiday work. It provided a useful, efficient way to make a quick reasonable amount of pocket or travel money. The *vendanges*, grape-picking season, was a time when students flocked to be fed and housed by commercial *vignerons*. I took pride in refining a skill that we called *faire suivre son rang* and it implied keeping a rhythm with your partner on the other side of the row. However, as I'd learnt in childhood, you have to be able to put up with being called names. Many country labourers felt threatened by the outsiders who appeared for the grape-picking season. In their eyes, those who were students would be useless at any type of manual work. If someone asked what time we finished work, one of the locals jeered, '*Une étudiante sans doute*, bound to be a student,' for not knowing about the long hours of farm workers. Englishness often provoked some sniggering. '*Un anglais encore!* An Englishman yet!' English people, the conjecture was, no matter how hard they worked or how much they spoke French, didn't burst out into the same hearty laughter in response to a French joke. To many French locals, they were the epitome of foreignness.

Back at the Petit Clos, a few months later, a customary follow-up visit took place. My family as well as my uncles, aunts and cousins took turns to drive back to Verteillac to collect wine from my grandfather. He fermented the wine into enough barrels to ensure equal amounts to each of his daughter's families to keep them in table wine all year. In the meantime, Mémée dispensed gifts of food from the farm to her daughters She wasn't just in charge of the farm. She did the majority of the work on it.

As we left the farm, my grandfather boasted, year after year, that his Dordogne wine was better than any of the clarets from near Bordeaux where we lived. Inevitably, he concluded with a joke that made us roll our eyes. 'Anyway, their Cheval Blanc – pffft, it turns out to be a red wine despite its name.'

Nobody took serious notice of his banter. In fact, Pépé, as my maternal grandfather was called, was a popular character in his community. He returned from the First World War missing two fingers on his right hand and he became the local postman, a public servant, instead of a farmer. By far the best storyteller of the family, he was famous for the great 1920s songs he entertained the family with at weddings and at Sunday gatherings.

Pépé could also whistle many fine tunes. He was famous for having a few drinks towards the end of his delivery round. One evening, he returned late, on his bicycle, from a string of visits to nearby farms. It was after dark and we heard him whistling before we could see him. We also heard the sound of his bicycle bell from the bottom of the driveway. As we looked up, we saw a beam of light going up and down the lane. He was waving his portable battery light to the rhythm of his songs. Because it was shining up and down and sideways, we knew something was unusual. He'd had a few drinks. To my surprise and for the first time ever, I heard Mémée raise her voice at him.

'So you stopped for a glass at each house tonight!'

He glowered past us, started to sing and walked into the beaten-earth cellar adjacent to the kitchen on the farm's northern face. There he kept enough of his wine for himself and his wife. They also kept what they called a safe there to protect some of the weekly food supplies from insects. *Saucisson,* pâté and *jambon,* sardines and the popular Camembert were stored there.

'It's to keep it from running off and down the road,' Pépé once said. Not sure if he was teasing me, I glanced at Mémée. She shrugged.

Pépé always projected a very traditional portrait of the early twentieth-century French soldier of the First World War and also the typical country character from the Dordogne. He followed customs thoroughly. At dinner time, if there was soup, he left a tiny drop at the bottom of the soup dish or *assiette creuse* and simply added a small amount of red wine, which made the finishing of the soup more palatable to drink off the plate. This is a regional French custom called *faire chabrot*, but better known as *(fà) chabroù* in Occitan.

Le Petit Clos consisted of a house, two barns (one for the cows, the other for the wine vats and farm equipment), an enclosed yard with a chicken run, a pig pen, a rabbit hutch and a well. Outside the fenced-up yard, there were several fruit trees, a huge vegetable and flower garden and a wooded field at the back. My mouth waters at the memories of the fresh hazelnuts and walnuts we picked off the trees. We ate them with bread and jam, as no one then had heard of Waldorf salads. The main salads then were lettuce salads, and when there were none we went out to pick a *pissenlit* or dandelion. We knew to pick those before they started producing crops of plain yellow flowers. I later heard that dandelion is also eaten in other parts of the world.

I recall the main room of the house, an old-fashioned kitchen with the open hearth facing the front door, where Mémée concocted for us the tastiest homemade soups and stews. I remember the strong tangy aroma of rabbit stews. I still savour how, to eat her famous *civet de lapin*, we'd suck and aspirate every last fibre off the small and juicy bones to make the rabbit stew last in our mouth forever.

Besides cooking, Mémée had other farm duties. She tended vegetables and fruit as well as kept a battery of chickens, and other yard animals. She force-fed the geese for valuable liver to make pâté before winter. She kept all meats ranging from geese to ducks and sections of pork, cut and quartered as *quartiers*, so they fitted in the storage jars next to the food safe in the cellar. Another custom was to make black pudding, which they ate cold, as you do salami, and a type of pâté of pork meat called rillettes, or of duck called *grillons*. After Mémée bled chicken necks quite neatly with a sharp pointy knife, she'd fry the blood that had been let out. She later served it as a delicacy called *la sanguette*. Rabbits she never had any problem with, stunning them on the nape in one blow. As for the awful squealing sounds of a pig being killed, it is a haunting sound that I avoid remembering.

I always enjoyed eating Mémée's country-cooked delicacies, possibly not fully appreciating the context of the local products or the unique skills that she used to produce her dishes. Nowadays, people write books about such cuisine, praising it and documenting it. They demonstrate recipes through cookery lessons and serve it in top world restaurants. Mémée practised it and, with amazing accuracy, used the slow over-the-open-hearth country cooking that used to be the traditional method before the advent of wood, coal, gas or even electric stoves and microwaves.

Mémée came into the kitchen with an armful of heavy logs she'd cut to even lengths at the back of the house, using a wedge against the blade of the axe. She crouched over the hearth, jamming extra logs at an angle across each other. She then gathered her pinafore around her waist from either side to make sure not to catch it in the fire. Sometimes she'd blow the fire to life or else used the bellows to get the sparky flame she needed. This usually marked the start of her cooking a meal. She got into position, facing the hearth to reach the ratchet from which she dangled the pots for boiling water or cooking a casserole.

Mémée liked to allocate tasks. She sometimes spent hours talking to whoever was in the kitchen behind her crouching body. Once, she sent Nanou on some errands without even looking at her. 'And before you ask,' she added, talking to me when I thought she didn't know I was there, 'Yayi,' that was my nickname, 'you are too small to go with her.'

Using either her pinafore or a couple of rags, she lifted or lowered the pots one at a time and moved them, altering the position of her cast-iron pots, placing the pots one at a time onto a different tooth of the dangling ratchet which she reset every so often: down for boil and up for simmer. This seemed to occupy her on and off throughout the day. She'd emerge from the hearth red in the face as if burnt. After dinner, as I kissed her goodnight on my way to bed, I noticed her wearily pushing a greyish lock of her hair to one side after it came loose from a hairpin. It must've hovered in front of her eyes at the end of a long day's work.

As an adult, I didn't attempt to replicate any of the hard work involved in cooking. I didn't even learn from my own mother's modernised yet delicate cooking. Was it because I couldn't make an omelette without mushrooms like the *girolles* or the golden chanterelles we used to pick from the field? Or was it because cooking as I saw it in my youth was demanding and complex? I could never romanticise barefoot pregnant women slaving over a hot stove. All I ever saw was a woman condemned to have a dangling ratchet hanging over her head. I felt pressured when assigned to any daily tasks. I resented it, fearing I'd be tied for the rest of my life to the same lacklustre situation my mother and Mémée had been caught up in. I yearned for freedom, for space and for action in life.

These early days of the southern agricultural French lifestyle made me feel cornered. I spent a lot of energy later in my student years trying to avoid the regular weekend visits that we often made out of duty to the extended family. My mother had set up home within an hour from her parents' farm. To compound this, my father's family also came from the same region. My parents' *raison d'être* was defined by Sunday drives across the Gironde to the Dordogne and returning via the Charente, where some of the extended family also lived, an eternal triangle that confined and defined their lives.

Just below Le Petit Clos, the road wound in a hairpin bend, continuing alongside the course of a clear brook below in which there was a *lavoir*, a sort of open-air village washhouse with a narrow tiled roof cover all the way around where the women did the family's washing in the water of the stream. One of Mémée's few domestic outings was to walk down to join them. They spent hours soaping, rinsing and beating clothes in and out of the water, talking all the while. It was quite a noisy social gathering. The first time I went with Mémée, I enjoyed the chatty and cheerful atmosphere. Yet with all the noise and my limited knowledge of Occitan, I couldn't be sure of what the laughter was about.

'What were the women going on about this morning?' I asked once we were home.

'Some things children don't talk about in the house,' she replied.

It was as though she wanted to keep me out of a conspiracy. When I asked if she'd take me again next time she went to do the washing, I could see her frowning.

'You are too young, and you ask too many questions,' she said.

The first thing you saw as you neared Le Petit Clos was a compact stone-built shelter with a low red-brick roof sticking out by the side of the front door close to the barn. It was a well. Some farms transported water, with an unstable horse and cart from the brook trailing back their barrels of water, which clattered along and overspilled onto the road. My grandparents prided themselves that they didn't need to go out and collect water from the brook. Their well didn't seem to dry up even in summer.

The well was so deep that voices echoed dramatically in it. I was scared of falling in, and it took some concentration to detect the water level and some weightlifting strength to bring the water up. To draw drinking water from the well, you clasped a bucket to a rugged metal chain with large rungs and lowered it until you heard a gulping sound that meant the bucket had reached the water. You would pull the chain up gently, even pausing sometimes so you could lift the bucket carefully as it became heavier and more unsteady. It behaved like a devilish creature determined to make you fail and get rid of the water before it reached the stone ledge of the well.

A balancing act ensued. I hated the challenge of leaning forward to grab the re-emerging bucket, and then straightening back up to keep it steady and avoid losing the precious water. The last step usually required an adult's help. While holding on to the bucket, you had to unclasp it from the chain and then lower it to the ground to carry it into the house. The grandchildren helped with this task in summer and the water well duties were kept going even after my grandparents had running water installed in the kitchen. As there was no fridge in the house, its cool water was welcome.

'Go and get some more.'

Why did she have to ask for more firewood, I wondered, when there was still a big log by the fireside. As a child, I resented the adults ordering me around. If I made a mess of it, I figured, they would stop giving me jobs to do. I was now watching Mémée ranting at me.

'I always have to sweep bits of wood after you drop them on my kitchen floor,' Mémée complained as she stood there, nodding to herself.

I was hoping to get a break from fetching firewood again. You could get into double trouble doing those jobs. You'd get a splinter, and then be ticked off because that was your fault. Children couldn't win, I decided.

Next, if I sat by the fireside reading my book, the adults asked me to stand up because I was in the way. That was a request even I didn't dare counter. My grandparents were more impatient with children than my own parents. Although I thought I was quick to comply with their requests, admonitions came thick and fast.

'Don't twirl a stick in the fireplace before bedtime or you'll wet your bed.' Mémée was watching over me again.

One afternoon, she started to instruct me. 'Close the shutters, just half joined together, on the catch, see…to keep out the heat and flies,' and then, 'Anyway, it's time to settle down to a siesta, and give us a break from that non-stop yapping of yours.'

I didn't like put-downs. Later, in my teens, she made another statement I hadn't expected from her. As I prided myself not to have to comb my hair because it was short, she said that a girl's beauty was in her hair. I remembered wanting to leave home at times like that, but my problem was that my grandparents' house wasn't my home, and it would take up to one hour to reach any other house. At times I felt these enforced so-called holidays could have been bearable, or fun. Not for long. Mémée soon reminded me of another chore. I was to shine my shoes. She said I'd need them on the Sunday for the four-kilometre walk to the church and back, cutting across country lanes. These were known to be full of fresh *bouse de vache*, cow dung. I obliged, wondering what the point was, especially as Pépé hated the church and priests and boasted of dropping spare buttons instead of coins in the collection box.

Extended families, although colourful and fun at times, could teach younger people tough lessons of life. You would learn not to ask too many questions or to repeat what you might have heard. At these times I thought I didn't like Mémée much and I felt I was being mocked or bossed around. So one afternoon, rather than sit in a close and darkened front room, I went outside to sit under a shade tree for a bit of peace. Mémée had a siesta but within an hour, she looked out for me. She delivered one of her didactic *dictons* or old wives' tales. On that occasion, I remember, she seemed to have found a new one.

'Never sit in the shade of a nut tree. You'll catch ill and you'll be sick,' she warned.

By the time I had finished hearing all the rules, I felt sick of being chided. I suffered from extreme boredom and grew more and more rebellious. I regret that, at that time, I wasn't aware of the significance of her statement. Her last-born, her first boy, at age two had died of measles with a high fever. She had tried to cool him under that tree before calling for a doctor.

Mémée possibly realised she needed to get me out of her way because one day she declared I was old enough to take the geese to feed in a distant paddock. I followed them out of the front yard, all by myself, with one long stick to drive them. That meant I was separated from my brother, sister and cousin. They were older and entrusted to take the cows grazing. They'd set off down the alleyway onto the sealed road following the cows *en file indienne*, in a straight line, for a while until they reached a very large paddock. Unknown to Mémée at the time, they were as rebellious as I was. They sat in one of my grandparents' fields nearby wasting valuable crops (even though some were for the pigs to eat). They pulled beets out of the ground, and carved them into shapes, like toy cars. Gérard once made me a mini toy bike and said, 'You're not to show Pépé. He won't like it.' When Pépé caught them in the middle of their artistic endeavour, my siblings suspected me of telling on them. I swore I hadn't.

Amazingly, decades later my own family and I were on a camping trip around Western Australia. One night, we set up tent late at an Albany campsite. The next morning a strange sound of loud cackling woke us up.

I was wondering what all the running around and cacophony was when all of a sudden, I sat up thinking, '*Des oies!* Geese!' Peering out of the tent quickly confirmed my guess that a gaggle of geese appeared to have taken over the campsite.

Kids were chasing them, then were themselves chased, all running in and out of tents and caravans.

I stood still looking around for a skinny fallen branch I could use. 'The geese took a wrong turn. Leave them alone. I'll have a go at sending them out.'

That sparked off a few comments from both my children.

'Oh no, what's she doing with that stick?' my son muttered.

'How embarrassing! I'm going back in the tent,' my daughter called out.

The noises abated and I started methodically and firmly to drive the geese out of the campsite. Quite simply, I pointed the long stick at eye level of the goose on the right-hand side, which made it veer towards the left. The others followed this inward move. I was ready for that and immediately showed the stick at eye level to the furthest left goose.

This redirected the group's move towards the right. Systematically, I pointed the stick to the front left and then to the front right, catching the side vision of the geese. This made the gaggle move inwards until I'd directed the group ahead to face the gates on the outside perimeter of the campsite. I saw them out and simply closed the gates, but I reckon I could have driven the geese all the way to Perth.

More noise. I turned around and saw my children with my husband leading the resident campers in a round of applause.

'They're just silly animals,' I said.

I was surprised how quickly the technique of dealing with nuisance geese had come back to me. In so doing, I impressed my family, who never knew I possessed useful country survival skills.

I developed another parochial pastime. Selecting the very point that was equidistant between Verteillac and the next village of La Tour Blanche, I lay down with my ear to the ground on the sealed road below Le Petit Clos. It was daring because that point was in the blind bend opposite the *lavoir*. I listened out for the one car that might drive along that road on that day. Hearing it approach made my day.

In spite of my dislike of the Dordogne, I can still recall a few entertaining activities. In summer, after a heavy storm, we used to go out and pick a species of mushrooms called *cèpes*. This beautifully scented delicacy is still my favourite food, pan-fried with garlic and parsley. Spotting *cèpes* in dark wooded fields was a skill technically mastered only by locals. Yet the amount of noise and boasting that went on after successful finds made it easy for anyone to catch on as to their locations.

The main reason I liked *la cueillette des champignons* was because during the annual mushroom-picking season, I got the chance to spend some time with my father, following in his footsteps, literally. I was schooled in scanning the undergrowth with a stick in hand, on how easy it was to get disoriented and about checking the sun's position, a useful early grounding for survival in the Australian bush. Crucially I learnt how to sort the genuine *cèpes* from many non-edible ones.

My father decapitated them to expose their discoloured poisonous undersides for all to see.

I didn't feel confident to transfer these valuable mushroom-picking skills, or the art of collecting *escargots* either, to other countries in which I went on to live. To play safe, I won't pick any mushrooms or snails that I don't know. Of course, snails were a lot more common and easy to find.

'*On va à la chasse aux escargots,*' Nanou said.

I loved it. There was no rebellion, complaint or annoyance on my part when it came to picking snails. We walked up to the nearest hedge after a night of storm and heavy rain, usually in August. We worked our way along, picking enough to fill a bucket. Then, and on our mother's advice, we soaked them in a vinegar solution for a couple of days to clean them out. We loved helping to prepare a mixture of breadcrumbs with garlic and parsley. However, their taste can't compete with that of *cèpes*, although they are cooked with the same ingredients. But pulling the flesh off the spiral of the shell with a two-pronged fork was great fun.

Truffles were another source of excitement for the family. Of course, they added a strong taste to bland or fatty foods, like foie gras or plain sausage minced meat, *les crépinettes*. But the smell of truffles I found unbearable. Pépé never said where he was going, but you knew where he had been on his return. One of the paddocks where the cows grazed was a few kilometres away. Adjacent to a neighbour's field, it boasted a beautiful oak tree. The tree had roots on his side of the fence. Pépé got dirty on all fours scratching under the tree till he unearthed some truffles out of the ground. He didn't trust pig or dog. Trying not to be spotted by the neighbours was wise, as the product of their tree really belonged to them. He didn't like to take chances.

'You can't be too careful with the neighbours,' he said, 'but once I've dug these out, nobody can get their hands on them.'

At the end of a day's visit, my grandparents gave our family two of their prized fifty-gram truffles. Although they were securely enclosed in a sealed jar, lovingly wrapped in a four-cornered checked tea cloth, placed by Mémée in a wicker basket and locked in the boot of my father's *traction-avant*, his old Maigret-style Citroën, the extreme aroma of the tiny truffles became overpowering. It wasn't discreet like the fragrance of a gentle perfume. It was pervasive and seemed to float above our heads in the car. The distinctive almost unbearable odour was nauseating. I felt queasy for the full hundred-kilometre trip home to Libourne.

Once home, we'd leave the truffle in the shed. The next morning, everyone swung into action under my mother's guidance. This was the start of an intensive week of goose liver pâté-making. My mother cut thin tiny slivers of truffle resembling black nail clippings. She then dropped no more than three to five in each section of pale yellowish goose liver slices that Nanou had been cutting for each tin. My role was to carry a basketful of unsealed tinned foie gras for crimping so it could be preserved. The one supermarket that sold open tins and lids was also equipped with a large piece of machinery, a bit like a soft drinks dispenser, which sealed the tins you'd filled up. Finally my mother boiled the tins in a special pot in the open garage. These tins of foie gras *truffé* were such a delicacy that they lasted a few years. My mother served them at significant occasions while my father opened some of the wine he hoarded for special gatherings, preferably of the year one of the guests was born.

Being brought up in an extended family, I tended to learn some of the essential skills of country life by watching. This provided in fact a formative preparation that helped me later when I worked with and lived among indigenous peoples in various countries such as Zambia, Papua New Guinea and Australia. I was naturally gregarious. But my own rural large family had taught me to understand that cross-generational interaction was a way of life. You listened to the elders and you spoke to the younger children the way you had been spoken to.

I always felt, staying with my maternal grandparents, that you had to learn the hard way. Relatives could be your mentors and your tormentors, usually both at the same time. My grandparents chided me often for asking too many questions.

I remember one day when Pépé appeared at the back of the house. Whenever he'd been out in the fields, he had a habit of raising his black cap, rubbing his forehead with the edge of it, as if he'd been sweating a lot, and then resettling it on his head. He was doing just that while signalling me over, calling out to me in Occitan, '*Aqui la gojata*. Here, child,' he said.

I ran over and saw in his *musette*, or satchel, massive magnificent brown *cèpes*. I must have jumped up and down asking where he'd found them and if we'd get more. '*Tu les as pris chez le voisin?* You picked them off the neighbour's?' I asked.

There he toned down the excitement and the boasting. '*Bondieu de drola, parla tròp!* Damned bloody kid, she talks too much.' he called out over his shoulder.

His voice echoed for all to hear, which they did and worse, because they all laughed. As a child, and as an adult later too, I always spoke out of turn, which led me into trouble. I remember the many reprimands I received for talking too much. Nicknamed *un moulin à paroles* or windmill, I was teased. Both my parents objected to children talking about their life to outsiders. But it seems that I was the only one to ever get caught doing it. It probably was because I'd quite happily embellish for my playmates basic stories about whatever went on in the home. I liked to twist the truth and pretend that exciting things had happened, mainly because I wished they had.

Then my father's voice came blustery from under his breath. 'She'll get us hanged that one.'

Of course, I knew that hanging had been abolished in France.

En solex
Riding a Solex

In France, most people go to state schools for a thorough education. A national programme was instituted in the nineteenth century to ensure equal opportunities for all. My first two years of secondary school were at a girls' high school called the Collège des Filles and located in a very old convent with an atrium in the middle. Everything there was old-fashioned, especially a famous deputy headmistress called Mademoiselle Sambucconi, who we suspected had no other duties except to check at the gates whether we wore our *bérets* and gloves. We didn't have to wear them all day, just when we lined up to go in and before going home. I hated it. I soon learnt how to hold one of my gloves as if I hadn't lost the other one!

A significant change occurred when the two high schools in town came to merge. The very old convent-style girls' college joined with the boys' old high school into a modern co-educational newly built Lycée Max Linder.

This gave a sense of excitement, enthusiasm and non-conformism to the girls and boys of the time. Erected along the town's main artery, the two-storey long set of classrooms dominated the centre. No school uniform, simply an option of overalls, pink for girls and blue for boys – how we loved to swap to preserve our clothes in classes such as science or art. I liked it there. The only rule I remember was that girls shouldn't wear pointy high heels to avoid burrowing into the newly lined soft corridor flooring. Fine for me who didn't identify with some of the well-dressed girls with high heels whom I considered bourgeois. I didn't empathise with their dilemmas on high-heeled shoes or make-up.

My longest-lasting friend in life came from those years. Dominique spotted me in the English class. She said she saw a girl over-committed to her studies who jumped onto her feet at every chance to give the answer to the English teacher's question. She sat next to me because she said she wasn't confident in English and she became my buddy.

We were part of a group of only four girls who kept on studying classics into upper high school, adding ancient Greek to Latin. For the Greek class, we fitted in a small old-fashioned study room with tiny windows. As people walked past our rooms, they peered in to watch us sharing in-class jokes. The word went around that studying Greek tragedies could be so amusing that we scrambled out of a two-hour class roaring with laughter from each other's company. And I did enjoy the Greek plays and poetry as well as my friends' company. The over-serious scholar in me succumbed to having fun with friends, but our French circle of friends didn't go as far as the characters in the iconic film *Dead Poets Society*.

Another feature of my French lifestyle was tasting a sense of freedom by riding the then ubiquitous Solex or Vélosolex. Forget the Vespa. This two-wheeled bicycle with a two-stroke engine in a black box sitting below the *guidon* or handlebar worked well as a handy vehicle. It could start if you ran alongside it, depressing the engine lever over the front wheel and simply jumping onto it as soon as the engine kicked in. The Solex was light and if it ran out of fuel, you could always pedal home. A great asset for a student. My home was situated midway between Saint-Emilion and Pomerol. As soon as I was old enough, I signed up over the summer holidays for grape-picking for a couple of months every year.

In my later teens, I decided, even against my father's veto, to acquire a second-hand Solex. I felt that ten years of a three-way child's bicycle share with Philipe and Nanou had been enough to limit my freedom of movement. On the gravel road, right past the windows of the gendarmerie, I had the first fall off my moped. The thought that my father and his colleagues might be watching made me even more determined to reveal no pain and to start riding again. I soon became confident to ride my Solex, using the back roads to the Saint-Emilion vineyards. The winery I went to, Haut-Segottes, was only about seven kilometres away from my home. Although situated across the road from the famous Cheval Blanc, it wasn't listed in the same *cru* and yet the terroir is similar. Of course, it is much less expensive than the Cheval Blanc.

I was in my teens and revelling in the feeling of getting away from home. By the evening, the physical exhaustion in all my tired limbs from grape-picking, combined with the most substantial of gourmet country cooking that we were treated to, resulted in my falling into a deep sleep of satisfaction for the night. I left home before the sun was too hot and sang my way there with insouciance. Later in my rushed adult life, when I have been depressed, I've often thought of the elusive quality of the perfect healthy living I enjoyed at that time. Over-commitment soon took over the well-balanced early phases of my life and various degrees of anxiety erupted. I didn't realise it was situational and feared my anxiety was due to my personality. As a result, over several decades my anxiety compounded into a chronic depression that I had to learn to manage.

One day, I knew I had left slightly later than usual when I heard the rumble of the early morning Micheline, the red railcar shuttle service that left Libourne at ten past seven towards Bordeaux. It was approaching a railway crossing that usually was clear when I reached it. As I got there, I hopped off the Solex seat. Seeing the barrier wasn't quite down and the train was still not there I decided I'd guide my Solex through the sidings on foot. In my mind, this ensured my safety because it would avoid any possibility of an engine breakdown across the rails. But the wind pushing against me slowed my down, so I started to run, or was it the train's incessant hooting that made me run? I can't remember. I just recall being panic-stricken and the train appearing closer and larger. I even saw the grin and gesticulation of the train driver before I hauled the back of the Solex off the track. This put a dent in the happy-as-I-go mood that had started my day.

These were the days of working against the grain, just to counter my parents' constant words of caution. So I often acted as the odd one out. I interrupted and asked questions out of place. I wanted to be heard but it was counter-productive to my wish to be popular. My mother said I was like my aunt Alice. I'd stayed with her in Angoulême, where she worked from home. A seamstress, she used to sing and whistle as she worked. I loved her chatting and laughter while we dressed to go out. She'd put on make-up and we'd go window-shopping, both activities my mother considered a waste of time. She taught me the cha-cha-cha, and I liked being with her so much that my mother said I took after her. Whenever my parents picked me up to go back home, they would ask, 'Did she break anything? Did she talk too much?'

My aunt once said to them, 'I reckon you must be right about her being restless, you know, because I keep putting her photo frame on my bedside and it keeps falling over.' Another excuse for the family to go on and on about my wayward ways.

Because I was labelled as 'awkward', I feared being rejected. I launched into trying to prove myself to my parents and to the world. I applied all my energies to my studies, thinking these were areas they didn't know about. My feeling was that even if I made errors, they probably wouldn't notice.

I liked English and gave total application to the subject at school. The teaching of languages, in those days, took place without any audio or visual resources. My first teacher had learnt from textbooks and she taught us by the same method. We had to read stories aloud before learning the vocabulary or parsing the sentences. In my haste to practise English, I launched into speaking it before I went to England. When I did meet native English speakers, I could listen and tune in to English accents and had no problem answering questions. By then it was too late to make major changes in the sound system I had developed when talking. So my marked French accent in English had become what linguists call fossilised. I focused instead on developing reading and writing skills in English, and on reading English novels like the work of Dickens and Thomas Hardy.

In the late 1950s, I surprised my mother by coming home late in the afternoons in the summer. While my friends went to the cinema, I'd hang around Les Allées in Libourne giving directions to the English tourists driving through and looking lost on their way south. Most of them were on their way to Spain, which was then the cheapest holiday destination in Europe. I didn't have to worry about safety as those were the days before the raging English hooliganism for which some English tourists are famous. Tourists in those days were likely to be the upwardly mobile British families who could afford a car to drive to the continent. I loved practising my English on them. I've often wondered if any of the British travellers remembered the French girl who directed them across the south of France into Spain – via the back roads. I thought they would enjoy the experience and I hope they found their way.

I like to think that I take after some of the Gascon characters that I used to read about in books as a child. The fictitious literary heroes from south-western France were famous for their daringness and their garrulous bragging. I perceived D'Artagnan in *The Three Musketeers* and *Cyrano de Bergerac* as typical characters that promoted anti-establishment sentiments. I felt that, like them, I loved speaking out and expressing my views in the open, no matter what company I was in. It felt that most of my life I had got into trouble for being verbose and too noisy. Although I had to control it, I found it hard to change that trait of mine.

About twenty kilometres east of Libourne, at the limit of the Gironde and Dordogne, was the Château d'Eyquem, the property of Michel de Montaigne. A philosopher and a contemporary of Erasmus, Montaigne lived there in and around 1550. Both a legislator and a writer, he is famous for the *Essais* which he wrote about the nature of humanity. He did most of his writing in a tower that still exists today. Determined to fathom the puzzle of human knowledge, he posed to all of us the question '*Que-sais-je?* What do I know?' There on the wooden beams of his study, he inscribed his favourite quotations in

Greek and Latin. Nowadays you can visit the long, narrow study at the top of his tower in which he composed his thoughts while pacing up and down. So detailed was Montaigne that his writing reveals the dimensions of his tower as well as the views he held on human nature. Possibly because I was the daughter of a gendarme, I liked to think of myself as non-conformist and a committed anti-militarist. My friends knew I always resented the authoritative system of Gaullist France. I disapproved of it with all the might of a provincial, and of a student.

Within a few years, I was specialising in English at university. At the same time, having passed the French national diploma as a librarian, I was running a Bordeaux branch library, part-time. A good career start, in a disadvantaged suburb on the other side of Bordeaux's railway station.

Echanges culturels
Cultural exchanges

My mother explained to anyone visiting our home that she should never have let me go on my first overseas trip to Bristol in England. 'That's when I first lost her,' she said. She paused, waiting for the visitors to stare, and then she went on to blame the perfidious Albion. '*Mais enfin pourquoi l'Angleterre*? Why did it have to be England, of all places?' Finally she uttered her punchline. 'And there to meet an Englishman, an Englishman of all people! As if there weren't enough French men, and we didn't even know anything about him or his family!'

In fact, my parents' lack of information about my future husband was to become a great advantage. If the details were scant about his family, there was less opportunity for my mother's comments about him or his folks. And that scenario suited me. In my youth, there were times when the thought of growing any older in the town of Libourne was unbearable. A vision of countless countrified expanses of vineyards surrounding the town's twenty thousand 'odd' people, with me stranded in the middle of it all, recurred in my daily musings as a dreary image.

When I was about fourteen, my English school teacher took me aside. She suggested, probably because of my devotion to English as a subject, that I should apply for a grant to enable me to join the popular Bordeaux-Bristol school exchange that summer. Many of my friends had signed up but my parents had said we couldn't afford it. I also knew they weren't keen for me to go overseas. When they eventually agreed to sign the grant application form, I could hardly believe it.

That night, I overheard my mother muttering to my father, 'No need to worry. She'll never get it anyway!'

Although they knew I was top of the class, they weren't aware that my application held strong on other crucial criteria. It had ranked high because my parents received one modest income providing for the education of four children. When I heard I'd been successful for the grant, I was so happy to get a trip away from home that I concentrated on getting my mother on side. I didn't consider any of the other issues. But it turned out to be difficult to place me at such a late stage. I joined the group as a paying guest whose family would be allocated on arrival. I felt that added spice to the excitement.

As the destination was Bristol, that first trip to England involved going to Normandy by train via Paris, an all-day rail trip. We then took an overnight ferry to Southampton. Although there was a lot of giggling all night, some of the girls had long faces. Some were nervous about living with new people, others were concerned in case they didn't find the fashion items they liked and complained that English fashion and food were boring. I had never gone overseas before and I was excited and pleased that there'd me no one from my family remonstrating with me.

Stepping off the boat onto the English shore in the early morning after a cooped-up train and boat journey was liberating. As I grasped my first breath of fresh air in England, my heart skipped a beat. I was on an adventure. I'd meet new people and try my English on them. As I looked around, I saw the symbol of Britishness, my first English bobby. With a group of girls surrounding the friendly policeman, my first move in England was to use my best textbook phrase to ask him for directions.

Next, we all scrambled in a rush to take a seat on the British train that the policeman had pointed out to us. How different the closed-in carriages smelled! There was a whiff of must.

'What awful cushions, so faded!' someone said as I plonked myself onto one.

'Look at the dust coming off the cushions,' said one of the girls who had been quiet until then.

Then we all screamed and jumped on and off the seats. It became a great way of releasing some of the tension and impatience.

'Why isn't this train moving? We've been waiting forever! Come on, let's plonk down again!'

So during their first hour in England, a group of French youths had great fun giving British Rail seats a good airing. But things weren't so funny for me when, hours later, the train arrived at Bristol Temple Meads railway station.

All the students who had applied early had addresses and photos of their exchange friends. The teacher organiser had told my mother, who was genuinely concerned, not to worry if I didn't have a contact address on departure. They had explained to her that several of the French students usually pulled out of the scheme and there would be English families desperate to pick up a French girl!

To this day, I don't remember what exactly happened. While most people were leaving with excited shouts, I stood on the platform surrounded by people walking about bearing tiny passport photos and looking anxious. And suddenly Mrs Chick, her husband and their two children had their arms around me. My own teacher had spotted a family that had been looking for me. The Chick family had been on standby for a last-minute arrival, as it happened every year. Their daughter, Stephanie, who was to become my penfriend, told me to start smiling because I was going home with her family. I was relieved to hear that. Standing there on the railway station platform, I had been dreading the thought that I'd be the one who had to select a family to go and live with, rather than the other way around.

Staying at the Chicks was great fun. When it was time to write home, I used my very first aerogramme – a one-page threefold blue piece of unlined paper with gummed edges that you sealed before writing the address on. I found it very practical. It was prepaid and cheaper than a letter. You couldn't, however, enclose any photograph in it, but in those days I did not own a camera. I liked using aerogrammes because they were faster, and they helped me limit my letters to one page. I kept using them for about thirty years until I moved to Australia, where contact by phone was easier.

Within the first week, a small group of French students, including me, organised an outing to the city centre by ourselves. We further experimented with other quaint uses of the transport system in England. Getting on and off buses without meeting a conductor who sold you a fare was the favourite challenge of that day. Coming from France, we couldn't believe how trusting the British system was. I mentioned this to my family in my next missive! 'The English have great respect for the individual,' I wrote. 'They trust people will do the right thing, like pay for their bus ticket.'

I found English people to be warm and hospitable. Although most appeared reserved, once someone invited you in, they opened their homes to you. This view of a warm and welcoming England has always stayed with me, yet when she heard this, Nanou was surprised.

'What's wrong with you?' she added in a note at the bottom of my mother's reply. 'Everyone else hates life in England and complains about the English.'

My host family lived in a working-class suburb of Shirehampton, Bristol's port near the mouth of the Avon River. As I attended school with my exchange friend, we boarded the bus in the mornings, Stephanie wearing the school uniform's blazer. As most students did, we favoured the top deck of the standard double-deckers. From my position at the top, I felt I could observe the English lifestyle. I saw workmen, with boots and all, with grey duffel coats carrying odd-coloured duffel bags. But I was flabbergasted to see flasks of tea peeking out of them, definitely something to write home about. 'In England, they drink tea all the time and even the workmen take a flask of tea to work, and drink tea over lunch, instead of wine!'

That didn't fit in with the image of the French working-class man that I knew. I found out the men also carried in their bags cut sandwiches, which certainly wasn't what French workers ate on building sites. I couldn't possibly be nostalgic for the noisy catcalls and swear words French workmen sprayed the neighbourhood with! Sitting up on scaffoldings, they'd hold on to the neck of their one-litre bottle of *vin rouge*, ready to take a swig. I could still see their wide open Opinel knives, rounding the bread and cutting it thick, then slicing their *saucisson*, only to slide a piece off the edge of their blades, straight into their mouths! That night in my room, I felt surprise at a hankering for the aroma of garlic-smelling *saucisson*. With my peers, I used to make fun of the old-fashioned long-distance traveller who used to settle down for a picnic of bread, sausages and pickles for their lunch, usually on the slow train to Paris. 'How parochial!' we'd say. But for the first time I was to learn how to jostle between my identity in France and the reaction that this novel exposure to another culture triggered in me.

So when my English landlady served nasturtium seeds picked from the front garden because 'you can eat them, like cress, and I couldn't buy any mustard seeds anyway', I kept a straight face and ate them. Another food item I found strange but had to swallow was the only macaroni to be had in the house. It came out of a tin and was baked in milk. I thought it had a sweet and sickly taste. But I ate the macaroni-in-milk because I didn't want to be someone who criticised English cuisine to their host. I was consciously avoiding making derogatory comments that would mark me as chauvinist. Not so my exchange English penfriend. Stephanie came to stay with my family for a month the following year. Apparently when she was very young, her parents had come across the English Channel with some friends and stayed in northern France for a few days. They had found that they could always buy her some bananas and order some chips at cafés. Stephanie had grown up protected in quite insular surrounds and wasn't very keen to sample any food she called unusual. To my mother's chagrin, when she first arrived, she would only eat bananas and chips at meal times.

Several years later, Stephanie's family and their friends paid a visit to my family in France. They travelled in two camper vans en route to Spain. My mother was excited to have overseas visitors. She put on a spread of her best traditional Southern French dishes: homemade *pâté de foie gras truffé*, preserved *quartiers de canard* and her so-loved *salsifis-au-jus*, a field vegetable called oyster plant.

Stephanie's family was overwhelmed. Wanting to demonstrate how appreciative they were, the next day Stephanie and her mother arrived from their campsite with the surprise sweet they had secretly prepared the night before. There it was, a bright red jelly that wobbled, indecently, adding to the decor of our family table. My mother was so puzzled that I had to translate the step-by-step process involved in making a jelly. After they explained how it was made of only water and colouring, my mother looked at me asking, 'Why do they eat it?' Then as we all laughed I realised that Stephanie wasn't the only one who was chauvinistic about which food to eat! In the meantime, my father being typically French, hovered over them waving, out of habit, the bottle of wine to fill their glasses. But they preferred tea.

Although my parents were usually edgy meeting new people, they became friendly with the Chick family. Several years later, one of my brothers, Jean-Marie, exchanged with Stephanie's brother. My parents eventually enjoyed a visit to their home when we also later lived in Bristol for a while.

When I went on to study for an English degree, the University of Bordeaux strongly encouraged their students to spend a year in England, preferably towards the end of a Modern Language degree. So a few years later, I went back to England, this time to Northumberland, where I was appointed as an assistant teacher at Tynemouth High School. Contrary to the initial advice I had received from Stephanie, I was to find my year there thoroughly enjoyable.

On hearing I was posted to a school in north-eastern England, she had written that she was devastated on my behalf. 'Don't go up there, you won't catch a word of what they say. They speak Geordie. We can't even understand them ourselves!'

Part of my contract was to attend a university course. Every week I'd catch the bus to Newcastle University. I'd find a seat on the rickety double-deckers from Whitley Bay to Newcastle-on-Tyne, while the Geordie conductor called out, 'Hold tait, luv!'

I made a point of standing near the front platform long enough to make sure I heard the then unfamiliar phrase. At first I had asked a few people what the conductor shouted as the bus took off. I could only hear its intonation. Although it was in a different dialect of English, it reminded me of an earlier experience in my days in Bristol. On the first occasion, I had heard the newspaper caller saying, '*Evening News*!' at Temple Meads railway station and had found it just as difficult to decipher his words. Adapting to the change of accent was a challenge, but it didn't take me long and it was fun.

In France, it is often said the further south you go, the more friendly the people are. I had the idea that this applied in reverse to the United Kingdom. People are perceived to be more open and easygoing the further north you go. As if to confirm this, I did indeed meet some pretty chatty and extrovert people who hailed from Scotland! On occasions, my landlady took in extra lodgers at my digs in Whitley Bay. To my surprise once, during the annual event Geordies called Glasgow Week when the Glaswegians came for their summer holidays, I found the two visiting boarders at meal time couldn't always understand each other. At one stage of a conversation I had to explain to a Cornish guest what the visiting Glaswegian had said and vice versa. They both thanked me.

'Oh! You know, for me, one English is as good as another,' I said. When I added I didn't think English belonged to the Queen any more, I saw the Scotsman nod his assent.

I was a lodger in Whitley Bay under a one-year accommodation deal organised by my university in France. Although I identified as Catholic when filling in forms, I didn't expect to stay in a home with devout churchgoers. The landlady introduced herself and her family as Roman Catholics. I hadn't heard of this phrase before. The use of the English term Roman Catholic with an added emphasis on the link with Rome reminded me of the rare and overzealous parishioner often satirised in France for being papist. In England, it surprised me that even government-run schools held prayers and hymns centre stage on a daily basis during the assembly. Students were to leave the room if they didn't adhere to the official Protestant faith. I felt relieved to have had a very secular education.

While I was there, I met some Catholic people who were forthright about their faith. Feeling that the rest of the community was against them, they developed their own networks and socialised at weekends with fellow Catholics even outside of church. Compared to what I'd seen in France, I found some aspects of Catholicism in the UK followed rigorously. Walking into my landlady's home, the first thing I saw, on the wall of the entrance hall, was a framed Indulgence from a former pope, Pope Pius. I had only read that some Catholics applied for Indulgences to do their penance ahead of Purgatory. I had never seen one before and expected not to see them again because the current Pope, Paul VI, had made Indulgences the first target of his reform.

In the dining room, there was also a statue of the Virgin Mary on the ledge of the bay window. There, I shared my meals with the other regular tenant called Daniel who, like me, was an assistant teacher from France. He was a nonchalant, guitar-playing, long-haired French student with a tendency to swear. Every time he walked in for breakfast or evening tea, he would walk up to the statue and steadfastly turn it half circle to face outwards. He claimed eating was a demure occupation and he objected to anyone watching him at mealtimes. The landlady went in and out, acting as if she hadn't noticed the statue was facing away from the table. The idea of the Virgin Mary on punishment in a corner made me giggle for the rest of dinner. There was nothing demure about my love of non-conformism.

One night in 1965, I went to a party with some friends who were teachers. We were dancing to Beatles tunes. Going back to our seats, a group of us was still singing, 'I don't care too much for money'. Just then, the door opened and a young man came in from the cold. He was waving a witch's hat, a bright red traffic cone. He plopped it in the middle of the floor where people had started to dance again and called out, 'No standing!' to no one in particular. I was sure I hadn't met him before, yet I was staring at him. At that point, he looked around with a laugh and just seemed to catch my eyes as I smiled. What a cool and unconventional thing to do, I thought! I found this tall handsome man fascinating.

A little while later he sidled up to me. 'Do you come here often?' he asked.

'What a great pick-up line,' I said, and we both laughed.

This bearded witty teacher, whose pinched upper lip displayed a cheeky smile, made a strong impression on me. He seemed to know everyone there, as it was a teachers' party and he was in his first year teaching in one of the schools in Tyneside. By the end of the evening, we had danced together and enjoyed each other's company. I thought he had said his name was Peter Smith. The next day, in the staffroom, when I told a colleague I had met someone I was thinking of going out with, she asked me who he was. She warned me that I might never see him again, as she was sure he must have given me a phoney name!

I wondered if she could be right. I had just left France, where we heard of social events in England involving mad groupies. Alongside the already famous mindless football fanatics, the Teddy Boys with their odd antics and sartorial manners had just emerged. This for me was in sharp contrast to the composed world of English literature where Bertrand Russell and George Bernard Shaw had dominated my studies. I didn't think I was a likely judge of character.

But Peter (it turned out to be his real name) and his friends had studied at Durham and were avid listeners to the radio programme *The Goon Show*. They were followers of Spike Milligan and his sense of humour. Instead of mad groupies, I joined in with a band of young English people who were different. Together with a sharp sense of humour, they showed great awareness of people's personal space and of identity. In my mind, England has always been a country of extremes, between the controlled stiff upper lip and the Beatles unruliness. I was to find Peter belonged to neither of these. He was clearly a sort of British *enfant terrible*, the witty, tongue-in-cheek and verging on satirical type, and he still is.

We soon started to attend folk clubs held in pubs all over Tyneside. We sang top Irish classics like 'The black velvet band', soon to be re-launched by the Dubliners, and 'All around my hat', to be brought back to fame by Steeleye Span. There were Scottish and Geordie songs too. I loved 'Keep your feet still Geordie hinney!' It is amazing how, even now, I can sing Geordie songs with a Northumbrian accent while I revert to my French accent for everything else.

When we were going out, Peter always rang the front doorbell at my digs. After he had done this a few times, my landlord asked, 'This Peter Smith, does he like to drink?' I instantly recalled the multitude of glass jugs with no beer in them lining the table when we left the pub the night before. 'Oh, yes!' I said, perhaps too promptly. Peter with a bunch of his hefty English friends had scrambled out loudly singing their way to the door, and it wasn't till their bus arrived that the excitement abated. My landlord was acting as my guardian. So the following weekend when Peter rang the bell, he took him into the front room. I had assumed my landlord was going to give him a talking to about not drinking too much, like my father would have, but instead they shared a beer together! It turned out that he was checking to see if Peter was a decent bloke whom he could trust with a young French girl under his care.

Peter shared an old-fashioned apartment with three friends in the main street of Tynemouth. Large Victorian armchairs made it difficult to move around and the fireplace was the only other feature I remember. Surrounded by the Sunday papers and the armchairs, the wood fire gave a welcoming warmth to the room. It provided well-needed brightness to a room that neither the ceiling light bulb nor the dirty window onto the outside could supply.

Reading the newspaper was a social pastime then, as well as hanging around bookshops, a routine Peter and I followed for the next fifty years. All these are activities we have continued to share with discussions and arguments in contemporary Adelaide where we now live.

One of our routine outings was along the coast from Whitley Bay to Tynemouth, where the statue of Queen Victoria in full regalia menacingly glared at the sea, as if to repel the piercing winds. I am of the view that not even a majestic queen would be able to coax the winds from the North Sea into any kind of calmness. It seemed to whistle shrilly around me, stinging my face with its sharpness whenever I was outdoors.

We took train rides on the loop line to Newcastle past our favourite pub in Cullercoats. I still remember going to the Tynemouth All Electric cinema to see films that marked our generation, such as *War Games*. Another favourite outing was to take a bus ride to the prolific Newcastle People's Theatre. There we saw some of the plays by Beckett, Osborne and Pinter, who were at the height of their popularity. It amazed me that such avant-garde drama was available in a regional theatre. The same wasn't true at the time in France, a country that was still centralised in the 1960s. Quality performances were rarely performed outside Paris, and aspiring artists, my eldest brother included, had to migrate there to make a professional breakthrough.

I have fond memories of a special theatre event. One Saturday night, we travelled south to Sunderland. Until then, I'd only heard of Sunderland's football team, which everyone said didn't rank as well as Newcastle's. We arrived as people were pouring into a large baroque theatre – the Sunderland Empire. They were in groups chatting and calling out to each other. As far as I knew, I was attending a one-man stage show in a venue that was out of the way. Once inside, the high level of anticipation in the audience surprised me. I had only heard about Spike Milligan from Peter and his friends and thought I might have seen him once on television. The theatre was packed. As it went dark, people started giggling.

The only thing I could see was some sort of torch shining from under the curtain. I hadn't reckoned on the fame of this actor. Unlike the people around me, I couldn't predict his grimaces or postures or recognise the range of voices his radio listeners admired. I wondered why a comedian was shining a torch onto his audience as a warm-up to the show. These lighting effects continued for a while intercepted with sounds like, 'Oh', 'Ah' and 'Ooh Aah!' At that point, the whole room erupted into laughter and applause while I sat still looking for meaning on stage and for the curtain to rise. It took me a while to understand that Spike Milligan was a creative artist whose improvisations were his strength. Later, I became familiar with his quirky puns and his poetry which has entertained generations of adults and children. But at the time, I didn't think that Spike's humour was something to write home about.

At Tynemouth High School, there was another assistant teacher with me, Rosario, a Spanish girl who hailed from Madrid. We both taught conversation in our respective languages. Soon Rosario and I became inseparable. As she was a city girl, Rosario had been quite unhappy on arrival in Northumberland. She found it hard to adapt to the English climate and to life in England and so, by the time the Easter break came, we both decided we'd use the time to escape the rain and wind and get away from what Rosario had declared, with vehemence, to be the 'depressing structures of North England'. She had been told Ireland was a green country and she knew it had been associated with Spain through history. We decided to make our way to Ireland to find out more.

I was looking forward to visiting Ireland, yet I found it wasn't an easy feat, as we'd have to travel across England from east to west. Because we decided to hitchhike, Peter advised us to make our first port of call Lincoln. Lincoln was his home town and, as he'd be there over the Easter break, he suggested showing us around the cathedral. 'Best example of perpendicular architecture in Europe,' he said.

An invitation for a guided tour of Lincoln sounded good, and free accommodation even better. But staying at his home? I was glad that I had a friend travelling with me and that Peter had clearly not said it was about meeting his mother. We had no problem hitching a lift south on the A1 to Newark. Getting away from the A1 became a bit harder but we managed to find Lincoln.

In Lincoln, the old mediaeval Stonebow was still overarching a main street. It was part of Ermine Street, the old North Road, which went through Lincoln on a direct line from London to the city of York. The soaring Gothic Lincoln cathedral, with remaining Norman features, holding one of the original copies of Magna Carta, impressed us both. Lincoln's castle, dating back to the eleventh century, was still partly in use as a court. Further along, there was some action with students working on excavations. There had been a discovery of Roman remains while building a new underground car park, so the town council started to dig in the hope of finding more.

But Steep Hill has remained the symbol of Lincoln for me. I enjoyed walking down from the castle past shops that looked like tiny cottages with timbered fronts and low roofs. We darted in and out of booksellers and antique shops, some still displaying heraldic signs that illustrated their trade. Although built on a sharp incline, this narrow and crooked lane was a source of great fun. I loved skipping on the uneven cobblestones all the way downhill.

It was the first time I had spent time with Peter without his circle of friends. Having one-on-one time with him was exciting. We walked hand in hand, beaming with happiness to be together in this beautiful town.

Not even Rosario, who walked ahead of us, could spoil this with her mumbling about miserable England. 'I could never live in this country,' she said. 'Look at this! It's already dark, and it isn't even four o'clock.'

She turned to look at us and we burst out laughing. Life was great.

Peter reminded us it was teatime and his mother had invited a few people to join us. When we got to the house, it was sandwich-making time, so I offered to help. Of course, I could butter bread. But how much butter do you put on bread and what do you do with a sticky slice of buttered bread? Place it on top of another one? But it will get butter on its underside! What will I do next with this pile of slices in front of me? Rosario had been very wise, saying she didn't know how to prepare sandwiches and she'd just watch. It was a relief when Margaret, Peter's sister, offered to take the pile of bread off my hands to do the filling. Talking to Peter's mother had been no problem, but from then on, I developed a mental block against buttering bread.

Although I was enjoying my time in Lincoln, Rosario was anxious to get to Ireland, which after all was our plan. To get across the country to the Irish Sea wasn't going to be easy. We organised railway tickets as far as Liverpool. Once in Ireland, we reasoned the real adventure would start again – we'd hitchhike and stay in youth hostels and generally enjoy our holidays.

Off the train at Liverpool, I went to ask a local bobby, 'Which way to Ireland?'

His repartee was quick. 'Straight ahead, luv.'

The English were funny and kept a straight face, I thought, for all occasions.

There was a ferry docked at the port but it could take us only as far as the Isle of Man.

'Great,' we said!

It was only after we disembarked on the Isle of Man that we understood the full restrictions associated with our ferry trip. The ferry line didn't operate out of the Isle of Man to Ireland until after Easter. Our only options were to ferry back to Liverpool or fly out to Belfast. Given our time constraints, we decided we'd just fly. There was no time to visit the island. We sat down that night and added up our many coins and the few banknotes we had in order to start the next leg of our adventure.

In the morning, we got up much earlier than we ever did during the holidays. We knew we'd have to hitchhike to the airport, as the fare for the flight had exhausted our funds. We stood on the road to the Ronaldsway airport thumbing a lift and smiling. Hitchhiking at the time was accepted in the British Isles, and yet gradually it occurred to us something was wrong with our plan. It appeared that the Manx people on their way to an airport don't pick up passengers, even when it rains.

Walking in the rain to the airport was long and distressing, but the most miserable part was having to drag our luggage with us. We arrived so late that we just had time to climb onto the aircraft dripping wet. It was so embarrassing. The other passengers had embarked. I made a point of not looking at them in case they jeered at us. In the 1960s, travel by air with a backpack and sports gear, compounded by being late and drenched, was unusual. The passengers all appeared to be be business people sitting up, strapped in and ready to start their busy days.

Rosario followed me into the aircraft.

As we sat down, I said, 'Look at these lucky people. They didn't get wet like us.'

My voice resounded and heads turned to look at us. That didn't make me feel any better. One person hadn't looked. The sight of the back of the head of a well-groomed fur-coated lady with hair daintily pinned up sitting just in front of me seemed incongruous. It helped to release my tension. I burst out into uncontrollable laughter made worse when Rosario joined in. We couldn't land in Belfast soon enough!

We were desperate to stop in town for a cup of coffee but we couldn't find anything open. It was early on a Sunday morning in a town where all public venues were shut. Everyone was meant to be at church. It was the first time I discovered that religion did interfere with the pleasures of life.

Our journey had started so strangely that we were able to laugh it off. We managed to find a bed and breakfast. On seeing one of the pamphlets on display, we decided to visit the impressive and massive Giant's Causeway further north. On our return, we got a lift into a town we hadn't heard of. When we arrived in Lisburn, people said it was the start of the Easter season.

Many towns in Northern Ireland held parades that commemorated historical dates and religious clashes associated with the rivalry of Catholics and Protestants. We had just missed the march but could see people milling about. There were drums and uniformed people of all ages. Everyone seemed to gather around those carrying bagpipes. In contrast with the deserted landscape on our arrival in Belfast, Lisburn was a lively place. There were people going in and out of shops but we were unable to find a space to sit down anywhere. Again we started looking for a cup of coffee. Impatient as ever, I thought I'd ask for directions to a quiet spot. We stopped a few people in the street. The response was negative and clearly we were unlikely to find one.

'Are there any other streets with cafés still open?' I asked.

'Yes,' finally a young man said, 'there is one more but it's full too.'

I watched him suspiciously. 'How do you know?' I asked.

'I've just left that queue over there,' he said pointing to another noisy crowd around the corner.

More people were lining up on the pavement nearby.

'Would you like a lift to my place for a coffee?' he asked. 'My mum makes good coffee.' He paused. 'We live on the outskirts of town but I could give you a lift there and bring you back.'

The idea sounded good, although strange and unexpected. He seemed genuine. We bravely agreed to get in his car. Although amazed by the hospitality, we didn't in fact have coffee there at all. By the time we arrived at his house, it was lunchtime. He had a large family. They were very nice people and insisted we stayed for lunch. We all enjoyed a homemade pie and mashed potato and gravy, and good conversation.

Given the tension that we had heard existed between Northern Ireland, Eire and England, all of which Rosario and I were visiting, we felt the very warm welcome we received everywhere remarkable. No one asked us about religion that day and we didn't ask them either. I still treasure the day as one of the most memorable episodes of unconditional hospitality.

Eventually this young man, whose name I have ungratefully forgotten, kept his word. He gave us a lift back through town and out of the city to the main artery that led to Eire, where we planned to keep hitching lifts for Dublin.

Hitchhiking across Ireland was strange, especially in the company of Rosario, who once took offence to the innocuous question a driver politely put to her. 'Are you from Madrid?'

Rosario turned in my direction and whispered. 'Why is he asking if I'm married?'

I was uneasy. A suspicious tone leading to a double entendre insinuation wasn't appropriate, I thought. At that point, I resolved to take the front seat the next time we got a lift. From then on, I took over the conversation about where we came from until we arrived in Dublin's Fair City.

I had been asked by some of my English friends, or foes, depending on the outcome, to go to O'Connell Street and ask the directions to Nelson's Column.

The woman at the newsagent hesitated. Then she replied sternly, 'Nelson's Column? Oh! It went boom!' she said.

Some of the customers in the shop stared at us while others appeared to scan their newspapers intently.

The 1966 bombing of Nelson's Column by republicans has remained of significance to both the Irish and the British. So we veered off history questions and Rosario didn't get to explore how close the seafaring relationship between Spain and Ireland had grown in previous centuries.

Before we left Ireland, which we both enjoyed for its greenness and cordiality, I declared our visit had been a pleasurable adventure with two exceptions. One was when it snowed outside Dublin at Easter, and the other was the most embarrassing and frustrating experience of not being able to understand a word of the question that a kind man from Cork driving a cart and horse had asked us. He was giving us a lift into Killarney. I was sitting next to him. He asked something. I asked him to repeat his question. For someone who was proud to practise speaking English all the time (and better than Rosario), this was a blow. I couldn't make out any of the sounds from his utterance. After he repeated it for a third time, I totally lost all confidence in my knowledge of English and withdrew from my naturally expansive mannerisms. Dejected, I sat in absolute silence all the way to Killarney, and nobody else said a word after that. The man from Cork had, however, understood us and he dropped us off just at the place where you could hire bicycles to go around the lake. Our stay there was great. Circling the water by bike across green expanses of grass was definitely to Rosario's liking. I eventually cheered up.

Our final stop in Ireland was to be the unmissable tourist spot of the Blarney Stone near Cork. My friends had said I didn't need to go there as I already had the gift of the gab, but I figured a kiss of the stone wouldn't hurt Rosario!

Eventually we left Ireland via North Wales. We chose to take the ferry to Holyhead as it was the shortest crossing distance. We had done very little research into travelling to Ireland, or back to the United Kingdom. Hence, our return passage to England revealed more unexpected discomfort. Unbeknown to us, the crossing is famous for being a rough strait of sea, so we had to submit to the sea's harrowing moods and motions. Massive waves pounded the boat and crashed over the front of the boat as well as over the sides. Even when the ferry was approaching England, the sea pounded the rocks so hard that we could only see walls of water before us. The water overlapped with such force that no matter how we attempted to disembark, we were drenched. It was so bad that Rosario and I changed our original complaint and claimed we longed to be back in cold, windy north-eastern England!

Un Anglais!
An Englishman!

On one of our walks between Whitley Bay and Tynemouth, Peter asked me to marry him. I had suspected he might and wondered what I would say. I was in love with him, but I wanted to make a decision that was also rational. A closeness had developed between us. The growth of our relationship was becoming obvious to us and those around us, yet we had only known each other for less than a year.

A normally impulsive person, I surprised him when I said I wasn't sure yet. I told him I felt it was a bit early to make such a decision and I had to think about it. Peter (and my children-to-be) were to realise later that when facing the more complex options in life, I always start my answer with a 'no' first. It allows me some space to consider any issue of importance. Perhaps not the best of ploys, but a strategy of sorts. Soon after, and I think it was on the very next day, I gave him the reply he had hoped to get: I would marry him. I felt my heart start pumping again, and a revival of my dulled senses, and we couldn't wait to start to make plans for the future.

Before we met, Peter had committed to spend a year overseas as a volunteer. Meanwhile, I needed to return to Bordeaux to finish the last unit of my degree. We decided that our separation couldn't last more than a year. So it became an easy decision to make. Although we would have a year apart, we decided that we'd get married in France when he returned the following summer. I was happy because it gave us another year to get to know each other, although our relationship would have to progress via letter writing instead.

Peter gallantly offered to write to my parents. I mentioned that writing to them might not be the best option and that he might have to meet my family in France. People in those days didn't travel as much as we do now. Neither of us had any money and no concrete plans were made. We also discussed the fact our marriage would be across two cultures. Peter, forever the historian, pointed out that our two countries had been at war for about nine hundred years. I said that wouldn't worry my parents, but their not knowing any English was more of a handicap.

The completion of my year in Tyneside was looming and I had to leave England by the start of summer. Although it was very hard for both of us, we trusted each other and went our separate ways. This sudden parting marked the start of a long written exchange between us that lasted a whole year. Peter and I had rejected the flimsy aerogramme and replaced it with the tiny postcard-size airmail envelopes of the day into which we had difficulty fitting folded pages of handwritten foolscap paper.

Peter's volunteer contract was with the British branch of Service Civil International (SCI) and he hadn't received any further information about which part of Africa he'd be posted by the time I left. Within a month, a letter came saying he was to lecture at a teacher's college in the west African country of Cameroon. Peter was also happy to announce that by chance Service Civil International was running a one-month volunteers' training camp in the French Pyrenees, on the border with Spain, not too far from my home. I was delighted and he said he'd try to visit my parents and me one weekend in September before they flew him back to London and out to west Africa. I was elated and couldn't wait to tell my mother.

When I mentioned this development to her, my mother looked away. 'I'm not sure if foreigners are allowed to stay at a gendarmerie,' she said.

Early one Sunday morning, my father was home shaving, and heard a knock on the door. One of his colleagues, the duty gendarme, was at the door.

'Phone call from the other office. They've got an Englishman over there. They reckon he wants to speak to your daughter,' he said.

My father asked which one, knowing neither of his daughters was at home that weekend. Because I hadn't heard from Peter about his intended trip, I'd gone to see Nanou in Bordeaux for the weekend. I didn't really think he'd be so brave as to appear at my parents' door. I was wrong. Peter had left his camp in the Pyrenees on the Saturday. He had caught a train to Bordeaux, not knowing that I was at my sister's.

My father called out to my thirteen-year old brother, who had just got up. 'Jean-Marie, bring your English dictionary and let's go over there, now!'

They drove to the old gendarmerie across town.

Although telephones existed in those days, they were neither portable nor accessible and the only number Peter had was my parents' in Libourne. His train arrived late at Bordeaux. He was to find that there was no further connection for the next thirty kilometres to my hometown of Libourne that night.

Peter learnt fast about French cultural habits. First he had left his passport at the camp for safekeeping, not realising that in France people needed to carry their identification all the time. Then he saw police patrolling the railway station area asking for identity cards. He didn't have any other form of identity on him, which was common among English people. Wandering outside the railway station, he pondered renting a room, only to find prostitutes hovered outside the doors of railway hotels, which they used as brothels. Anyway, he didn't have enough money on him to rent a hotel room and couldn't have done that without identification.

As a result, he spent the night roaming the streets of Bordeaux. He figured a middle-of-the-night telephone call was hardly the best way to introduce himself to his future father-in-law. He had a sleepless night wandering tactically around to avoid the *agents de police*, the prostitutes and the homeless, who he said had lamented his lack of money on several occasions. In the early morning, he took the first train that brought him, unshaven and with sore feet, to the steps of the old gendarmerie, the police barracks where we used to live in the

1950s. He wasn't to know there were two gendarmeries in Libourne, and he had gone to the wrong one.

My father, my brother and his dictionary eventually made their way back to our gendarmerie with Peter. I have never had any detailed information about my mother meeting Peter for the first time. I imagine that they shook hands and that she went back to the kitchen pretending he wasn't there.

My father, on the other hand, swung into action and enjoyed making an early-morning phone call to Nanou's flat in Bordeaux. He was fully aware that both his daughters loved to sleep in on weekends. Nanou's telephone was an old black heavy contraption with a hearing device, called *l'écouteur*, that could be detached to allow another person to listen in to the conversation. We woke up to hear our father proceeding to give us instructions for the day. We were to stay put, he said. He added they were coming over with my two young brothers, Jean-Marie and four-year-old François. They were bringing that Englishman, Peter! I had my ear stuck to *l'écouteur* and my face lit up at the thought that Peter was at my parents' and that they were accommodating his wish to visit me. He then said they'd pick us up at Nanou's flat before noon. We'd all have to pile in with them – the days before seat belts – as they planned to go to a beach for lunch.

Much later, Peter told me of the intense flurry of activity that ensued at my parents'. It consisted of my father finishing his shave, then him lending Peter some of his shaving cream and a razor. In the meantime, my mother apparently had rushed into the kitchen and started to boil some eggs for a picnic. She then sent Jean-Marie and Peter to buy a couple of baguettes at the *boulangerie*. Meanwhile, my father went to buy fuel so that the car was ready for a return trip to Arcachon via Bordeaux. The journey wasn't much more than two hundred kilometres return, but he felt he also had to check the oil. The car was a square-shaped Peugeot which Peter said was used as a popular taxi in Cameroon. I still think it was bizarre to see them all arrive at Nanou's with Peter beaming away despite suffering from sunburn from the first week of his camp. I felt so sorry for him because he only had a woollen pullover to use over the blisters on his arms.

From Bordeaux, we drove to Le Bassin d'Arcachon in no time. My father seemed proud to give Peter a guided introduction to this famous haven off the Atlantic coast. A safe holiday destination, it is a large bay area well known for its quality oyster farming. Of course, he was unaware that Peter had never tasted oysters before. Next we went to one of the worst ever picnic venues on top of the Dune du Pilat, where people always end up eating more sand than bread. This, however, was a popular spot. The height of fun for children consisted of rolling up and down its sandy one hundred-metre-high banks. I have often thought this landmark would erode under the numerous visitors' footprints. Recently, I watched video segments posted on YouTube for posterity. People are using this natural two-kilometre-long sandy space for paragliding and other acrobatics.

The following year was strange. I was busy finishing my degree at the University of Bordeaux, and Peter was in Cameroon teaching African history and geography. Our relationship became an intensive year of writing love letters to each other. My mother was disappointed she couldn't read them and my friends at uni rushed to bring me my mail so they could claim the colourful Cameroonian stamps.

I also started working on the paperwork and plans for our marriage. I took on the responsibility of getting all Peter's documents translated, because the French administrative requirements are strict and complex. I had to have all the translations certified and formally accepted by the equivalent of a justice of the peace. Each transaction was costly and because Peter was overseas I had to pay for all the paperwork for our marriage contract. I like to say that I paid for him and haven't asked him for a refund. To my surprise, the paperwork in triplicate was less hassle than obtaining contraceptives. But it was more expensive.

The era when Peter and I first met in the north-east of England was what people still consider the adventurous 60s. Peter and I have now spent decades together and we still don't think they were special.

The only major advantage of the era, I felt, was that the contraceptive pill came on the market and was accessible in the UK, although not so readily in France. There, anyone wanting to be on the pill had to satisfy a range of medical criteria. You needed to find a medical practitioner to prescribe it, and you had to have given birth to at least two children to qualify. French women, like all women, shared information by word of mouth. There in the confines of the kitchens where men of that generation never thought of disturbing them, they passed on the names, phone numbers and addresses of doctors who were approachable. Fortunately there were a few doctors who were willing to write prescriptions for the contraceptive pill. I nicknamed them 'the underground network of Catholic doctors'.

I felt the scientific reasoning of some medical practitioners who happened to be Catholic had won over their personal adherence to religious dogmas. I thought that Catholic believers were becoming more flexible and making adjustments to meet their modern needs. At the time it was hoped that with Pope Paul VI phasing Latin out of the Catholic Church because it was outdated, he'd also allow the use of contraception in a more modern church context. In the heady 60s, the whole world was expecting a pope's encyclical to ratify the use of the contraceptive pill, and it still is. It hasn't happened but I suspect many Catholics have acted as if it had.

With the changes of the Fifth Republic, General de Gaulle, as president, announced incentives to achieve a population of one hundred million 'Frenchmen' by the year 2000. Not everyone embraced this wishful population explosion plan despite the financial bonuses to families. At a time when the state and the church seemed to be in line with one another, individuals started to resent the outside interference of the church on the ever increasing population. In fact, I personally opted to get the pill while in England and then to marry my English husband in France, because it meant fewer constraints on me.

Peter and I both decided the ceremony should be a low-key event, partly because we didn't have any money, also because of our ambivalence about church and formal occasions. We didn't want a large wedding, and ended up with about fifteen people. We already knew Peter's mother couldn't come over to France. She had never travelled overseas before and it was an expensive journey. So Peter had written from overseas to tell his family and his friends he was off to France to get married and we'd try to catch up after summer. He invited a friend from France whom he had met in Cameroon, the only person on the groom's side, as his best man.

Peter, a non-practising Methodist, had agreed to a wedding in a Catholic church. With the support of an ex-school chaplain, we composed a service with readings of our choice, doing away with Saint Paul's misogynist text from the Corinthians, about women having to remain silent. We chose a non-conformist format that Peter referred to as a 'hymn sandwich'. It consisted of a Bible reading either side of each hymn. This was very different from the usual service but it wouldn't worry my family, as no one but me, a casual churchgoer, attended church. The changes in the Catholic Church had passed them by. Yet my grandfather was quick to remark that the priest neither spoke Latin nor squirrelled money off us.

Our wedding day was undramatic up to a point. Peter remembers how at ten o'clock one Saturday morning we went into the smaller side altar at l'Eglise St Jean in Libourne while the main aisle was being arranged for a funeral ceremony. In fact, the priest had explained to me that the coffin would arrive before we did so as not to disturb our event. But my uncle, who had been smoking outside, opened the door to the main aisle, and at the sight of the coffin swiftly retraced his steps to the side door to find us.

Next, because in France marriage requires a state signing ceremony, separate from any religious service, we made our way to the imposing entrance of the Libourne Town Hall. There, we stood and waited at the steps of the Mairie while a clerk asked if we had paid extra for a traditional trail of laurel leaves. This leafy streak was one metre long under the imposing archway to the modern double sliding door. We weren't aware of the option and we certainly had not paid extra. We stood and waited while we watched the clerk call for the duty officer. His job was to sweep the leaves off from under our feet and place them against the wall of the archway.

We entered the mayor's chambers and a display of antique furnishings, wall hangings and assorted swords surrounded us. But the real formality of the event struck me when the assistant to the mayor appeared in a tricolour sash to perform a swift wedding ceremony. As we left, Peter and I found it funny to watch the same duty officer outside, broom in hand, busily sweeping the same old leaves back on to the arch's path for a couple who had paid for a trail of leaves while they stood waiting to go in to get married.

My parents chose a nice country restaurant for the reception and I was relieved that no one noticed I had forgotten to comb my hair that morning. The only other drama was that there was apparently an earthquake in south-west France that night. We never noticed.

In spite of our massive one-year correspondence, I didn't realise at first how much Peter's French had improved. Our relationship had started in English, and that had become our language of communication. I was very happy with that, as I just liked speaking English. At the end of a year in Cameroon, where some volunteers were French-speaking, Peter's fluency in French had progressed radically. It was unfortunate, I felt, that it allowed him to follow the lecture my father chose to give him on the perils of dealing on a daily basis with this *têtue* daughter of his, the stubborn one!

As a newly married couple, we rented our first home in north-east England, back among the Geordies, in winter. The house was located in Whitley Bay and we rented the second floor of a house from the owner who occupied the ground floor. There were top-floor tenants whom we never saw but we heard a lot. The freezing wind from the North Sea howled across the town and the bitter cold caused the clothes to freeze when I left them hanging to drip dry over the sink. After the owners explained we were entitled to weekly access to the bath, we realised the onus was on us to purchase a bag of coal for the landlady to heat up the water. Thursday was our day and the English stereotype of the once-a-week bath became a reality for me, yet not a pleasure as the bath water was never hot enough. Using an electricity meter came as another shock. The control was in the room and it used power by the shilling. You had to organise enough coins to match the type of current you needed every time you were in the house. At any time that you were not watching out for it, power would get cut.

In friendly Northumberland, I worked in a public library where I had to answer the telephone as 'This is Mrs Smith speaking.' With my French accent, phonetically that was nearly as much of an ordeal as the sibilant tongue twister 'She sells seashells on the seashore.' I was proud to take on the challenge at Gateshead public library. But as I mangled 'Zees eez Miseez Smees speaking' on the enquiry line, I puzzled over the reasons that made women do away with their maiden names.

As a child in a large family, I always feared I wasn't being heard, and I felt my views were mostly ignored, hence my efforts to be funny to at least be noticed. This need to be heard recurred after I moved into the Anglo-Saxon world through my married and travelling life. At socials, I tried to catch on quickly to the topics under discussion. I liked to join in but sometimes my responses were like an afterthought to the conversation. I was always slightly out of touch with my comments yet I became quite at ease with my new personality. I had spent my youth looking for acceptance, challenging the authorities and wanting to be different. In the English-speaking world, I didn't have to boast about how different I was because I was as un-English as my accent.

The challenges of my life became more demanding, with longer-term decisions to make. Life in west Africa had been fun for Peter. I had heard his stories of camaraderie as well as makeshift resourcefulness in the classroom. When he returned, Peter had applied for a position as a fully fledged teacher in Africa, a posting which came under the British government scheme to support its ex-colonies.

When we heard that Peter's teaching job was to be in Zambia, I knew how unusual our next move was because I knew little of the country. It was newly independent and its name had changed from Northern Rhodesia. Even in England, there were no more than three books about Zambia that we could find in either libraries or bookshops. Atlases were the best source of information. I enjoyed all the preparations during the few months before I left the cold, temporary flat I had come to resent.

Peter and I had one last visit to France to farewell my family before we set off. It was important to say goodbye to some of my friends. It felt strange seeing them again. In fact, I had a bizarre experience when saying goodbye in France. One of my ex-university friends called in to see me.

'*Je pars en Zambie*,' I said to her.

'Oh!' she asked. '*Tu pars samedi*? You're leaving on Saturday?'

The word Zambie was so unfamiliar to her that she reinterpreted it as *samedi*. I felt it was quite a misunderstanding between friends who were speakers of the same first language. '*En Zambie*' and '*samedi*' weren't connected. The confusion, however, was from someone looking for meaning, expecting a date of departure and making out that meaning from the sound she had heard. I learnt from this that in the search for meaning, good pronunciation isn't always the cause of errors or inaccurate interpretation. A lack of familiarity with the information can also be a serious handicap in communication. Later I found this was a common feature for second-language speakers of English.

Leaving France for the second time since I got married wasn't so distressing for me. My parents and siblings, who were the ones staying behind, felt the separation more acutely than me and I didn't understand at the time what removing myself from my home country for several years meant. Nor did I realise until six years later that my youngest brother, François, who was only six years old at the time, had cried to see me go. My mother and I wrote to each other using the now almost defunct aerogramme quite regularly but she only told me about my brother's sadness much later. François explained recently to me that the reason he cried as a child was because our mother was deeply saddened and tearful at my departure. I believe them both now that I have had to let go of my own children and I have a fuller understanding of separation myself. I have also come to terms with my origins and admitted to a strong attachment to my south-western French personality.

Zambia

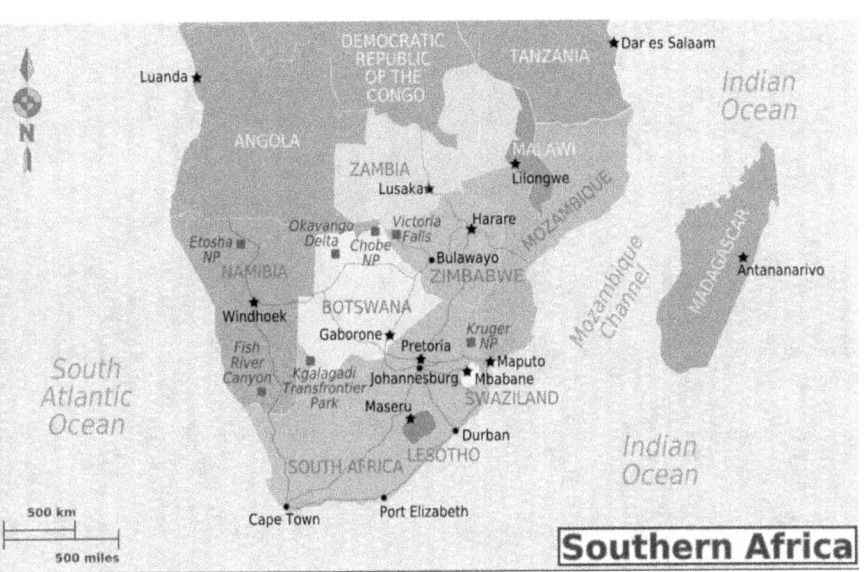

Southern Africa including Zambia.
(https://wikitravel.org/en/Southern_Africa)

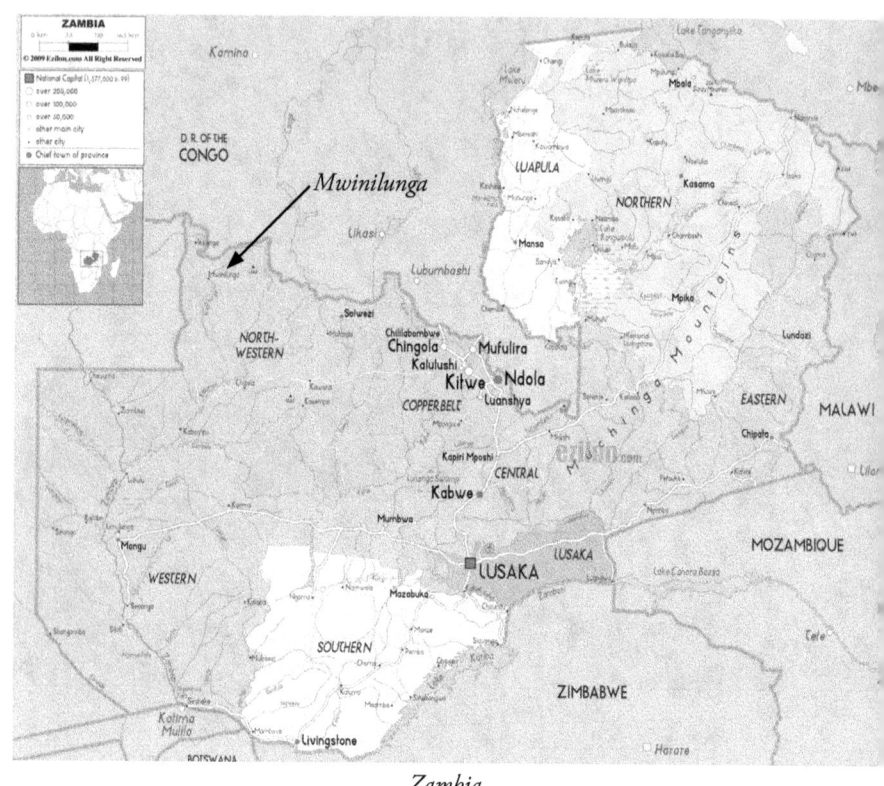

Zambia.
(http://www.ezilon.com/maps/africa/zambia-maps.html)

En brousse
Life in the bush

The sun and the sounds of daybreak woke me up. It was early one Tuesday morning in February. Cheering at our passing truck, small groups of children, silhouetted against the dust, were racing along and chanting. We were on the way to Mwinilunga, a small Zambian town located five hundred kilometres away from the sealed roads of the copper mining centres. We had left Zambia's main copper belt town, Ndola, the day before and had been on the road for one day and one night. We had journeyed deep into the north-western province of Zambia, Solwezi, its regional capital, a few hours behind us.

We had yet to see our school. Sitting between Peter and the driver in the front cabin, I could hear our suitcases rattling on the back of the truck. A pile of school desks and some office equipment held them jammed behind us.

Straddling the crown of the corrugated road with skill, the Zambian driver rode over the ridge of sand creating dust clouds behind him. He managed to wave in the direction of the scores of children hailing us from the edge of the road. The sound of their voices echoed the excitement I felt as I sat in the morning sun warmed by the brightness of my early-morning vision. Then there was a lull and the children seemed to have disappeared. One of the many tracks that led to a primary school, although hardly visible to us from the truck, had swallowed them and their happy sounds into the nearby bush.

'Not far now. Take a look at that bridge. What a hazard! Many have fallen off their bikes and died in this river,' the driver said, 'and there was a terrible car accident last year. A new doctor, the poor man just arrived from India! He drove off here and drowned.'

Dumbstruck, we stared, first over the lack of parapet, then at the derelict tracks ahead. The two main planks across the platform needed securing and there were gaps between those and the next section of planks. Serial loose bolts protruded upwards through some of the perished wood. A train would've derailed, but not our driver, who made his truck hurdle across to the other side. He was anxious now to deliver us, and his goods, to our destination, Mwinilunga Secondary School.

We knew the school year had started without us. Stranded in Lusaka for a fortnight, we had endured an impatient wait for an education department truck that was due to take us to our school with some supplies. But there had been some delays. What an anticlimax for Peter and me after months of expectation! Ready to go and teach in a remote Zambian government school, we had despatched some of our luggage by sea ahead of us before catching a British Airways flight from London to Lusaka.

While we were there, some newspaper headlines had startled me. I read that there had been a student revolution back in France. How I wish I'd been part of the action, digging up the cobblestones with my friends! But our lift arrived the next day and took my mind off what was happening in Europe.

I felt we had progressed well along our bumpy, lengthy trip. We were very close to the end. Safely past the bridge, the driver had put his foot down and our truck wobbled as it overtook a long bus spewing dust in all directions. On its rack, next to boxes and trunks, stood a heap of bread loaves, tied with a rope over a dusty cloth, which flapped in the slipstream.

'You've made it on time for this week's bread,' the driver said. 'Lucky it didn't rain yesterday. Make sure to get a loaf today before the shop runs out.'

I eventually worked out that the amount of mould in the sliced bread was a fair measure of rain precipitation in Zambia's north-western province.

I went quiet for a change, trying to imagine the kind of shops that I'd find there. But the sight of some huge anthills diverted my attention. It started with a large quantity of rugged brown mounds appearing on one side of the road. Then when you thought they were gone, a single mound of a lighter hue of brown broke the low-lying landscape. This time it was as pointed and tall as if it was a tree and yet resembled a man-made sculpture.

Before I could ask questions about these anthills, the driver had dismissed them as 'Just old termite piles, full of soil,' and, pointing ahead, he called, 'Here is the *boma*.'

The administrative headquarters was a low unassuming office block that looked like a community centre. A few green bushes sticking out from the red beaten earth contrasted with an array of purple flowers jutting over a signpost in all directions. I'll never forget that first view of a Mwinilunga bougainvillea. I found both its colour and shape enchanting.

'Of course, you've missed the start of the rains. But you'll soon make up for that now, plenty to come yet,' Mr Sutton-Smith, the deputy headmaster of Mwinilunga Secondary School, said as he showed us around the school premises which were to become our new environment. Past the office block perched on a rise there were two rows of classrooms facing each other.

'Wait till you taste the flying ants at dusk,' he said. 'They're quite a delicacy around here and, by the way,' he added, 'make sure you buy enough spare mantles for your Tilley lamp.'

Although I could understand his words, I couldn't make out how what he said related to me.

'Mind you don't slip on the mud! We're still building part of the school,' he said. 'Make sure you step on the stone path here…'

Further over, between a brown patch and some very green grass, I could make out a blank wall.

He pointed in its direction. 'We've nearly completed the girls' dormitories,' he said.

I started to wonder where the girl students slept in the meantime, and I felt sorry for them before ever meeting any of them.

Next, Mr Sutton-Smith said he had found a house for us. He proudly listed the facilities we were to expect: running water, a kerosene fridge, a Tilley lamp, a wood stove, furniture – beds, tables and some chairs. At that point, he explained how cutting wood and lighting the stove was necessary for hot water, cooking or boiling a kettle. He added that the fire in the wood stove had to be roaring before you could have a hot shower. Then he uttered another of his puzzling statements. 'Anyway, you'll have a queue of people who want to cut wood, keep the stove going and cook for you outside your house first thing in the morning.'

How would all these people know where to go before we had even been to the house? So I asked him what he meant. He explained that we were strongly expected to employ a servant he called a houseboy from within the African community. He said it helped the local economy. He confused me further by saying there were no schedules of rates for their wages, however.

The next day, someone told me of the putzi fly that sometimes laid eggs into all clothes that had been placed outside to dry. The larvae then burrowed into the skin. The only solution was to use a hot iron on clothes. At that stage, I purchased a charcoal iron and handed the housework over. Unlike Mémée, who could wedge a log and bring an axe down on it, I was committed to going out teaching during the day. So I swallowed my reluctance to follow the colonial model and employed a servant. I believe it worked out well. Melleck worked for a wage that included leave pay whenever we were away. He worked for us for six years. No matter how much I tried to minimise it, I always felt guilty that it was exploitative of him and his family,

And getting used to the lack of electricity wasn't too hard. We supervised the homework evening class by Tilley lamps. We marked by candlelight at home, often handing students back their workbooks with wax-stained pages as well as coffee marks. All the teachers lived on the school campus in houses clustered and situated just past the classrooms and dormitories. Two years after our arrival, a generator was installed for the whole compound and power came on after dusk from about six and went out at nine. It took me a while to get used to light switches again.

Mwinilunga was so remote from the centre of government in Lusaka that both our combined salaries were delayed, Peter's by six months and mine by a whole year. Our first year at school wasn't easy, as we had to run a debt at the local mission store. We survived the year mainly by living off a diet of rice and corned beef. They were cheap goods and were always available at the store. Of all the shortages we endured in our life overseas, a lack of fresh food and of reading matter were the worst. It was true, however, that we pined for books more than for fruit and vegetables, all of which we found difficult to obtain where we lived. These for us were worse deficiencies than the lack of electricity.

Our dental health was another casualty of our remote lifestyle. In the village close to the *boma* was the government clinic. A low elongated house, it had been converted into a primary health centre. Peter had a tooth abscess one day and the new Dutch doctor there had to extract one of his molars without anaesthetic. That was a first for Peter and a few days later the doctor told Peter that pulling the tooth had been a first for him too.

These were remarkable events. Small issues also, like my termite mounds queries, were resolved over time. Some adventurous person dug out a hole in one termite hill and made it into a baking oven. This became our local bakery. That, I felt, was appropriate technology, but the experiment only lasted a year. Good for our taste buds!

Zambia had been independent for a few years and Dr Kenneth Kaunda led the country as the first president. He was the founder of Zambian Humanism, a type of African socialism. He was respected and the Zambian people we worked with often expressed their pride in their country and its aims. I am still in awe remembering how the students sang the national anthem so well in front of President Kaunda when he visited our school that he promised the school a piano. One year later, sandwiched between the weekly supplies at the back of a truck was a piano. A truck driver spotted it on the road and sent word of its arrival ahead.

'The man's kept his word. The piano's on its way!' the students chanted.

Down the road and up the hill was the head office of Plymouth Brethren missionaries. In colonial times, they had established a chain of stations along the slave route through Angola and into the ex-Belgian colony of Congo. It passed through the far north-western corner of Zambia, at the source of the Zambezi. They had set up a boarding school past the source of the Zambezi near Kolwezi in Congo-Kinshasa. It took in the children of all Plymouth Brethren missionaries across the borders of Angola, Zaire (the new name for Congo-Kinshasa, later changed to DR Congo) and Zambia. At independence, the missionaries, anxious to keep their contact with the Zambian population as well as their commitments to neighbouring countries, had retained a base in Zambia, where the mission continued to offer services in and around the area.

The Ikalene hospital, where our son was born, was situated at the source of the Zambezi. At Mwinilunga, there was a mission shop and the mission headquarters. The latter consisted of a vast residence which featured a beautiful view and a rare swimming pool, which I was stunned to hear their faith prevented them from using on Sundays. On Sunday afternoons, there was a discussion of the Bible followed by a prayer, and some of the teachers were invited over for tea. I was always very self-conscious of my background. Being brought up a Catholic, I felt quite intimidated the first time we accepted an invitation. However, I started to relax when the pastor's wife offered me a second cuppa with home-made drop scones.

'Oh, I do like your droppings!' I said.

'Oh dear, we call these drop scones in English,' she replied.

That was by far my greatest social faux pas in life, let alone in English. It often comes back to me as a cringing reminder of my fallibility.

As for religion, I found to my surprise there was some not-too-subtle infighting between creeds. The Plymouth Brethren had been the first group of missionaries in Mwinilunga by about a century. Then at about the time of independence some Catholic fathers had opened a mission in the *boma*. I heard that soon after he arrived, the Italian Catholic priest was reported to the authorities for carrying a bottle of vodka while travelling. The Plymouth Brethren were concerned he might be guilty of drink-driving. The Catholic priest told the story with much glee. He said that he wasted no time waving the vodka bottle under everyone's nose at the police station. It turned out to be filled with spare fuel for his motorbike.

At the same time, the Vatican's Second Ecumenical Council sparked internal disagreements among Catholics because it made none of the expected changes.

A progressive Dutch priest who was building a church showed us how he was including a very large confessional. 'We can use it as a spare room for visitors, once the pope has abolished confession,' he explained. He also played tricks at his Italian colleague's expense. He took all the statues out of the church every morning and left them in the middle of the flower bed outside the church. Every night, when we sat with friends on our veranda for a sundowner, we could hear the Italian padre mumbling. That was the time when he replaced the statues safely back inside the church.

One day, three Russian teachers, two named Vladimir and one called Nick, arrived as USSR aid teachers in Zambia. It was interesting that just as we had found little information about Zambia in Europe, our USSR colleagues had arrived with even scantier intelligence about the country. Because our school was near the borders of Zaire and Angola, they worried that when jogging they might cross a border and not know which country they were in. As we all did, they had to wait till the first term break before they could purchase in Lusaka their own map of independent Zambia. As expatriates of non-Anglo-Saxon background, they had a harder task than most. As well as adjusting to their students, they had to adjust to the different Western concepts of the syllabus and of their new surrounds.

Nick always requested information using the opening phrase, 'One more question'. Every so often, he came up with questions to do with culture as well as language.

I remember him knocking on our door, with his friend Vladimir, brandishing an outdoor brush.

'One more question,' he asked. 'What do I do with this? Do I broom or do I sweep?'

But any difficulties soon faded once they picked up their guitars at night. Nickolai and the two Vladimirs expressed the joy of their culture in front of everyone, and we all shared in it, to the rhythm of the Russian song 'Kalinka'.

With colleagues from Russia, India and Canada, we felt the swinging 60s helped us build bridges and make our generation open-minded. We danced hectically, arms wide apart mimicking the sound and movement of aircraft. Later, when the night was no longer young, we fell back on the routine of rocking and rolling. As baby boomers, our trademark was to articulate the words of 'Ob-la-di, Ob-la-da' and 'Maxwell's Silver Hammer' in chorus and with rhythm. We wore flares. I loved to wear a brash orangey stretch trouser suit that I hoarded and kept for years. I regretted letting go of it. As for my miniskirts, they have been back in fashion at least twice over.

As a newly arrived staff member, I had to hold my own when Mr Sutton-Smith suggested I should become a domestic science teacher. 'English is my area and I couldn't possibly teach domestic science,' I said. So I taught English. And although I didn't think the role of housemistress suited me well, I had to accept the extra weekend duty. This consisted of performing the morning inspection of the girls' dormitories on Saturdays.

I didn't enjoy on a weekend morning to have to rush early out of my bed, which then remained unmade for the next day, and, bleary-eyed, risk losing my balance while dragging my way across a muddy construction yard to the dormitory. By the time I got to the dormitory, my lethargy soon gave way to curiosity. I could hear the students' cheerful voices as I approached.

As I stepped in the door, the group of girls called out in unison, 'Good morning, Mrs Smith!'

Each one of the girls was standing by her bed. They had folded the bed linen in uniquely styled origami and displayed photos of their favourite personalities, which they had cut out of magazines. The area was bright with purple bougainvillea branches snatched from the bush and placed inside green empty cans of cocoa powder. Embroidered cloths covered their suitcases and trunks, which they used as makeshift bedside tables. These were the same trunks they had carried on their heads a few months before in the humid January weather when they had trudged from their villages, through bush tracks for scores of kilometres, to attend high school, some for the first time.

During the week, I went to the local store where I had spotted a small pair of gumboots. They were not a heavy work boot and they were bright red. Just the job, I thought, as I signed off for them on our account at the mission shop. On the following Monday, I noticed two of the same first year girls who had stood at attention that morning walk into my classroom, proudly sporting a pair of bright red and yellow gumboots each. I asked what was wrong with their flip-flops and the class burst out laughing.

I feared, however, that I failed my students both as an English teacher and as an educator on the day of the broadcast of the first landing on the moon in 1969. Because it was a major event, I was anxious to involve my students and departed from my usual routine. I entered my classroom with a two-band radio already programmed to the BBC World Service. The plan was for all of us to witness the momentous event of the US of a moon landing. However, the crackle and interference was so bad that no one, including me, could follow the American commentary. As my radio was also programmed to a French-speaking station, I switched over. Straining to hear the radio announcer's voice through the static, I was able to hear the French version of the astronaut's words. Dutifully, I translated back into English for my first year students what Neil Armstrong, an American man, was saying, 'One small footstep for man and a giant footstep for humanity.' The class cheered, not at my free translation, but because Neil Armstrong was on the moon.

During the mid-year break, Peter decided to try our new silent eight-millimetre camera to film the approach to Mwinilunga that had made such an impression on us. He filmed the treacherous bridge and then started to capture a shot of the *boma* and nearby offices, such as the clinic and the police station. As he focused on the buildings, a police officer came into his view blowing a whistle and gesticulating in his direction. As Peter approached him, his signalling became clear. He was telling Peter to stop filming, then demanding that Peter hand the film over. Baffled, Peter asked why, and the police officer told him that foreigners weren't authorised to take photographs of the police station. It was a confronting encounter and its main outcome was to stymie Peter's filming career for a while.

Meanwhile, I ventured past the police station where the road widened. There in front of a couple of shops a few scattered stalls formed a small open-air mini-market. The villagers sold a variety of goods like locally grown maize, cassava and leafy vegetables. The usual tropical fruit, like pawpaws, bananas and guavas were plentiful but there was an abundance of pineapples, as they happened to thrive on the acidic well-drained sandy soil in this subtropical region. It was so fertile that a cannery was established near Mwinilunga a decade later. I can't resist the sweet scent of ripe pineapples. There I watched while the store holders demonstrated that the fruit was ripe by gently releasing a leaf off the top. I have since used this clever leaf-pulling trick to choose the pineapples I want to buy in supermarkets around the world.

Often I went out walking because I liked to observe the people around me. I was surprised to see that, regardless of the setting, people spent a long time greeting one another. Traditional greetings were a necessary part of the social norms to maintain relationships with relatives, friends and any of the elders. The ritual involved a complex set of body gestures. Formal greetings required a gradual bending at the knees in a sort of downward bowing movement by the person who wished to show respect. People had to keep their head lower than the party they deferred to, especially when facing a chief. The participants then engaged in a simultaneous clapping of hands, performed at a slight distance from one another. Sometimes, modern technology disrupted the formality of the ceremony and it was curtailed faster than was intended by custom. Once, I saw two villagers greeting each other standing on either side of the dirt road while traffic roared past. No one heard the words that accompanied the polite gesturing as the trucks beeped both villagers back towards each kerbside, showering them with dust.

We were to find that greetings for the *muzungu*, whitefella, also involved a similar long drawn-out and sophisticated routine. After the initial traditional bowing and *chilunda* greetings, another formal introduction took place, sometimes in English, and with some shaking of hands but not too much eye contact, especially to or by women. On one occasion when we were invited to a village, our host remained standing while someone brought two low hand-crafted stools for us to sit on. We felt awkward about it until we understood that because he was an elder we were meant to keep our heads at a lower level than our host's. The villagers had been wise enough to assume that white people weren't very skilled at crouching for long while talking to a chief.

I didn't take long to get to know my neighbour, Eileen. In the following months, she gave me interesting insights into some of the common African customs. Eileen and her husband were schoolteachers in what was their home country, Rhodesia. They hailed from Bulawayo and were from the Ndebele nation. Through a mission scheme, they had received further training in the United States of America. On their return, they had volunteered as a couple to be posted in Zambia for a while on a government contract scheme. Living in southern Africa at the time was difficult. African people south of the Zambian border were severely restricted in their movements. Whether Eileen and her family had gone back to Rhodesia or lived under the apartheid regime of South Africa, they knew that people of 'colour' in those countries were subjected to atrocious segregation in their daily life.

Eileen didn't speak much about the difficulties they had encountered yet she recounted how startled they were the day they had first crossed the border into Zambia at the Victoria Falls. She said they had selected a café with an outdoor veranda, unsure whether black people were really allowed to sit in tourist cafés in Zambia. While they were still nervously perched on the edge of their chairs, not knowing if they'd be served, they saw a white family approach their table.

'We watched them. As they stepped on the veranda, we expected them to tell us to go sit on the grass further away, instead, they simply settled down at the table next to ours,' Eileen said. 'We couldn't believe it.'

The idea of 'mixed colour' customers sitting near one another was a scenario completely unheard of in Rhodesia and was illegal in South Africa.

Eileen and I became good friends. She taught me how to use a sewing machine and we giggled at my vague attempts to make curtains like young sisters do at home. One afternoon when I visited her, she was getting ready to go to the clinic with her baby on her back. I asked her why she used a towel instead of the usual stretch of *laplap* or cotton cloth. She said that towelling was more absorbent for extra comfort, for both her and her baby. I learnt a lot from her. I even came to observe her child's language-learning steps. When her baby made a type of click sound, she explained it was one of the early sounds Ndebele children often made because it relates to the phrase Ndinxaniwe meaning 'I'm thirsty' which uses a click 'x' sound in it. It is one of the several sounds many people associate with the southern African click languages. Eileen soon became a mentor for me, especially when my first child was born.

All of us expatriates had a lot to learn about various aspects of cultural protocol. We tried our best. Soon after arrival, the new expatriate teachers got to mix with the African community. Because the school campus was close to the *boma*, the expatriate teachers could socialise with villagers, officers and professionals. Some chose the local bar, while others interacted through the church. Many preferred music and dance. We loved spending evenings with friends. We shared stories of fun, failure or commitment and often discussed various aspects of African culture, and occasionally we admitted to the inadequacy of our understanding.

The worst scenario I recall is our reaction to one of the students' illnesses. Even now I doubt if I would gauge it right. At the time, a student's health issue caused deep concern to many of us. Within a few weeks, the young student had wasted away and dwindled down to half the size he used to be. Although this adolescent had asked to go home, which was miles across the stark open bushlands, he was advised by a nurse to wait till the end of term instead before going, and we as teachers had agreed to that suggestion. According to one of his teachers, he had presented with a 'supposed' perception of being 'sung' or bewitched by some of his relatives. He believed he needed to go home. One day two weeks later, that belief had become an immediate emergency for all of us to see. He came out of the dormitory in such a feeble state that he was rushed to hospital and sent home. It was dramatic. On his return the following term, he said he was better. He looked well and, we were happy to see, had no further health issues.

A travers l'Afrique
Across Africa

At the end of the first year, when I received my one-year-late pay packet, we paid off our debts and then bought a box-shaped Renault 4 car and travelled south across the border. From its source in central Africa, the Zambezi, one of the longest rivers in the world, crossed multiple countries and language groups to reach the Indian Ocean. It took us three separate journeys to gain insight into the backdrop of southern African life.

We first camped on the Zambian side for the night at Livingstone to see the Victoria Falls. It was enjoyable until baboons descended on us. They came down from the tree above us looking very tame and sophisticated but soon took over the campsite. In front of us, they polished off the inside flesh of the orange peels we'd discarded on our campfire as if to teach us not to waste food. I believe they did that with most campers, but although they looked 'cool', they became aggressive at times with those tourists who tried to befriend them.

To get to Livingstone from Mwinilunga, we had driven for two days through tracks across a large area that later became safari parks. At one point, we made out the shape of some elephants at the same time as they warned us with their trumpeting. But I felt it was less of a threat than our daylight encounter with the rogue baboons.

At the Victoria Falls – named Musi-Oa-Tunya in the Zambian Tongan language, meaning 'the smoke that thunders' – my heart didn't stop pounding. The falling waters roared so violently that nothing else could be heard. At twice the height of Niagara Falls, the Musi-Oa-Tunya falls are one and a half kilometre long. We tried to walk a section but had to give up because we were drenched. The Victoria Falls also marked a significant border point with Zimbabwe, which was then called Rhodesia. At the time, Rhodesia was restricted by international sanctions because of its political status. Its leader, Ian Smith, had declared a unilateral declaration of independence (UDI), seceding from Britain to avoid the possibility of a handover to a majority African government.

The next morning, we made for the border post. There, a Rhodesian customs officer offered to issue us a visitor's visa on a separate page of our passport. He explained that a visa into Rhodesia in our passport could compromise our chances to visit other countries. Our discomfort grew at our very first stop at a café, where a handwritten placard announced, 'This is not a multiracial cafe.' We had just ordered a coffee when someone sidled up to Peter. We realised later he was the owner and had spotted the Z for Zambia on our parked car's number plate.

'Northern Rhodesia,' he said. These were days when people from Rhodesia still thought of Zambia by its old colonial name. 'What's it like up there?' he asked. The fact that Peter said nothing negative about life in Zambia prompted an instant racist comment. 'Might be OK for you,' he said, 'but I've got three daughters, you know what I mean.'

We didn't stay long at the café.

Before we made for South Africa, we had to keep a promise. We had offered to visit our friend Eileen's family, who lived outside the town of Bulawayo. It had sounded simple. We had a sketch map to get to the farm owned by Eileen's parents some kilometres outside the town. As we were unsure of the directions, we asked an African man if he'd heard of that farm. He said he'd be right back with a friend who knew the family well and we went into a hotel bar to wait for his return. After a while, the head waiter came over to say two people were asking for us outside. It took us both a while to realise that the African men weren't allowed in the premises, and that we had to step outside to talk to them. The friend gave us clear directions, but he declined to come with us. He said he didn't want to risk being seen in a white people's car.

We arrived outside the farm in the afternoon. It was a pleasure and a contrast to be made welcome into an African home after the reluctant reception we had been subjected to by the white community. Eileen's parents showered us with cups of tea and scones. We hadn't been able to bring any goods for them across the border but we had brought their daughter's good wishes. We heard later that Eileen's mother had to mourn two of her sons who died in the civil war that ensued.

A few years later, we paid Eileen a visit in Botswana. We travelled the areas around Lobatse where she'd moved with her husband and children and then went to its capital, Gaborone. Its buildings offered an incongruous contrast with the bush savannah and the flat sandy ridges of the dry earth around. The landscape there reminded me of the backdrop displayed in the cult film *The Gods Must Be Crazy*. For the first time till I moved to Australia, I travelled across a hot and arid land. It was strange to find out later the iconic African baobab tree had a family relative in the boab trees of the Kimberley in Western Australia.

On the return trip, we drove to a small isolated border crossing so far away from anywhere that even the South African customs officer looked desolate. When he asked us if we had any subversive literature on us, I was about to declare a one-month-old copy of the *Times of Zambia* in which I had wrapped my boots. But Peter asked what he meant.

'Pornographic literature, like *Playboy*,' he said, with a smirk.

I later heard this border point was a main point of entry for white South African men to spend time with women and gamble in some Botswana hotel casinos which apparently weren't available in puritan apartheid-controlled South Africa.

Racism in South Africa had become institutionalised. In Johannesburg, I saw African people veer either left or right in the grid-patterned town at the sight of anyone in uniform, no matter how distant they were. My friend Eileen explained that people tried to avoid delays having to show the pass they needed to carry for being in the city. So black people or coloured people weren't visible in the streets. Neither did they seem to climb any of the steps of any of the Johannesburg public buildings, because their presence was illegal there. This was clear to us when I saw the large lettering stating WHITES ONLY displayed on the steps leading to the railway station. We circled that station several times without finding a back door, or a side entrance or a labelled hatch for non-whites. There was a 'goods only' heavy trapdoor which a person needed to step over and stoop into all at once. I feared that must have been it. The tagging of public toilet doors must have presented South African citizens with many dilemmas. I figured you might try and hold off going to the toilet, but if that was impossible, decide which side of your family to embrace or reject by choosing 'Coloured' or 'Indian', for example. I felt that with complex rules, people try so hard that they often make the wrong decision under pressure.

We took several days to drive back home over corrugated roads and dirt tracks in our Renault 4. Being stranded was common on those roads. Large cars with low suspensions could remain stuck for a long time. Our small car wasn't fast but it was light. It was also high off the ground and could be lifted out of the soaking terrain. This was a regular event in the rainy season. Wherever you travelled, you had to take an axe and a spare fan belt for the engine. The axe came in handy to bring down tree branches. You then had to place the wood under the wheels so the car could grip onto it while one of you was revving and the other one pushing.

Travelling north-east of Zambia was an appealing venture. To go to Lake Victoria or to see Mount Kilimanjaro in Kenya, you'd drive through national parks in Tanzania whose president, Julius Nyerere, had led an African socialist movement called Ujaama from the Swahili for 'brotherhood', which was based on communal village life.

The main problems we expected were the road conditions into Tanzania. Affected by restrictions over Rhodesia, landlocked Zambia needed access to Tanzanian ports. Tanzania, together with China, had started a phase of joint ventures incorporating a line of rail between Zambia and the Tanzanian ports near Dar es Salaam on the Indian Ocean. However, there were major delays in the 1,800-kilometre

Tanzania Zambia Railway project. The unsealed road was waterlogged, slippery and broken up by the wheels of heavy trucks. When a North American firm started work on sealing some sections of the highway into Tanzania, the Zambia and Tanzania Company, nicknamed ZamTan, started running its trucks on it. The road went into such disrepair, and the trucks were so poorly serviced and dangerous that drivers called it the Hell Run. So as we set off, we expected the journey on the highway ahead of us wouldn't be comfortable.

The road to the border post into Tanzania was manageable. The guard took one look at our passport and asked why we had visited South Africa. We had to explain that we'd driven through South Africa for a few days on the way to Botswana, and that we were aware of international sanctions against South Africa.

The worst section of road was the two hundred kilometres of semi-sealed road once we crossed the border into Tanzania towards Mbeya. The road had been cut to follow the contours of the numerous ups and downs which peaked, ridge after ridge, with ravines on one side or the other. We felt pleased to have driven quite well so far in spite of some uneven and narrow road sealing. Chugging along with our reliable front-wheel-drive five-door Renault, we noticed the road begin to climb very steeply again. Attempting to overtake the slow double-articulated ZamTan truck ahead of us would be difficult, as we had no vision over the crest of the road, so we waited for the truck driver to signal that the road ahead was clear. Peter overtook him just before the top. We waved back to him as we motored down the steep slope and I remarked how lonely the truck drivers must be on this Hell Run.

At that point, I saw Peter stare at the rear mirror and then I heard the loudest hoot of a large truck. The same driver and truck were speeding down the hill towards us. By the time we wondered how we'd provoked this reaction from the driver, I turned around again and saw his face grimacing, while the sound of the horn became louder and more insistent. This short episode made no sense to me. I thought he must've gone mad.

In the meantime, Peter had accelerated hard towards a bridge at the bottom of the slope. He saw the truck's grille in the rear-view mirror. Just as we reached the bottom of the hill, it smashed into the back of our car, and that fortunately bounced us forward. We must have been going at the same speed at the time of impact. The moment the truck hit us square on the tailgate of the car, a tiny track forked off to the left and Peter shot up in its direction. We were both unharmed. The rear lights were smashed. The tailgate had caved in and a large dent had forced the back door off its hinge, leaving a gaping hole.

Meanwhile, the truck had careered up the main slope. We heard some heavy screeching as the truck jackknifed halfway up the road. We walked up towards a frantic but apologetic truck driver.

'The brakes, they failed. Sorry, sorry!' he was saying. He asked Peter to test the brake pedal, which was totally loose and unresponsive.

We figured then that the truck driver had suffered a much more traumatic time than we had. He knew what was coming. He could probably see the bottom of the ravine on the right while descending at breakneck speed. It was fortunate that Peter had kept his cool and taken time to concentrate on the speed and the terrain, which meant the truck only hit us once.

We managed to drive on as far as Mbeya, where the ZamTan head office was. The driver had given us the contacts we needed for insurance purposes and said his company was used to claims as they didn't maintain the trucks properly. The office was closed when we arrived and we had to spend the night in Mbeya. The next morning, we joined the queue of complainants at their office door. When we reported the accident, the supervisor suggested the driver was at fault by saying he must have been freewheeling. Peter told him how he had tested the brake pedal and that it hadn't responded at all.

While standing in the office, I noticed that a blackboard covered the wall behind us. On the board were lists of dates, places and names of people, with a wide column listing compensation keywords. Some were for hospital fees, others for funeral fees paid to families. We grimaced at each other, happy to have survived.

The one garage in Mbeya was closed down, and the only source of Renault spares was in Dar es Salaam situated 900 kilometres down the coast. The gap in the back door sucked copious amounts of dust into the car, to the point that we saw little of the mountains or wild parks we passed. As we arrived at a hotel in the town of Iringa, the porter made a point of walking our suitcases back out onto the porch and wiping off the thick layer of dust that had accumulated during the journey. We felt embarrassed until we realised that we were both encrusted with sandy and grimy soil. This time we laughed.

In Dar es Salaam, I experienced for the first time a tropical humid climate similar to what I'd encounter in Port Moresby in Papua New Guinea a few years later. Peter said it reminded him of his year in Cameroon. We stayed there for a few days until the car was fixed. Because we used most of our travellers' cheques to pay for the car repair, we couldn't drive on to Kenya. A trip to Zanzibar was tempting but we couldn't afford it. As our room wasn't air-conditioned and the fans didn't keep us cool, we spent the days on the beach. We sat next to a private beach which cut access to the sea by means of a wall enclosure which sheltered some of the wealthy tourists and their boats. I still remember alluring beaches and very tall palm trees.

We stayed in Dar es Salaam during Christmas before returning to Zambia. On Christmas Eve, we walked to a Catholic church where the only seats we could find were towards the front. We took our seats only to realise that people had left a respectable distance behind the family that sat in the front row ahead of us. President Julius Nyerere's face wasn't just on the money in my pocket but at an angle ahead of our pews. As we sat down, Peter started to wrestle, saying he felt itchy. He found out later that somehow a tiny gecko had made his way up his leg, and was crawling around inside his underpants. As Peter wriggled, the congregation rose to sing a Christmas carol. I knew the tune and, seeing the lyrics provided, I joined in. It was 'Silent Night' and I sang it in a language I didn't know of yet, Swahili.

Mama-Patrick
Mama-Patrick

The early 1970s in Zambia were turning points for newly married expatriate couples like us who set about having their first child. Difficulties in becoming pregnant created restrictions to our own planning. I went off the pill and I didn't become pregnant till two years later. By then, I had started to think we would never have a child. It was a stressful phase which made me miserable. There was no way I could access support through IVF. I realised how distressed anyone who couldn't have a baby felt. It was a turning point in my life. That was the first of many times I was given tranquillisers by a doctor.

I worried about other home issues as well, including how to introduce French at home.

One morning, à propos of nothing, soon after we had arrived in Zambia, Peter said, 'Why don't we try it?'

'Oh, not speaking French on Sundays!' I said.

Peter was getting desperate, I could tell, wanting to practise his French. I realised I wasn't putting much effort into making it work but I didn't really want the constraint of rules about French in the home to take over our life. We'd tried to speak French on Sundays but failed. I felt it was as ridiculous a suggestion as going to church or having sex on say...Wednesdays. Knowing, however, that Peter was patient, I came up with an idea that might work.

'I'll start speaking French at home when we have a baby!' I said.

After two years of trying, I was told that I was pregnant. At last, our plan to become parents was to come true. I went through the initial excited phase of wanting to stand on the house roofs and shout out to the whole world about it. It was exciting and we started doing some planning.

'Here's what I feel like doing,' I said. 'I'll start speaking French at home on the day this child is born, and he'll learn it as he grows up, and you can just join in. That will be easy for father and son!'

Somehow, I had decided I was expecting a boy. I must have been homesick for my brothers – I was eighteen years old when the youngest one was born and had spent quite a few weekends at home in my student days playing with him and watching him grow.

At the time of my first pregnancy, I hadn't yet studied how children learnt languages. For want of other choices in literature, my bible was Dr Spock and the generic advice he offered. Dr Spock's book was the only thing I could find in a bookshop in the mining town of Ndola, one of the bigger towns in the area of Zambia called the copper belt. I did well to find it, as it was the only bookshop in a 300-kilometre radius. I didn't resent his style too much at the time. I liked it best when I got to the end of the chapter where there was a caveat about trusting one's own judgement. Being told what to do by anyone had always worried me. As I had always done with foreign concepts, I only took what I wanted from his book and left the rest out. Just as well, since I heard later of people whose childrearing went to pieces because they took this so-called expert literally.

It was 1970. I was twenty-six. I was three months pregnant. My mother was back in France and the last thing I'd ever consider discussing with her would be pregnancy, or child-rearing. My mother's style was traditional. She was devoted to the children yet always strict. She used to say, '*Plus tard. J'ai quelque chose d'autre à faire maintenant* Later. I have something else to do now.' That model of motherhood where, whenever you wanted to talk to your mother, she was always too busy, didn't appeal to me in the least. I intended to be more interactive with my children.

Although I did miss her, it wasn't easy to share my worries with her or tell her of my strange dreams. I figured that if I wrote about my dreams in my letters, she'd think I'd lost my mind. For example, I had a recurring nightmare about ants marching through the house under the front door, straight across to the kitchen. It wasn't until they'd cleared all the perishables that had been in the fridge that they'd leave the house out through the back door. Someone had told me this tale as a true story, the clearing of food in a house apparently being one of the ants' most impressive achievements. I couldn't tell my mother how I had chosen to set the baby room as far as I could from the fridge. She wouldn't understand that.

Still, I enjoyed writing to her once a month from my home in the heart of Zambia. As Peter had renewed his contract for another three years, I planned to interrupt my English as a second language teaching for a year around the baby's birth and go to Europe to introduce our baby to the family.

We weren't the only young expatriate couple on the staff of the school attracted to an African adventure and soon we weren't the only couple expecting their first baby. Mwinilunga only had a small government health centre and, although there was a mission hospital nearby, its resources were limited. There was a staffroom story that one of our colleagues' babies, her third, had popped out in the women's toilet, and we debated how to avoid a similar ordeal. As a result, many of the first mothers-to-be planned to fly ahead of their confinement date to give birth in the mining town of Chingola. Being expatriates, we could apparently use the fully equipped mining hospital so long as we found a place to stay in town. One of my colleagues, Anne, made contact with a family in mining and when she was seven months pregnant embarked on an early transfer to Chingola. She had booked her trip on the weekly single-engine mission aircraft. On the morning of her departure, we were horrified to hear that the plane had overturned on take-off. Anne stayed suspended upside down for about twenty minutes while a group of four-wheel drive vehicles cut a path through the savannah grass near the airfield to reach the downed aircraft. Once she was rescued, the head missionary took her to the mission pilot's house for a rest.

As a fellow pregnant woman, I went to offer support. I arrived there a couple of hours after the accident and asked how she and baby felt.

'I'm less worried,' she said, 'now that the baby has just started to stir again.'

Anne flew safely to Chingola the next day and gave birth to a healthy baby girl. I have often puzzled how someone from the mission could have taken her back to an empty house, given her a cup of tea, and left her on her own in a spare bedroom for hours. Anne admitted to having had a tense time and doing nothing but pray and drink tea.

The magical effect, for some Anglo-Saxons, of the perennial cup of tea still amazes me, for it has never worked for me. I suspect this is because I'm not a believer in its powers, a perilous downside of not being culturally Anglo-Saxon enough.

As I didn't have anyone to stay with before giving birth, I'd decided to fly to the mine hospital in my last month of gestation. We had planned for me to catch a flight to Chingola in March 1971. So, in early March, eight-and-a-half months pregnant, I was still in Mwinilunga helping my colleagues to organise a most momentous party for the end of the teaching term. 'Let's make pineapple the party theme,' somebody had said.

Given the constraint of distance, such a complex project would take about a year to put in place. In the meantime, all the teachers and friends had fun planning the party. The lead-up had lasted several months. The more adventurous had extracted pineapple juice and set about brewing varieties of potent pineapple-based punches and wines. Our group, in a state of excitement, prepared pineapple fruit salad and pineapple skewers. I remembered someone calling her dish 'Yellow Submarine'. As my *pièce de résistance*, I had carved out whole pineapples and then refilled with chunks of the same fruit.

The party took place on a Saturday night and I was careful to imbibe only the non-alcoholic concoctions. Whether I achieved that or not, I clearly remember sitting for hours resolute that, given my condition, I should avoid strenuous movements. By about midnight, everyone seemed to have collapsed from exhaustive drinking and dancing. At that point, the only person left on his feet, John, a young Canadian aid worker, called out, 'Has everybody given up then?' He took over the floor just as the tune to Zorba's dance started to play.

Well, there I was, a southern European, having spent three years in an Anglo community and in the main starting to feel like I'd missed all the fun! I jumped up and joined him. 'I just have to dance to this!' I said. To this day, I felt I executed a very skilled version of the steps to 'Zorba the Greek'. I noticed an English overseas volunteer's Polaroid camera flash at me. I still own the photo, a weird set of half-bent legs in mid-step with a forward-pointing belly.

As I finished dancing, the whole room watched while I lowered myself on to a chair, panting for breath while John called all of us party poopers.

Soon, Peter said it was time to go home.

As we drove back, I must have regained enough breath to ask, 'Why didn't you stop me from jumping to that crazy tune?'

'As if I could, even if I'd tried,' he answered. He knew me well indeed.

However, he wasn't ready, and neither was I, for the shock of the explosive sound when my waters broke – a premature membrane rupture – five hours later. It was a rude awakening for both of us on that Sunday morning. It took me a while to accept that the boom wasn't part of my dream sequence, in which a drunken John was starting to pound on a traditional African drum.

Complex negotiations ensued after Lisa, my new African neighbour, came over to give me some well-needed guidance. 'First we remove the bed sheets,' she said, 'as they'll need a wash.' She then sent Peter to locate the clinic's four-wheel drive and instructed him to make sure the stretcher was in it, as she knew it could double-up as a makeshift ambulance.

The strangest part of this episode was when I had to wait for the agreed time of departure outside the small clinic. The night nurse assigned to travel with us was the same one who'd just completed his night shift. He came over to the vehicle. 'I'm just tidying up from the night, and then I'll have a coffee before we set off,' he said.

For him, the slow drive over many a pothole on a dirt road during the rainy season would be a welcome relief. It would be a two-hour chance to catch up with his sleep.

We had to travel from Mwinilunga to Ikalene. The Plymouth

Brethren mission hospital was located close to the source of the Zambezi, the border point between Zambia, Zaire and Angola. We had already witnessed Zaire's dramatic internal warfare the year before. We knew Angola in the west was still a Portuguese colony and troubled by freedom fighting but hadn't seen evidence of this yet. That day, on the way to the hospital, the shell of a newly blown-up bus, abandoned on the Zambian roadside just over from the Angolan border, was a reminder of how close to us the fighting was. The thing I clearly recall, however, and still talk about is how during the journey to the hospital I loved going over the potholes. I'll recommend to anyone the experience I benefited from during that phase of labour. In the Land Rover, I was lying on a stretcher with my feet behind the driver and my head towards the back door. So every time we emerged out of a deep puddle while the vehicle pulled up slowly, it placed me in an inverted posture. This had a great soothing effect on the back pains that were becoming more and more regular.

'When is the next pothole?' I'd ask, and Peter replied, 'Not far to go!'

In retrospect, I wonder if the worst ordeal for me during that eighty-kilometre drive through the bush was the strange recurring thought that I wished I hadn't been brought up a Catholic in France. I couldn't decide whether to feel alarmed or reassured when I recalled the Plymouth Brethren doctor's words at one of my check-ups. 'Of course, if ever you came in an emergency, we'd take you in,' she had said. I was worried that the two-hour drive meant the doctor and nurses would all be at church by the time I arrived in labour, which they were.

This was premature labour. I was about two weeks early. I'd been due to fly three days later on the weekly Wednesday mission flight to give birth at the mining hospital as planned. I should instead have been concerned that my baby was going to be small. And he was. He weighed below two kilograms, at three pounds and fourteen ounces.

Someone must have been there to open the door of the delivery ward. It was a sort of long skinny shed. A nurse said that the mission hospital on a Sunday was short-staffed and that the doctor would come but that she was due to go on a holiday the next day. She then reminded me that the baby was to be small and said she'd give me an injection to slow down the labour, which made me sleep for a few hours.

Peter asked if he could go with them into the delivery room, and they agreed provided he'd give a hand. While they were strapping my feet to the bed, they asked him to stand behind the head of the bed and hold my hands tight, as if they were tied up, when I went into the final phase of labour.

Although he felt reluctant to take part in such restraining practices, he duly obliged. The only thing I remember was waking up after someone had shouted 'Push' and, in a semi-dream state, I had called back 'No'. I then woke up feeling as if my face was being slapped. I opened my eyes to see the nurse gaping at me:

'I'm sorry I had to slap you,' she said. Then she started applying a cold flannel to my face, trying to keep me awake.

At that point, the midwife mentioned my blood group could be an issue and explained that the mission pastor's wife was on standby as a donor. My blood group was the rarer O-type Rhesus negative. There was a further complication. Because my husband's blood group was A positive, the baby's blood group could turn out to be positive. If that was the case, the doctor explained to us that antibodies could develop the need for me to have a blood transfusion. She said that in some cases they had flown patients to the Chingola mine hospital, where I had planned to give birth.

It was only a week after I gave birth that a nurse unravelled the full scenario for me. She said that because I'd given birth on the Sunday afternoon, any help from the mission flight would have been unavailable till the Wednesday. It would have been too late to either bring medication for me or to take me away in an emergency. 'Had there been complications with blood groups within the crucial first seventy-two hours, that flight would have been twelve hours too late. It had been stranded in Zaire and would've had to fly to Chingola for the anti-D serum first,' she said. 'The plane wouldn't have delivered the serum in time,' she added.

It was fortunate that I didn't need a transfusion. And I didn't receive the serum to avoid the build-up of antibodies until after I gave birth to my second child, who was also Rhesus positive. On that later occasion, I discovered other dangerous health issues I'd surmounted at the Ikalene mission hospital. One was that I'd experienced child bed fever, a complaint I had heard of through old wives' tales in France, and from my readings of 19th-century novels. I didn't believe it was a contemporary illness that could crop up in cases where the entire placenta wasn't cleared at the time of giving birth. Although it was more than three years since I had first given birth, I recall how throughout the early weeks I had been quite ill. I had assumed I had malaria since I was taking medicine 'for the fever'. I found out much later that the feverish state I was in wasn't due to malaria, but that I had suffered from puerperal sepsis.

Peter and I named our little boy Patrick, as he had been due to be born around St Patrick's Day. The name existed in both French and English. As he was two weeks early and premature by size, the doctor said I had to stay in the hospital. Consequently, we stayed for three weeks in the hospital with African mothers who'd walked in from the bush. However, I was placed in a separate wing to the African mothers and was told it wasn't to separate me from them but simply because I didn't eat the same diet. After tasting the British gravy-laden starchy food, I must say that I hankered after any other diet but I was in a foreign and religious milieu and not well enough to pick an argument about food or race.

On the first day, I was told that another little boy had been born who weighed just below three pounds. Later that week, when I enquired about that small baby, the nurse said his mother wasn't so lucky because he hadn't survived. She explained that some African babies sometimes died in cases where the mother suffered from malnutrition or some other serious ailment.

Baby Patrick had to be vacuumed out because he was so small.

The doctor gave me clear directions. 'He really needs to be in an incubator, but you'll have to make do with a hot water bottle to keep him warm,' she said, adding, 'You'll have to feed him every two hours.'

I didn't see her again, as she went on leave. Later, I heard that she had been suffering from depression. I reasoned that my ordeal was a one-off but that, for the young doctor, running a small hospital in isolation and with scant supplies must have been a serious challenge. I didn't envisage that in later years I'd develop some similarly depressive anxieties in my own life.

On the first morning after giving birth, when I saw the nurse glance in the baby's direction as she opened the curtains to start the day, I asked her, pointing to the cot, if he was still alive.

'Yes,' she said, and she seemed to straighten herself as if jerking back into her uniform, 'Of course he is!'

I didn't need to discuss my concern for having to care for such a tiny baby. I knew then that this little being needed someone to take care of him. It wasn't a feeling of maternal instinct, it was a response to reality, compounded by some awareness that he was small.

In the short while before I could fully breastfeed, the nurse used a tiny syringe-shaped glass tube with pointy ends as a mini-milk bottle. She made him up a light milky Nestlé concoction. Then I fed him whatever milk I had managed to express using a manual suction pump, resembling the type you use for blocked sinks. Finally, to stimulate further milk supply, I had to put him to the breast. This sequence lasted about ninety minutes and left me just enough time for a coffee and a toilet break before I'd start the whole routine again.

After a few days, Peter had returned to work for a week. On his second visit the next weekend, he smuggled his way into my hospital room to spend the night with us. That was a pleasant two-day interlude, then he had to leave again. At that point, the rainy season had fully started and the roads that were open the previous week were flooded. Peter couldn't travel back for another ten days. By then, I was feeling low, sick and isolated and I felt abandoned by him. Instead, I found I bonded with the baby. This lasted for three weeks while he started to gain on his birth weight and I dutifully took the medication against my child-bed fever.

I eventually took Patrick home because he'd started to gain weight, although he was still below five pounds. I kept on feeding him every two hours for another three months but that seemed easy after the difficulties of the early months. Swathed in wrappers, my baby looked like a mummified version of Gandhi. Cleaning him after a nappy change became a nightmare, as some of his skin came off with the body lotion.

When I got home, Patrick gained strength from day to day. It was bewildering to watch him making any progress at all. Once, I walked him near the *boma* and a man I hardly knew greeted me as 'Mama-Patrick'. Not sure what to make of this new title, I chose to accept it.

I had a scare about three months later. I was taking Patrick for a walk one afternoon. It wasn't a hot day and I was walking in the shade. All of a sudden, I noticed his face had gone bright red. I thought he looked like a crayfish that had just been plunged into boiling water. At the Mwinilunga clinic, the nurse said it was likely Patrick had 'caught up with his calories'. I already knew he had caught up in weight with another full-term baby of the same age, but this was an unexpected development.

Researching it later, I determined that it meant from that day he would no longer require extra calories to help him catch up with his body warmth, although I often found his lips went blue very quickly when he became cold. It didn't last and I was pleased to observe that he developed as well as children of his age group. For the first time, I witnessed the ugly side of competitive parental pride. On some occasions, I overheard parents boasting, 'Ours could blow his first candle' or 'Ours could walk before his first birthday.' I felt that it was a miracle ours had a birthday at all. This realisation came to us gradually. I was amazed how much Peter and I had achieved as parents with so little knowledge.

Zambia had been good to us for six years. I'd managed to give birth in the remote bush while also teaching there. It was time for our family to return to England. Peter had obtained a grant for postgraduate studies for a year at Bristol University. Back to Bristol! I was pleased to return to the very first place that had welcomed me in England in my youth.

It was important for us as we had become a family now to set up home, and doing so in England I thought suited me fine. I planned to be the main income-earner, while Peter did his research. We'd wanted another child, but I realised that, like many women of my generation, I could never give birth when I wanted to. It seemed that the more intent I was on falling pregnant, the less regular my ovulation cycles became. I wanted to avoid the tension generated by thinking about it all the time, as had happened to me before.

At the time of packing some time before we left Zambia, I made a point of parting with all baby equipment and toys, a practical plan for downsizing back to Europe. I wanted to believe that scientifically the rational need for me to support the family would override my wish to have another child and that we were to have an easy and economically viable move back to Europe. We flew back to Europe and stopped in southern France to visit my family before relocating to Bristol. There, we bought a left-hand drive car which we drove to Calais and put on the ferry to Dover.

Even before landing, I realised I had become pregnant because crossing the English Channel had never made me seasick before. The surprise pregnancy was welcome but meant we'd have to adjust our plans. Because I had qualified as a librarian alongside my main studies for my degree in English in my early years at university, I decided to work part-time in a library until the birth and we'd have to manage on a lower income.

This pregnancy was different. In contrast with the days I'd been indulged as a different patient, and yet not being told what was going on in the mission hospital in Zambia, I entered a new world of prenatal treatment. At Bristol Maternity Teaching Hospital, there were class loads of students and professors who seemed to want my case to feature in their assignments. They held their tutorials at my bedside. The medical students took turn measuring me to see if they could verify my approximate date of delivery. The professor rejoiced every time they were wrong. I became a guinea pig as they gathered around my bed while the surgeon lectured us all explaining that, in my case, the baby was under-size by four weeks because of several factors.

'She's a smoker, and small size is hereditary as well,' he asserted with smugness.

Back in Zambia, soon after I gave birth, I'd written to tell my mother about Patrick. In my first letter to her, I was careful to tell her that my newborn had started to put on weight. Only in my next letter did I mention he had weighed below two kilograms at birth. Obviously I hadn't wanted to worry her. On hearing about it, she wrote to say that she too had only ever had small babies. Admittedly, hers had been all around the four-kilogram mark.

I felt I'd started to work out for myself that heredity was a factor in newborn sizes.

In Zambia, a nurse in attendance tried to encourage me not to be too concerned about my small-sized baby. 'Tropical climate and the height of the plateau above sea level,' she said, 'are two factors that influence birth size.'

Those theories I have yet to hear confirmed. Heredity and smoking were definite constant factors, I felt. I then found it handy to use the size of my firstborn as an excuse for keeping on smoking during my second pregnancy. 'I don't think I could manage to have a large baby,' I argued.

This time, I went to full term. Apart from repeatedly telling me that I'd have a small baby, the midwife said the baby was presenting as breech. The rest was fine, and in spite of all the fuss the hospital had made, Nathalie was born within two hours from the time I left home in labour soon after my membranes broke in my sleep, again.

We took nearly an hour to get into the centre of Bristol. The baby was still in breech position although, during my last antenatal visit, the midwife had attempted to manipulate the baby to turn it around. Peter drove the left-hand drive Renault 4 with me stretched on the back seat. It was like being in an ambulance, but without any of its support service, or any potholes to relieve the pain. Peter, wanting to alert the hospital of our arrival, stopped at a phone box, but said there was no answer. He was so nervous he must have misdialled.

Once we arrived, I could hardly walk into the lift. As soon as a midwife was able to examine me, she mentioned that the doctor lived out of town and we'd have to wait about an hour for him. On this occasion, contrary to the first time I was giving birth, I was told not to push. The problem was that, as the birth was breech, a doctor had to be present because technically a breech is an operation. This rule also meant that Peter wasn't allowed in the delivery room. Our daughter appeared into the world feet-first, performing a little dance, and was larger than her brother, at four pounds twelve ounces, just over two kilograms.

Nathalie was dark-haired with brown eyes, like Nanou, while Patrick was blond with blue eyes, like my brothers. I was one week overdue and, although all the equipment seemed on standby for her and they did place her in an incubator, she didn't need the extra warmth, and the crib's top remained open. On the evening of her birth, I went to see her in the premature baby unit only to find she was bright red, like a crab.

'She's caught up with her calories instantly,' I said.

The nurse agreed and then asked, 'Would you mind if we used your baby to demonstrate bathing in the premature unit?'

I had become the expert mother of premature babies, and Nathalie became the demonstration baby.

On the next day, however, I became worried. I approached a nurse to ask why I wasn't passing clots of blood as I had done after my first child was born. That question led to an instant visit by yet another nurse – the typical British dragon of a matron you see on television hospital soapies. She said that I shouldn't expect any, and if I did pass blood clots, I was to call her. The matron's questions uncovered the issues surrounding Patrick's delivery in Zambia. I must have retained some placenta and that had led to my suffering from child-bed fever.

Before she left, the matron stood up as if to deliver a pledge and said, 'In this country, we like to look after you, dear!'

Her tone and words frightened me even more than the blood clots had.

Peter's mother, Doris, had come over from Lincoln and was a great help in the time before Nathalie was born, and during the coming home phase. She was a person who was always aware of people's need for space and looked after Patrick at this crucial time. When she brought him to the hospital, she said he'd spent a lot of time watching some tadpoles we kept outside our back door. I explained that we had just acquired the tadpoles to help Patrick cope with the death of his goldfish the week before. I'd told him my unborn baby was like a human tadpole maturing in my womb. So we all agreed Patrick was obviously coping quite well with the thought of the new baby, especially as he didn't remark on his sister not resembling a tadpole.

New challenges came with a second child. Patrick had been a quiet baby but Nathalie wasn't. We gave her a bilingual name too. It was based on the title of the popular song by Gilbert Bécaud, hence the French spelling. Like the singer, she made sure she was going to be heard wherever she was.

Peter was by then studying for another year for a master's degree and with no further income we were living off our last savings. He managed to earn some cash for a few months doing some part-time marking but I hadn't yet gone back to work. I worried about financial constraints over the baby's first years and I regretted having parted with our baby goods before we left Zambia. After years of struggling to obtain baby clothes and goods because of a shortage of shops in the bush, it was ironic that I found the range of retail options on offer in Bristol overwhelming. I felt as if all of a sudden I'd stepped out of my closed-in cocooned earlier life and had choices to make, but no money to realise them. The temptation to go into baby shops seemed to spring out at me at every street corner. This was the era when modern and accessible shops like Mothercare were opening everywhere in England. We'd managed to acquire some quality second-hand educational toys and I'd sourced some of the discarded books from the library where I'd worked. All very useful because, after Peter's mother left to go back to Lincoln, I found it hard to go anywhere with two small children

For me, it was hard, and depressing that we all had to dress warmly in England and at all times. We had enjoyed the tropical climate in Zambia, where we simply put on our sandals when we left the home. I had forgotten how long clothes took to dry in England. It was a considerable advantage, I felt, that Patrick was nearly of school age. This allowed me one-on-one time with Nathalie and, on his return from school, Patrick and I then shared her company. He readily made space for a crawling baby as well as moved his Lego pieces off the floor and out of reach.

His sister was certainly not short of toys as I'd feared she might be. Although I chose to avoid buying too many girlie dolls, she ended up with a room full of soft toys, dolls and other fancy animals our relatives sent her. The tiny baby room was but a cubicle but what a warm niche it was in the house!

A few months before she was born, we made a wise decision. Planning for the family's future, we had put some savings into one of many newly built houses in a sort of dormitory estate, outside Bristol, around a village called Yate. A first investment bargain, it was what Peter called a 'two-up, two-down' house, while I referred to it as a 'box'. Because it had a tiny baby room as well as two bedrooms upstairs, we figured it was adequate. Along with other houses situated in a half-circle within other half-circles, our home had the classic bay window design of many houses in England. But it had an extra feature which I loved. This was new technology in England at the time. The house had a system of central heating installed under the floorboards. We were pleased with our new warm house. We chose to paint the staircase rather than lay carpets. It was a bright and practical home to live in. We stopped short, however, of inscribing a romantic name on a plaque over the front door.

We didn't develop a great affinity with the premises, the suburbs or the people around us. Socialising with residents or even finding a network group within this dormitory estate was not an easy task. I used to have the knack, arriving in a new place, of making the acquaintance of interesting people. Unfortunately, at first, the people I met were the ones selling basic household goods. Soon after, they would move on. The majority of the residents there although new to the suburb had come for the long-term, gave their house a 'Sweet Home' sign and installed their first lawn. They didn't want to hear about overseas places like Zambia,

France or Papua New Guinea. Talking about the iconic theatre in the city centre, the Bristol Hippodrome, was the limit of their conversation. Early on, I had mentioned my state of pregnancy, hoping that the topic was a standard universal that anyone could relate to. But none of these exchanges went any further than over the washing line! Good at talking to people as I thought I was, this time my skills failed me. Could it be that these neighbours were wise and spared their own energy, figuring we weren't going to stay in the housing estate for very long?

My parents' visit to Bristol marked a short but significant landmark for my family over the two years we lived there. They came from France for Nathalie's christening. Again, my brother, this time François, followed my father with an English dictionary. My parents wouldn't have visited us if my sister and another brother, and probably their neighbours, hadn't volunteered to water their garden plot back home. It was my parents' first ever trip to the United Kingdom and my father was very keen on seeing Wales, 'never mind England', because he admired the Welsh at rugby. We had hired a larger car for the occasion and with the two children travelled to Heathrow airport to welcome them.

My father enjoyed the trip. What he couldn't make sense of, however, was the non-alcoholic beer he drank at a service station on the motorway between London and Bristol. It was summer and we were thirsty, so we stopped off the M4. He tasted his beer and then turned to Peter, 'It's OK,' he said, 'but why do you drink it if it doesn't have alcohol?'

I was fearful that my mother, on the other hand, would comment on my lack of housekeeping skills. Of course I didn't polish parquet floors on my hands and knees as she did. In my youth, I had resented having to slide across the floor from the front door on a pair of *patins* to my bedroom so as not to mark the floor with my school shoes. These *patins* were sole-shaped and made of felt and a pair stood by the door to be used by most visitors, except the high-ranking select few my mother wanted to impress.

As we walked into our Bristol home, my mother said, 'These windows will need a good clean.'

We knew that she'd love to take over the housework, so Peter and

I had carefully planned our strategy. We diverted her attempts to do household duties by organising frequent and interesting outdoor trips. We started the sightseeing by taking her to the famed Roman sites of Bath. And not far from our dormitory estate of Yate, we explored some of the small villages such as Chipping Sodbury.

My parents also enjoyed day visits to Longleat Lion Park, the Wye Valley, Tintern Abbey and the bridge over the River Severn that marks the Welsh border. My father spotted the Welsh flag draped over the bridge and was proud to say he had just about set foot in Wales. His excitement was so palpable that Patrick spoke later of how well he remembered the fuss and the exclamations over what seemed to him to be just a green flag. As he was only four years old at the time, it must have created a great impression on him.

Nathalie's christening was important, not as a religious event, but in the sense that it brought us together. Peter's mother came and we were also able to include my first English family, the parents of my Shirehampton exchange friend Stephanie. My parents hadn't seen them for nearly fifteen years.

Family gatherings are the essence of my culture, and I realised how much I enjoyed them after having been away from home. This was another turning point for me, in which I started replicating the standard family gathering that I had once hated so much. What I have always loved is the coming together of people, and I made this happen in many of the community groups I belonged to later in my life.

Peter had taken care to reserve a famous Cotswolds restaurant for the christening meal. The menu was partly in French, which is common in English haute cuisine, so my mother was suitably impressed. By the second main course, she declared, 'They don't eat as badly as all that in England.' Obviously, she uttered these words as if to contradict all the prejudicial comments she'd heard about English cuisine before she came to England. It turned out the 'haute cuisine' resided more in the terminology of the menu than in the food. The *terrine de pâté* was more like *pâté ordinaire*; slices of oranges decorated the duck in a main course of *canard à l'orange* which had been roasted like any regular poultry. Fortunately, the typically British creamy and milky tasting ice cream, which both my parents and François loved, accompanied the tinned fruit dessert. The drinks, like the wine and the coffee, weren't remarkable, they said, but the beer was good. The 'olde worlde' decor, with a rose garden, had character and the staff were friendly.

We had a good time and my parents never said a bad word about Bristol, Chipping Sodbury or the Cotswolds. These became the happy reality of England for them. I believed I had passed a test of sorts when introducing my parents to England. I also felt that was the point where as a couple we were treated as adults for the first time. I believed that my mother accepted the fateful fact that her daughter was an adult and her son-in-law was English. I also realised that she didn't think me important any more as she transferred her full focus entirely to her grandchildren from then on. Although when I first left home for university I recognised that my world had become dissociated from the one my parents lived in, I didn't realise that my children would react the same towards me after they left home.

Refining my approach towards my adult children has been an ongoing process. It took energy and flexibility to follow their interests, to keep up with dancing and football as they became young adults. What I found the hardest was to absorb what I came to call their Australian lifestyle, the informal and laid-back approach to their routine. Then when it seemed I had reached an understanding of their new way of life, they turned the tables on me and demonstrated a vitality and strength that reminded me of Peter and myself in our youth.

The ups and downs of parenthood were surprising. In the early stages of their development, it was only after the event that I became aware of which specific phase the child had gone through. This applied to things like teething, the weaning off bottles or the fear of strangers, all of which I felt I came to understand too late.

Then towards the end of the pleasant Bristol interlude, Peter was offered a position in Papua New Guinea.

Four months old with mother, gendarmerie front yard, Libourne, France, 1944.

With Nanou (left) and Philipe, Libourne, France, 1945.

Mémée and my mother, 1954.

Peter balancing a bidon (plastic can), Cameroon, 1966.

Wedding, Peter and Anne-Marie, France, 1967.

With Peter, Mwinilunga High School campus, 1969.

The Lunga bridge, Mwinilunga, 1969.

Mwinilunga High School staff, 1969.

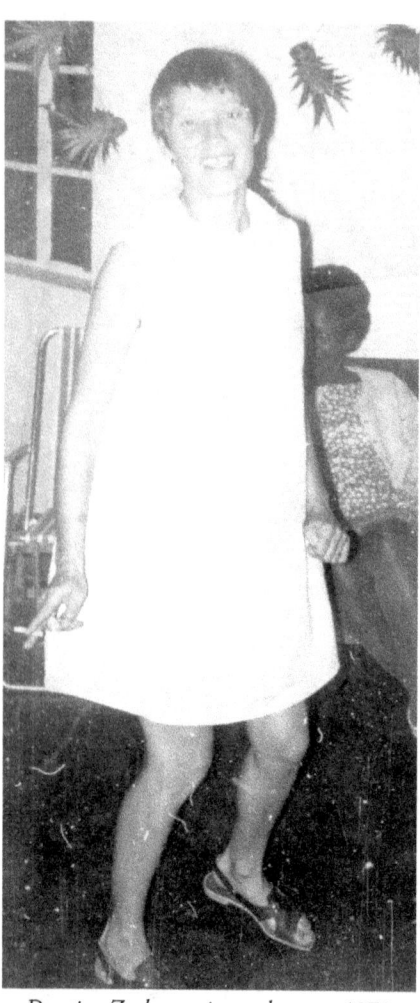

Dancing Zorba at pineapple party, 1971.

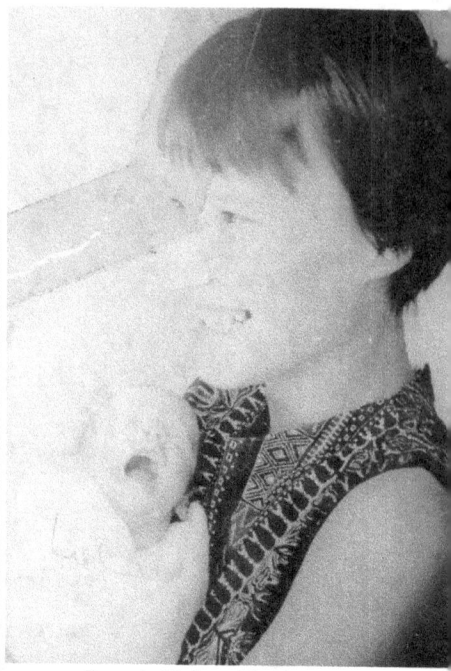

Patrick, Ikalene, Zambia, 1971.

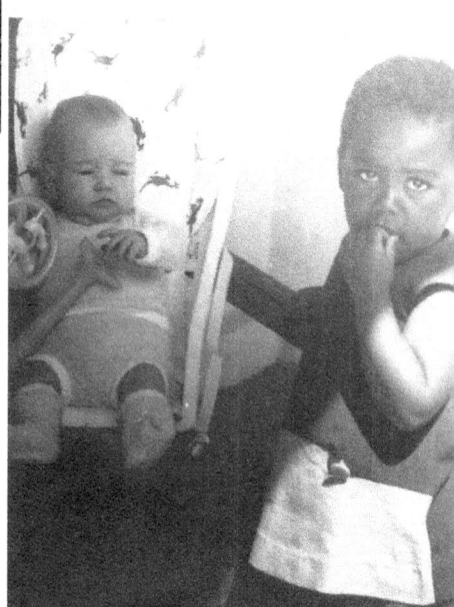

Patrick with Malaika, Mwinilunga, 1971.

In our Renault at Victoria Falls, 1973.

Patrick plays boules, Zambia, 1973.

Nathalie near Bristol, England, 1975.

Nathalie (front R) and Bubu Lili (back L), UPNG Daycare, 1976.

Philipe and Nathalie, Libourne, 1976.

Nathalie with recycled sign, 1979.

L-R Nathalie, Vanessa, Matthew, Patrick, in Tenth Street, Waigani.

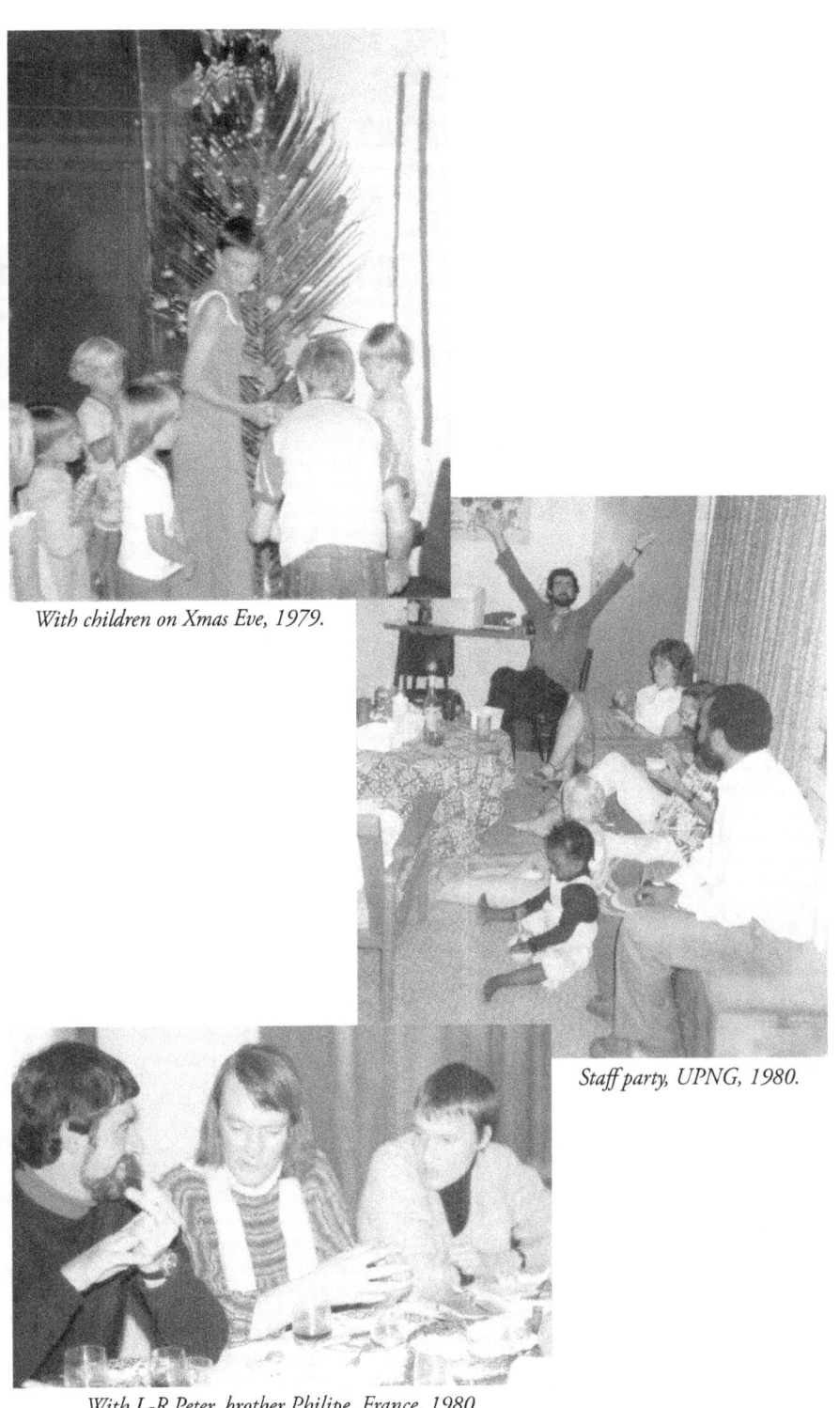

With children on Xmas Eve, 1979.

Staff party, UPNG, 1980.

With L-R Peter, brother Philipe, France, 1980.

Peter & Patrick, Tapini, 1980.

With Patrick and Nathalie at Goroka market, 1982.

UPNG 'Kanaky' group and friends, 1983.

With my children, nephews and nieces, Libourne, 1984.

With friends on canoe to Yule Island, 1984.

Going pinis (leaving) mumu, Port Moresby, 1986.

With L-R Nathalie and Beatrice, 1984.

My father & mother and nephew Stéphane, with my brothers Jean-Marie & François, Libourne, 1988.

With my father, France, 1988.

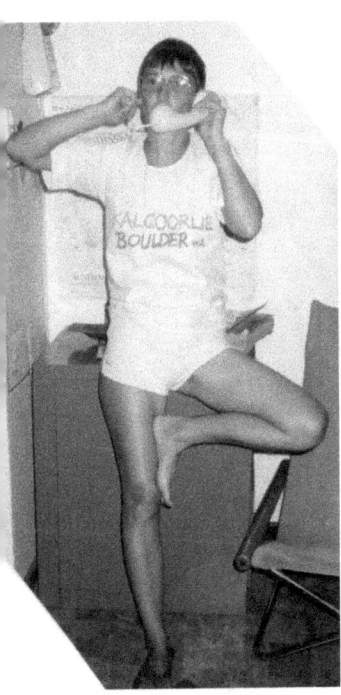

Calling France, 1988.

Peter, his mother and a camel, Coolgardie, 1988.

With Carol, Kalgoorlie College, 1989.

With Digna & friends, Migrant English Centre, Kalgoorlie College, 1989.

Barbara (R) at Kalgoorlie College, 1991.

L to R Patrick, Nathalie & Peter, Nullarbor Plain, 1992.

Hearson's Cove, with Eric the dog, 1995.

Peter and Eric the dog overlooking Karratha, 2000.

Peter, Nanou & her husband Michel, near the Pinnacles, WA, 2000.

Miriam's citizenship ceremony, Roebourne Shire, 2001.

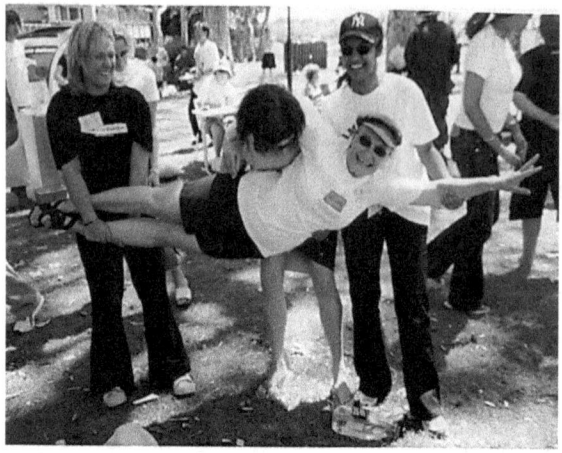

With Zulfah and friendly volunteers at Amnesty International WA Freedom Festival, Perth, 2003.

With Nanou, Bordeaux, 2008.

Culture is… launch MWAA with authors and Wakefield Press, Adelaide, 2008.

At Nanou's with her grandchildren, with nephew Manuel (centre), 2008.

With Patrick, Hango, Finland, 2009.

With Nathalie, Helsinki, 2009.

With one-week-old Zara, Canberra, 2010.

Grandchildren L to R: Maija (front), Zara, Samuel and Erik, Adelaide, 2014.

Joint fiftieth wedding anniversary, with Peter, Michel and Nanou, France, 2017.

With my family, Messanges, France, 2017.

Papua New Guinea

Papua New Guinea.
(http://www.ezilon.com/maps/oceania/papua-new-guinea-physical-maps.html)

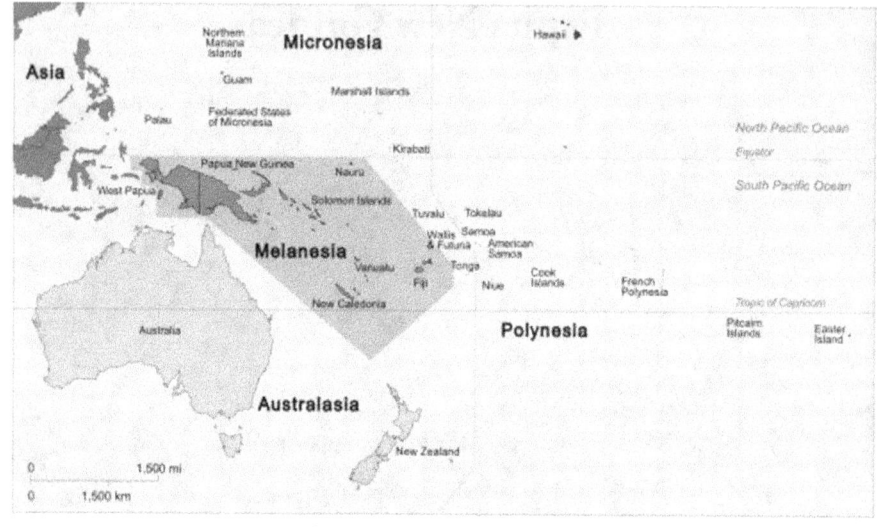

The Pacific including Melanesia.
(https://en.wikipedia.org/wiki/Melanesia)

Arrivée chalereuse en PNG
Warm arrival in PNG

Our family landed in Papua New Guinea (PNG) in July 1976. Nathalie, at the age of one year and two months, had a very distinctive smile with her lone tooth, which she shone at everybody we met. The customs officer loved her for it and waved us through with words of welcome. She spent her formative years and the whole of her childhood in PNG. By the time we left, she was eleven years old, attending Boroko East Primary School, while her brother was in year nine at Port Moresby International High School.

I remember the contrast between the noise and rush of Hong Kong airport and Port Moresby International Airport. The warmth of tropical humidity enveloped us and so did the kindness of the Melanesian staff on duty. People smiled a lot and that made me feel welcome. I needed that because the heat was overpowering us and we had to stand in a long queue in an open-ended hangar to go through customs. The only source of ventilation seemed to come from a half-dozen overhead fans desperately trying to pick up the outside breeze.

Apart from the warm welcome, there was a tremendous sense of patience exercised towards the new arrivals queuing at desks. The airport was busy but there was no tension. Several groups of people had disembarked with us. There were new expatriate families like us who stood in silence watching. Some of the expatriate men consisted of self-assured men signalling their confidence by greeting one another as if they were brothers. Some wore short-sleeved shirts, and long shorts with long white socks, while others had long ponytailed hair and Hawaii-style shirts over casual pants. It took me a while to realise it was

English they were speaking. This must have been my first encounter with Australian English.

It was fascinating to see Papua New Guinean women around me wearing clothing that I wasn't familiar with. Some wore blouses with a blend of red and yellow flower designs over long and bright wrap-over skirts. Another type of dress was a one-piece colourful overall top or *meri* blouse. I would wear one later with pride and on special occasions after an islander friend gave me one as a present. The Papua New Guinean men seemed to be more formal in their style of clothing. Some favoured the long-sleeved business shirts and trousers that many expatriate men seemed to have done away with. Most surprising for me was that people chewed what I thought was red gum, as I hadn't heard of the traditional red-staining betel nut or *buai*.

The sound of languages spoken was also a puzzle to me. For the second time in the last ten years, we were arriving in a newly independent country for which English was the official language, but this time English shared its status with two widely spoken Melanesian languages. Hiri Motu was spoken along the coast near Port Moresby, and Tok Pisin in most of the country, but there were also approximately eight hundred languages in PNG.

As Peter had applied for his job from England, the university provided us with a house and travel allowances to return to Europe every few years. Peter had signed a three-year contract, which he could renew if the conditions suited us, and the university could also terminate it if necessary. I was looking forward to applying for work locally, which as his partner I was allowed to do.

An Australian lecturer called Barry, from the University of PNG, or UPNG, was at the airport with a 'Peter Smith' placard. His role was to greet us and take us, with our two children, who were by then heat-exhausted and thirsty, to the university main campus. He said we'd move into a house there in Waigani. All the way there, he talked about nothing else but the type of car we might wish to buy. It is always easy for second-language speakers to close their ears to some sounds. I had certainly not come to PNG to listen to conversations about the Holden versus Ford dichotomy, from a long-socks-wearing old-expatriate man. His style and conversation reminded me of the settler colonials I used to avoid in Africa.

Next to the house stood a small frangipani tree, a welcoming reminder of the tropical vegetation of Zambia. Even more appreciated was the cold water in the fridge that someone had kindly placed there with other essentials. I put on the overhead fan, as we all needed fresh air, and went to check the other rooms. I heard a sharp scream from Nathalie. Barry had taken it upon himself, as many men tended to do with children in those days, to amuse the youngest child in the family. He had picked her up and thrown her in the air above his head to make her laugh. But when she was up close to the ceiling, one of her legs had touched the fan and stopped it mid-whir. Although the jolt shook her badly, she wasn't hurt and didn't cry for very long. The mechanism had stopped the movement of the fan, as it was meant to do. I think the shock was worse for Barry than for Nathalie. He apologised and said he would go home. I talked of how jet-lagged we all were. It took a few days before we met again.

That first encounter had alerted me to a fact which I hadn't felt so acutely in Zambia, although it had applied there as well. No matter what we did, we were to live in a neo-colonial bubble, although some fellow academics were careful to refer to themselves as post-colonial residents. There was the advantage, however, that the Waigani campus accommodated most of the university staff. Although Papua New Guinean staff were still in a minority at the time, the allocation of housing was designed to ensure expatriates like us weren't more than three or four houses from a PNG neighbour.

The first thing I learnt when meeting Papua New Guineans was how people told me about their place of origin, which Tok Ples, or which language, they spoke at home and how you'd be welcome there if you were to visit. They talked about their lore and language stories. When I was new in the country, I couldn't always be sure which region the person was referring to. When I asked, people didn't often answer in terms of provinces or of compass directions. They might point in a northerly direction. They talked about crossing the sea or *solwara* if they were islanders, or mentioned a well-known town with a market if they were from inland if they were highlanders. But I found that the geographical location of their *ples* seemed less important to them than talking of their village or tok ples.

Most people I met appeared to miss the *ples* or home they belonged to. They had left it behind because of the necessity of obtaining an education and then work. Many had their own families with them. Others had married outside of their ethnic group. This meant the language they spoke at home was often Tok Pisin. This language had started as a colonial contact language combining English vocabulary and Melanesian grammar. Once it was spoken at home, it developed as a Melanesian language and became an official language of PNG, together with Motu and English. The number of small languages had started to decline with mission influence, and because fewer people spoke them. PNG had around eight hundred languages at independence, but many have died and some are still dying. A couple may adopt a lingua franca, a common language for ease of communication, most often Tok Pisin, and their children may not have the fluency in their parents' language. In a way, this is what happened in my family over the Occitan language which I could follow, but didn't speak.

Gradually we met up with Papua New Guinean families whose children were at school with ours. I warmed very quickly to the extended family that surrounded my children's friends. It seemed to make up for our own lack of relatives. Having grown up in a family of five children with about eight sets of uncles and aunties and more than a dozen close cousins, I missed the wide companionship that used to surround me.

Our children often asked when their grandparents would come to visit. It was a hot humid climate where you had to take malaria tablets and older relatives from other parts of the world found the environment harsh to sustain for long stays. Peter's mother had visited us in Zambia, which was more temperate, and visited us later in Australia, but she was wary of the humidity. My parents didn't know how to navigate across continents, and they only spoke French. Some of the grandparents of other families who hailed mainly from the eastern states of Australia came for short stays, which was a big event for the particular family.

At the Waigani day-care centre, Nathalie had a supervisor whom the children called Bubu, as that was the Motu word for Grandma. She was popular and known as Bubu Lily. We still have a photo of her with all the children around her. I made up a lullaby in which her name rhymed with Nathalie. It also included the name of one of her friends there, Johnny, whose mother was one of my students. This is how it went:

Nathalie *li- li*	Nathalie li- li
Et Bubu Lili	And Bubu Lili
Nathalie *li -li*	Nathalie li- li
Avec son ami	With her lil' friend
Son ami Johnny	Her lil' friend Johnny
Elle s'est endormie	She fell into sleep

I was aware that the university campus provided us with a sheltered life. We made up babysitting rosters and all the children enjoyed the privilege of knowing the babysitter and their children. To transport our children to their international schools, we set up a car pool. I hated the sticky plastic Toyota car seat when driving in the heat with the window open. It was my turn about twice a week and I didn't enjoy putting up with the noise of children from the back seat while my face was streaming with sweat at the front.

At Boroko East International, there was a wide range of children from diverse nationalities and language groups. Papua New Guineans who had studied or worked overseas sometimes placed their children in international schools. Many children were also from families whose first language wasn't English. The university and the government tended to recruit staff from the Pacific, India and parts of Africa. Our children at school learned the greetings from up to twenty languages. It made a long list on the classroom wall and was a great education for them.

As a parent, I was aware that life in PNG was to be different for my children from my own early life in France. I knew for example that celebrating birthdays differed in various customs. Definitely the French customs differed from the British one where birthday parties were major children-centred events. I was from a culture that invited adult friends and children rather than children only to birthday parties, like many PNG parents did for their children's parties. Nathalie's best friends were twin girls whose parents hailed from the New Britain islands. I enjoyed chatting to Donna, their mother, at one of the parties. There I heard that my daughter didn't abide by my efforts to embrace the Anglo custom of eating sandwiches for lunch. Donna teased me that I should prepare double lots of sandwiches because her twin girls were fighting over who should swap Nathalie's sandwiches for their rice dishes. Two sets of truth here: Nathalie was one for trying new things and I have always had a problem making sandwiches from my early days in England.

Port Moresby was a pleasant spot to bring up kids. We had fun as a family there even in the years when we, as parents, became weekend taxi drivers, carting our children from aerobics and ballet to soccer and swimming. Over the many years we stayed in Port Moresby, we lived in a house in which our children grew from toddler to teenage. It has symbolised the formation of our family and I decided that number 13 on Tenth Street was a good luck location. It had an unusual design and a lot of character.

Peter and I had to find a balance while learning the art of bringing up children as well as relating to indigenous cultures that we didn't know or understand. Although our own two cultures were compatible from a Westerner's viewpoint, I still wrestled with attempts to merge French and British customs. Reaching agreement wasn't, however, always easy. I followed the classical principles I'd learnt. It was simple

– an idea, once clarified, was to be acted upon. That was logical for me. Peter, on the other hand, followed the pragmatic approach of assessing a situation for its practicalities before we'd get to what he called a consensus. That was too drawn-out for me. It seemed to require compromise, a concept I've always resented. So we had to make constant adjustments as a couple about child-rearing.

At an intellectual level, we both tended to react in the same manner to some established traditions. We were both typical rebels of the 60s, baby boomers, wanting to progress and very keen to be avant-garde. The theatre of the absurd was my credo and Peter's was the kitchen sink theatre. Yet we carefully distanced our personal lives from the practices of modern mayhem. Peter and I always tried to avoid a group mentality with any neighbours or friends. We both believed that educating children in isolation and in far-flung locations was a feasible venture, and we always kept to that principle. For our family, Home was a place where we lived for between six and ten years. It was a place where we kept close to each other, reinforcing the lifestyle that had sustained us.

Every so often when someone left the campus, the children suggested we moved to the newly vacated house for a change. However, I resisted the idea of moving house because I felt living in a foreign country took enough toll on our identity as a family. Our home was the middle one of only three houses of the same design. Built slightly offset from each other and in parallel positions, they were shaped like long rectangles. Both of the long sides, flanked by patios built from extensive sets of breeze blocks, were closed off with wooden gates at either end. These created safe outdoor areas especially for children, dog, pet turtle and a couple of bikes. In the driveway there was a huge mango tree, some of the fruit from which Nathalie picked, often before they fully ripened, while waiting for her lift to school. The house gave us plenty of indoor privacy, yet living on the Waigani campus gave us access to a great social life.

The backyard led through to a preschool playground where all the kids from nearby houses met in the afternoons. From the patio, you could hear children playing. I could hear the sound of various languages, mostly Tok Pisin, alongside English. The children said '*Olsem wanem*. It's all the same,' of each other's games, clothes and toys if they didn't fall into arguments over them. Our neighbours, the Hegartys, originally from Melbourne, became our friends. They used their yard as a makeshift cricket ground where everyone joined in. All the children in the street had a go and great fun. On weekends, we met their visitors, several of whom were PNG politicians. One friend of theirs, John Kaputin, who was to become Minister for Justice, was quick to join in for a cricket session.

The other neighbour, a Yorkshire man, played classical music or jazz on the piano while his wife regaled us with Filipino-style spring rolls and seafood delicacies. Alongside families from PNG there were also children whose parents were from Sri Lanka, Tonga and Namibia whom our children later met in Australia. Life was good on Tenth Street.

Overall, we were a close family and a bilingual home. In fact, there were up to four languages spoken in the home. Nathalie spent ten years in Papua New Guinea, and spoke Tok Pisin with many other children when playing, and understood Hiri Motu from Helen her babysitter.

English was the dominant language of school, and French was the language of home. At one stage when I was researching psycholinguistics, I made the deliberate decision not to analyse what my children's language learning habits were like. I thought that wouldn't be right. From a sociolinguistics angle, however, I witnessed much switching and merging in and out of languages. This was true for both of my children, and even myself.

I recall how Nathalie once switched from French into English at the juncture of two clauses. When I came home from work one afternoon, I chatted with Nathalie in French. As I picked up a mat and some toys to go and sit outside on the lawn, I asked her what she wanted to do once we sat on the mat outside. '*Qu'est-ce que tu veux faire dehors?*' I asked.

Her reply still rings in my ears. 'I wanna...*lire un livre*,' Nathalie said. Her choice was clear: she would read a book.

I was amazed she had split her sentence after the first clause 'I wanna' so distinctly that she expressed the second clause in a different language.

On another occasion when we were all at home, I was cutting some flowers from the back garden to put into a vase. '*Porte ces fleurs à la maison, et donne-les à ton père. On va les mettre dans un vase,*' I said to Nathalie in my native French.

'*Wanem samting yu makim nau?*' Helen, her babysitter, asked her in Tok Pisin what she was doing.

'*Maman i tok olsem yu karim em bilong haus na givim* Peter,' Nathalie explained. Running into the house, she called out to her father and told him what she'd just said in Tok Pisin to Helen. 'Maman told me to give you these flowers to put in a vase,' she said. By the time she told Peter of her mother's request, she was expressing it in a third language.

Patrick's bilingualism on the other hand made me think that in his early days he didn't know where one language started and the other one finished. While with us, he used the language of home. Once outside, he spoke with the language of school or of friends. I wonder if this is the way most of us speak even within the one language.

Once, Patrick's friend Luke came to the door. 'Can I go out and play football with Luke?' he came in to ask me.

'*Tu sais bien qu'on a promis à ta soeur d'aller à la piscine cet après-midi. Dis-lui que tu ne peux pas sortir maintenant, peut-être demain.* You know we promised your sister we'd go to the pool this afternoon. Tell him you can't go out now but maybe tomorrow!' I replied.

He went back to the front door. 'My mother says No,' he said to his friend and closed the door.

It meant a lot to me that both children had a common language with me in the home. I encouraged that practice as a parent and not as a linguist. These bonding sessions always started after school, when we prepared for the evening meal. There was a well-established custom that we all spoke French during mealtimes because that was the family special time when we regrouped around the table and spoke about family-related issues.

While cooking, I asked the kids, 'Bring me the casserole,' meaning the saucepan, and told everyone, '*Les pâtes sont cuites*,' when the pasta was cooked, followed by the popular call, '*A table!*' when it was time to sit down for dinner. Then '*Fais passer le beurre…tu veux du fromage?*' I was offering butter and cheese options for the pasta dish. That is when a real family *franglais* argumentative interaction started.

'*Non*, I don't like *fromage*,' said one.

'*Oui*, I want *tout le fromage*,' the other said.

'*Ah non pas tout…mais laisse la cuillère, prends ta fourchette et ne chante pas à table!*' I was imparting my usual instructions about table manners to Nathalie.

'But I was singing *avant de m'asseoir* (before sitting down),' she called out!

'*Alors assieds-toi et ne chante pas à table!*' I said.

Peter could keep control of the distinction between languages, and always spoke in complete sentences, summarising what I had said. 'Sit down and don't sing at the table!'

'*Demande à Peter s'il veut du sel.*' I was giving directions again, about passing the salt.

'Peter, did you want some *sel avec tes pâtes?*' asked one, while the other passed him the salt to go with his pasta.

When going on holidays in Europe, the children had the benefit of speaking French with my relatives. Once, after a stay with my family, we'd just started our long drive across France on the way to England. Suddenly the children made up a singsong about traffic lights and it was in French. It seemed loosely based on the Monty Python 'I like Traffic Lights' sketch that Peter used to sing to them while driving. They even got it to rhyme and with the emphasis on the final syllable they replicated the southern French pronunciation they had picked up while staying with my family in Bordeaux:

J'ai-me voir les feux	I watch traffic lights
Avec mes grands yeux…	With my eyes so bright…
Et s'ils sont rou-ges	Red…it's too late
Person-ne ne bou-ge	Everyone wait
Et ils passent au ver(t)-re	And when green they go!
Vite! Vas-y mon pè-re!'	It's 'Go Daddy Go!'

Later on, as we were about to drive the car onto the ferry to England, Patrick told his sister of his language-switching strategy as they left their grandparents in France to visit their grandmother in England. 'Let's put the French in the back and bring the English to the front,' he said, pointing to his forehead.

One home rule, however, could never be switched. As they grew older, and they studied formal languages at school, I still spoke French to them as much as possible. I didn't mind which language they answered me in, so long as they never ever called me 'Mummy'. I said I was no 'mummy'. They still only call me *Maman*.

With a coral reef protecting the Papuan coast around Port Moresby, the blue sea was attractive and it also offered the scope for safe activities. There were no predators or dangerous waves. Even children could snorkel over the coral and spot multicoloured fishes and molluscs. Yet our first serious misadventure occurred there.

We'd heard of a seaside spot for weekend picnics called Idler's Bay. My friend, Andrea, had heard that it was a small bay that was apparently good for parents' peace of mind. When we reached Idlers' Bay, with Andrea and her family, it seemed like an ideal weekend picnic area, if somewhat restricted for shade and rather wild-looking. On arrival near the beach, we parked the car further up a track in full sun and carried eskies and bags with us back to the water's edge. There we squatted under a scraggly bush. It was a skinny, ragged pandanus branch, shaped more like a mangrove than a tree. I thought all would be fine so long as we huddled around it, following its shade.

In the meantime, Nathalie set off to play with Jamie, Andrea's toddler son. Armed with plastic spades and swimming aids called floaties, they stepped towards some of the low sea puddles.' We remarked with pride about their developing self-confidence. I watched Nathalie throw her tiny self into the salt water. But, before I could see what was happening, I heard her screams.

Within seconds, she emerged from the water screeching in absolute agony. 'Ça pique. It stings!' She stamped her feet as if to shake off an invasion of mud crabs.

We ran to her, but had no idea why she was crying, what was making her body quiver or how she had been stung. When we got closer, I made out an angry intrusive red mark on her tiny torso.

Not until that traumatic moment did I know of the existence of the nasty box jellyfish or of its sting. I'd find out later that poisonous jellyfish come to the edge of the sea in the warmer months of the year. Yet people said, 'The children will love it at the beach there.' In my state of shock, I couldn't imagine what sort of creature broke through the reef stinging small children who were simply frolicking about in the water.

Aside from food and drinks, we had brought the usual paraphernalia of sunblock cream, a first aid kit with plasters and antiseptic cream. However, these supplies were inadequate for such a crisis. Andrea, recently arrived from England, had done some research about various stinging creatures and had packed a tube of antihistamine cream. At first the cream seemed to soothe the pain, and at least I was able to do something for my howling child. Later I learned that vinegar was the best remedy for the sting as it put an end to the biting which can occur even after the jellyfish has dropped off its prey.

A biologist friend of ours who was interested in the box jellyfish came over to see us. He started to speak in a neutral tone. 'And of course your daughter is going to be in pain for quite a few days.'

I looked at him in distress then turned to my family and said, 'We'll take her home.'

As we drove off, we had to negotiate the bumpy and busy one-way track, dodging families in cars who, unsuspecting of jellyfish stings, were making for the bay. A massive octopus-shaped stain covered Nathalie's whole body. The mark had grown redder.

Hearing of other jellyfish stories later in Australia, I have thought either this one wasn't venomous, or Nathalie escaped the worst fate. She shook and sobbed all the way home until she eventually dozed off. For want of knowing what else to do, I must have used up all of my friend's antihistamine tube. The pharmacy was closed on Sundays and she didn't seem feverish enough to go to the hospital. The pain continued for a few hours into the night. It left a smear on her for days, with visible red marks where the jellyfish had attached its tentacles to her tummy. When she was older, she said she remembered. 'The pain,' she said, 'just didn't stop and it was all over me and touching it made it worse.' What had shaken me was to realise that the sting marks covered the whole of her body because she was so small. From then on, I carefully inspected beaches for signs of jellyfish even on the southern coast of Australia.

Another of Nathalie's early memories in PNG was how a bucket of sand made her go blind. One afternoon, I was in the house while all the kids were in the playground at the back of the houses. Some children were shouting. A mother somehow always knows when it is her own child screaming. No matter how distant the voice, how high-pitched, whether or not it is mixed with sobs, you know that it's your own child's. A cacophony of voices guided me through the path towards Nathalie.

A group of kids were running either side of Patrick as he carried his sister on his back. I grabbed her off him while they both talked in one voice. It was hard to catch what they were saying with a mob of children running and chattering behind us. What was that word they kept using? Was it Sam or sand? It seemed to be both. The sand was in her eyes, she was rubbing them. Yes, it was Sam who had tipped a full bucket of sand directly onto her eyes. She remembered coming out of the play tunnel. Her friend Sam had called her name and she had looked up. From his vantage point above the end of the tunnel, Sam had poured a bucket of sand onto her expectant face.

She described what happened to her. 'I remember it (the sand) falling. I saw a face. It was him – Sam.' It seemed they had had a fight about taking turns in an earlier game. 'I first thought Sam looked at me in the eyes because I had done the wrong thing before,' she said, 'but my eyes couldn't open and I screamed. Patrick came straight to me, put me on his back and ran. I was crying all the way home and I remember him reassuring me, it's OK, Nathalie, nearly home.'

It wasn't until the middle of the night that I had a reaction to seeing my child in pain. Nathalie's eyes were red, irritated and clogged up. Standing her in the shower didn't ease the sting. Water didn't clear the sand in her eyes. Peter reminded me how breast milk was supposedly a good cleaning agent.

'I don't have any,' I replied.

He said he'd get some milk. He went to the fridge and brought some of the long-life milk. As Peter walked past Patrick's room, he said he glanced in to see Patrick with his back to the door chucking darts at a one of his cushions with all the strength of his frustrated feelings. We started to clean her eyes with milk and cotton wool.

She was sobbing, and there was still sand in her eyes. 'I can't open my eyes, they keep on scratching,' she yelled. Five hours after the incident, she still couldn't open her eyes. Exhausted, she cried herself to sleep.

Suddenly shaken from our sleep a few hours later, we all jumped out of bed hearing the shouts from Nathalie's bedroom, 'I can see! I can see in my room.'

I couldn't figure what she could possibly see, as the house was in the dark. Peter warned her to beware as he was putting the light on. He did and there she was, with a bright smile on her face and eyes, repeating, 'I can see you.'

A queasy feeling came over me. I had to sit down as I felt faint. I think of that basic emotion every time I hear of people suffering shock. I can't fathom the various stages of how people recover from major traumas.

The next morning, Nathalie's eyes were so crusty that the lids were glued shut. When we managed to clear them up, we took her to the doctor's to have her eyes checked. To our great relief, the check revealed no scratch marks on her pupils.

Although I've never been very keen on pets, twenty years on I admit having had fun with those we acquired. Getting a pet often happened to a newly arrived family like ours who had no household goods yet. The first people we met were people *going pinis,* as in 'leaving for good' to work in a different country. Their addresses appeared in 'for sale' public notices. While we negotiated the purchase of essential household goods, like a fridge for example, their child mentioned to yours the plight of their friendly dog which they couldn't take overseas because of the horrendous rules of quarantine.

As we left with equipment sticking out of the open boot of our car, they called out, 'And let us know what you decide about the fridge and if the children are still interested in the dog!'

I looked to the back seat.

'And his name's Karlis,' the children said.

That was the first I had heard about a dog. Most parents know how hard it is to counter the insidious emotional blackmail their own children could exercise on the family. The kids, so keen on getting their way, made sure to enlist Peter's agreement and at the same time, reiterate the message to me.

'Well, he's called Karlis, and he isn't that big. He's got friendly eyes and he's well-trained.'

'I'll think about it,' I said.

At that point, the family had gained a pet.

I still wonder how over a period of twenty years we gathered at home a goldfish which committed suicide, some tadpoles, five dogs and a turtle. The latter was a contemporary of Jack, a young pup who decided to play with it. So playful was Jack that he took a chomp of its poor shell, while nudging the turtle. I tried to revive it in water, but it drowned as it was a land turtle. Then, as Jack was still a pup, we tried to train him not to chase madly after cars. We failed and he came to a sad accidental death. We had to bury him in the back garden near the house. Soon after, one of our friends, a Papua New Guinean artist who was going to study in the UK, asked us to take over his dog called Hot Dog. It was a long lanky hound and already famous in Port Moresby, as the artist had used him as the subject to illustrate one of the early school readers. We discovered that Hot Dog was also well-known at the beach where he raced after everyone's frisbees. There was no shortage of good homes with frisbees for us to hand him over to when it was our time to *go pinis*.

Culture moderne en PNG
Modern PNG culture

It wasn't until two years later when with my family I managed to take a trip to the Goroka market that I gained a more complete insight into the cultural life of PNG. The inland regions, in great contrast with the coastal regions and other islands of PNG, had mountainous highlands. The larger town at the centre of the eastern highlands was Goroka. I believe that even before we reached the entry gate into the market I was absorbed by its dynamic ambiance. The place was a feast of noise and colour.

I first walked around the array of *bilums*. I was captivated by the handwoven colourfully adorned bags which were designed from continuous threads of natural fibre. Then there were massive amounts of fresh fruit and vegetables displayed by colour and size in immense rows that stretched across the length of the market. Villagers grouped vegetables and fruit by size, by their round, oval or conic shapes, and in small piles at set prices. Although not as colourful, piles of the main staple, the sweet potatoes or *kaukau,* together with yam, were stacked into high mounds not unlike the way the French display garlic at annual market fairs.

Many cultural words for food came from PNG languages including Tok Pisin and merged their way into the variety of English spoken in Papua New Guinea. They followed the grammatical patterns of the English language. A *mumu* was similar to a Maori *hangi* and people said they were *mumuing* when cooking a pig or chicken in the ground. In PNG if a friend went to the market to buy fruits, they could also say 'I am going for *kaikai*, food.' This phrase was equivalent to the

Singaporean idiom 'going for *makan*', or the Australian going 'for a feed'.

The word *kaikai*, borrowed from Tok Pisin, had become a generic word for food especially during a *mumu* which captured the attractive aroma of the tasty food on offer at an open-air food gathering. Coastal or Islander-style *mumus* were a treat with meat and vegetables wrapped in banana leaves soaked in coconut milk. It was such prized fare that even people who lived in the city could produce delicate dishes by wrapping the ingredients in foil and cooking a feast in their oven at home, *mumu* style.

Cultural terms from many parts of the world have often fused their way into the vocabulary of English. In Zambia for example, a popular mealie-based home brew was called mealie-meal, while at the market in PNG you often saw a couple of *wantoks* (relatives, people who spoke the same language or mates) standing together and chewing *buai*. The drinking of *kava*, however, was more common to the people of the Pacific islands of Vanuatu and Fiji.

Outside the market you saw clusters of men and women squatting at regular intervals along the lines of display that seemed to form a permanent structure in the venue. Some men walked around in full formal face paint wearing plumed headdresses and kept appearing and reappearing at the many intersections that shaped the extensive market area. These elders, whose skins shone from shades of ochre, red, yellow and black, looked to be permanently about to start performing a traditional ceremony. We couldn't wait for them to seize their spears, *kundu* drums, whistles and multiple shaker accessories and to begin their chants.

On that occasion, we were also lucky to witness a traditional dance by a group of Asaro mud men. At one stage that morning, there was a commotion when everyone ran towards the market's entrance when those dancers suddenly appeared. Because their bodies were totally covered with a greyish white clay, their outlook was distinctive from any other group of dancers. They performed a dance and, with the appearance of eerie ghosts, they circled their audience. You couldn't see their heads, as they were totally enclosed in huge clay masks that looked rather like divers' helmets. The Asaro are said to have retained these mud men costumes because when they very first appeared daubed in mud, they totally frightened their enemies, who thought them to be spirits and ran away.

Another striking feature of the highlands is the care people take of pigs, which often moved with the family as domestic pets do. Pigs to the highlanders and many other regional groups were more than mere food. They were used for compensation and ceremonies. Traditionally, pigs had high value as currency in marriage payments. They denoted the wealth of a family and were part of the dowry for a future bride.

Goroka, situated at 1,600 metres above sea level, was accessible by road to many people who hailed from the various regions of the highlands or the northern coast. As a result, a variety of family and regional groups arrived together on market day into an atmosphere of fresh food and fresh mountain air topped up with an added matting of man-made dust that enfolded all its visitors with commotion and clamour. While all these men and women dominated the sound of the air waves calling after each other with the voice of authority, an elder whose headdress displayed bird of paradise feathers with a headband covered with cowrie shells came near us beating the rhythm on a drum just for the benefit of our enchanted children and smiled while we took his photo with them.

When we left, we withdrew along a path out into a thick vegetation of palm, banana trees and coffee bushes. The noise and movement gently abated and by the time we arrived back in the built-up area, we were once again facing large government houses displaying deserted stretches of manicured lawns that reminded us of the early days of colonial settlement.

We'd love listening to Helen, the woman who worked in our house and looked after Nathalie when I was away. She came from Tapini and could play an instrument made of bamboo called the *tutap*, a two-tone music maker which was a sort of hand-held mouth harp. Another

Tapini man we knew used to sit under a tree and smoke from a hand-carved bamboo pipe consisting of a long tube with a carved hole half way down its length. He inserted perpendicular to this hole a shorter tube which he pushed in an out to activate as people do with pan pipes.

Tapini was a small village situated in the mountainous area west of coastal Port Moresby and near the central highlands of PNG. It was known to be a place where traditions were strong in spite of being so close to the capital, so we tried to drive there for a short visit. We set off with friends in three vehicles because we were warned of the difficult terrain. As predicted. the road was impassable and we ended up camping in the open bush some way before we could get there. The roads were so bad that any of the younger people from Tapini who came to the coast to look for work had to make their way by foot down from the mountains.

Back in the early days before independence, the colonial government had made the installation of airstrips a priority in places like Tapini for which isolation and lack of supply by road made life difficult. Access to or from that airfield was known to be treacherous. Some of our friends on their return from a flight to Tapini told us of a popular guest house.

We decided to try again by braving a flight, despite the many stories of hair-raising flights we had heard, and decided that a trip in an unusual light aircraft was attractive enough for us to give it a go.

Landing there was the very first ordeal in our adventure. The twin-engine aircraft had to circle down a valley to reach the start of the airstrip, then it bounced on the gentle rise into the plateau. Finally it relied only on its brakes to stop abruptly at the end of the runway. The airstrip was devised to terminate on a slight upward incline which helped slow it down until it faced the edge of a steep cliff.

As we disembarked, we saw people busying around the aircraft. Some were greeting passengers, yet many were there to help offload the luggage. The guest house manager was at the head of a chain of people shouting directions to his sidekicks downloading beer, wine and cigarettes. I was sure I had seen the seat behind me on the aircraft stacked high with cigarette cartons. I couldn't help but imagine that the reason a passenger was turned away before we left Port Moresby was that the plane was hauling all the bar supplies that the pub needed on time for its weekend action.

On the next day, we went to watch the moves the plane followed at the point of take-off from the runway, which we could only compare to a short aircraft carrier. We squinted into the sun as the plane lurched off the end of the airstrip, then dipped out of sight into the valley only to re-emerge into view parallel to the foothills. It then appeared to follow, as if at eye level, the mountainside four-wheel drive track which wound its way up the hillside above the deep gorge.

In spite of the many concerns people have about the difficult position and layout of the Tapini airstrip, data suggests that it has suffered very few cases of accidents and that they were mainly due to bad weather and poor visibility.

Most of our week was spent looking out for snakes when taking walks and watching the twice daily landings and take-offs. It was a fascinating spectacle from the veranda of our guest house. Yet something extraordinary happened to make our trip even more memorable.

It was the most remarkable *singsing* or demonstration of traditional dancing and songs I saw in PNG. This mesmerising event took Peter and me by surprise one evening. At first, the only thing we heard was like a rustling sound outside. As we stepped down from the veranda, we realised that the bushes were all alive with voices and surrounded by people.

Quickly the atmosphere built up to sound like a warm-up to a battle rather than to a dance event. Across the whole village, the reverberation of the chanting could be heard. It was accompanied by the tapping of bamboo sticks and spears and a jingling sound which kept up the rhythm into the early hours of the morning. The vibrant pulsations projected throbs and vibrations of a very different character from the controlled demonstrations of drumming we watched at later festival events.

The next day was very quiet and, perhaps due to a surge of fresh outdoor air in Tapini, Peter and I gave up smoking. Well, Peter gave up smoking for good and I stopped for a whole seven years. We never went back to Tapini, where our cigarette packs abandoned in our room may still languish on the very top of the wardrobe in the room of our guest house.

There were some occasions when people's actions showed that while they were keen on following their traditional lifestyle they could at the same time find ways to modernise the practices that customs demanded.

Before the onset of mobile phones, the most modern item of technology in the 1970s was the pocket calculator. During my visit to Goroka, I was astounded one day while standing in the post office at the sight of a PNG man ahead of me in the queue. I took him to be a coffee owner who'd come in to do a business transaction. I first noticed him ahead of me because of the dominant stature of his headgear colourfully decorated with traditional bands and bird of paradise feathers. I hadn't seen anyone in Port Moresby wearing a full headdress while doing business in town. At that point, I also realised he was wearing nothing but a sporran held up by a woven belt. As he approached the teller's booth, his hand went to the side of his belt to reach under it for the plastic calculator that he had tucked against his bare skin. His practical bearing stood out in complete contrast with the backdrop of a uniformed postal clerk whose name badge was hardly visible behind a high office counter.

Independent as PNG had become, there still seemed to be times when its citizens needed to work through the effects that church and state had imposed on their language and customs during the colonial era. I found it interesting, however, to observe how a PNG sense of ownership could easily be superimposed on the more recently introduced customs. In fact, a direct return to cultural ways was at times openly on display.

On one occasion after a visit to a Jesuit Catholic mission centre near

Port Moresby in Sogeri, Peter and I were invited to join its community for afternoon tea to welcome some church dignitaries. When we arrived there, it was clear that the festivities would go into the night. Leis of red bougainvillea and white frangipani flowers were pinned to long stretches of bright bunting. Coloured lights were leading the path to a covered hall where massive amounts of fruit and food trays were piled up on trestle tables near the refreshing drinks standing in long rows of iced buckets.

While I was looking around at a few young women putting finishing touches to the side of a curtained stage, an unexpected sight caught my eye. I saw a Papua New Guinean Catholic nun swinging her hips while she wore a grass skirt she had secured over her grey habit. She wore a lei of frangipani strung around her neck and a red hibiscus on one ear. It turned out she was practising her steps for the traditional show that would welcome the new bishop at Sogeri.

One of our neighbours hailed from the large island of New Ireland. With his family, they'd set up a magnificent garden consisting of an array of banana trees, corn, greens and root vegetables in what for them must have seemed a tiny plot alongside their house. Their crop was ample enough to feed their own family and friends. I used to relish the corn and spinach they often gave us. Sadly, they were hit with a family crisis which they had to resolve in urban Port Moresby far away from their home.

At work, we heard that the father of that household, who was a UPNG staffer, had suffered a sudden collapse. He'd been rushed off in an ambulance but was pronounced dead by the end of the day. He'd been a healthy-looking man and his death came as a shock. The widow and the children were distraught and the whole family was wailing. When we offered our services, we were reassured that members of the local New Ireland community had already stepped in to help the family through their ordeal. We were told how customs around grieving were very specific for each community. Apparently, back in their village the bereaved families followed the tradition of burning and destroying the dead man's homestead after his death to appease his spirit, and that included his house. The family then moved on and rebuilt a home somewhere else.

One afternoon the following week on my return from work, I was faced with a disturbing sight. The garden belonging to that family had been totally burnt to the ground. It had become an empty plot, with no more vegetation in sight except for several branches of banana trees lying uprooted just above ground. There was a pungent smell and a haze of smoke hovering around our neighbours' house, which although left intact now looked gaunt and puny. The whole family had left.

My other PNG neighbour, who was from Lae in the Morobe province, told me how one of the New Irelanders, a *wantok* of that family, had seen them off to the airport and they had all flown to bury the deceased man in his home village. She also explained that his widow knew she would have to move back to the province of New Ireland because her husband's housing was allocated with his Port Moresby job. So the family in their bereavement had made the major decision to abide by their tradition and destroyed the fruit of the man's labour, which was represented by his garden plot. They'd left the university house standing, as it wasn't built by him or by his relatives.

Near Port Moresby and only thirty kilometres inland was the Sogeri plateau. The Laloki River, although not the largest in PNG, had such a fast flow downhill that it formed impressive gorges and was spectacular at the Rouna Falls. Barrages were built along the river to supply water and electricity to the capital. It was a place we visited on regular occasions with our children and friends. We went for picnics to a nearby cascading stream called Crystal Rapids. It was such an appealing spot that sometimes we also camped there. Emerging even before daylight, the sharp chirps of birds woke all campers to the start of a cheerful day under the cool shady trees. Because the area was close to the paths that marked the start of the Kokoda trail, we encountered many PNG and expatriate families there who also came to visit this famous spot.

The home of the Koiari people, Sogeri was a very active centre. It had one of the four prestigious senior high schools of the country. From that school, students went on to tertiary studies and attained high-level occupations. One of them was Michael Somare, who led PNG to Independence and later returned twice as its prime minister.

Our weekend outings to Sogeri and the foothills of the Owen Stanley Mountains instilled in our children and their friends a love of jumping over stepping stones in and out of cascading waters. They became practised at diving into swift water torrents. I realised later how popular swimming down fast-flowing rivers had become in PNG.

A few years on in the early 1980s, we went on a trip with our PNG friends and colleagues, Andy, whose family came from the Simbu region of the highland, and her husband John, who was originally Australian. Setting off from the northern coast town of Lae in the Morobe province, we first stopped in Bulolo, where we had the chance to meet her mother who lived there.

The drive down to Bulolo turned into a daring event for Andy. We had left Lae and had just settled in the car admiring the open view over the wide river bends which ran parallel to the fast-flowing Bulolo River when Andy in the car ahead stopped the vehicle. I wondered if she'd found the ideal picnic spot or planned to show us a significant landmark. As we approached her car, I could see we were very close to the river. She was pointing down towards the wide grassy river verge. I was surprised when I heard her say she'd ride downriver for a stretch of the journey. She was in the middle of explaining to John where the next large bend in the road was and asked him and all of us to watch her start and then drive ahead to collect her a few kilometres further downriver.

At that point, she went to the boot of her car, from where she pulled what looked like the inner tube of a large car tyre and, with a cheery wave of farewell, she made for the riverside and jumped into the water, trusting that we'd find the river bend at which she'd told John we should meet her.

So we all followed the next stretch of road and wide-eyed were able to witness this amazing PNG river sport in action. Called *gumying*, after Tok Pisin *gumi*, the word for tyre and rubber, it consisted of people travelling down the river astride a rubber tube. It was an astonishing acrobatic feat at times which required a strong sense of balance and familiarity with water. It seemed dangerous to me, as it lasted for several kilometres and you could lose sight of the participants for some time. John had no problem locating the major bend where roads and rivers became close again. Once we got there, I realised we weren't the only people whose role was to pick up water adventurers, the majority of whom were young Papua New Guineans like Andy.

After a soothing tea break with Andy's mother in Bulolo, we drove further south on a road that took us alongside the MacAdam National Park, which was home to very rare pine trees, birds and tree kangaroos on the way to the old town of Wau. We'd heard that Wau had been a busy gold mining centre from the early 1920s. However, very little was left of this once active centre. The Wau Institute had remained active as a museum of insects and butterflies and was still able to host research conferences. Apart from that, the only other remnants of this goldfield were two massive semi-derelict unused dredges on the edge of a dry riverbed. Although it was an eerie and deserted area, a few people had found their way to the riverbed and were busy panning for gold. They worked totally unaware of the tourists' movements around them in the old mine site.

We arrived in Papua New Guinea at a good time. It was an exciting, newly independent era for Papua New Guineans to thrive, and for us in terms of personal development and career. It also turned out to be an ideal place to take young children on great camping expeditions.

We liked to travel with several families for a few hours along the Papuan coast to a beach near the village of Gaba Gaba. We carried ample food supplies and jammed the car boots with camping gear. We organised lights to see through the night, spare water, wine and bread galore. On arrival as we all poured out of the cars, we split into two groups, one playing cricket, a sport I still had problems understanding, while some of us opted for volleyball, a game that I'd played many a time at the seaside in France with siblings, cousins, uncles and aunts in my youth. I remembered how we had all travelled in the one family car and taken over the nearest beach by storm to start a volleyball game, with or without a net.

On our first visit, in the afternoon of our arrival the villagers from nearby Gaba Gaba welcomed us. They surprised us by leaving some watermelons and home-grown vegetables just outside our tents while we were playing ball games on the beach. Volleyball over, we were hot, sandy, sweaty and desperate for cool drinks. The ice had melted in our eskies. With the sun high in the sky radiating over the white long open beach off the bright blue Coral Sea, the only thing we wished for was a slice of the juicy watermelons that stood by the tents. We couldn't wait any longer. With a huge knife in hand, we worked through one of the massive fruit. It wasn't the first we had sampled but it was the best.

Hooked on thirst-quenching watermelons from then on, we planned all our camping trips by number and size of the juicy fruit. This was a novelty, and in direct contrast with some years later when I heard some my Australian friends planning a trip by the number of 'coldies' or cool beers they needed to get there. Later, when our family moved to the north-western part of Australia, I was surprised at the answer I received when I asked about the distance from Karratha in the Pilbara to Broome in the Kimberleys. I was told it was measured by the numbers of cartons of beer required!

At Gaba Gaba, the first night at the campsite was always a lot of fun, with the fire crackling through the still night and Peter reading Dr Seuss's *Green Eggs and Ham* to the children by the firelight. This meant we would soon put them to bed, and the adults then took over with their own storytelling. Some liked boasting of their student days and drinking patterns, as well as their knowledge of the stars, each one trying to impress the others.

But for me, the experience was a dilemma. I liked the fun and reverie but spoiled its enjoyment by starting to plan and prepare for the next day. When I attended parties, I really had somewhat of a reverse social hang-up. I wanted to start talking, loudly and non-stop, whereas many people said they only managed to do so after they had their first drink. I felt I was different. Instead, I needed to wait for them to have downed a few drinks and, as their inhibitions lowered, I could at last let go of my natural voluble personality. I was then able to talk freely and incessantly without anyone objecting to it or calling me a chatterbox or any other nickname.

Joining in with the group banter and laughter was very cathartic, as it helped rid me of my tense mood. However, it was also when my other habit, the one in which I fretted about things, started to take over. I began to busy myself around the campsite checking that everyone was kept happy. Then after a while, I would retire to the tent and start puzzling over the next day's tasks. Would we have enough food to donate to the villagers in return for their gifts on the last day, or what would be the best activity to amuse the children with in the morning?

On that first evening at Gaba Gaba, I must have gone to sleep, because I woke up to some blurry sounds that I couldn't quite make out. It sounded like whispering and tittering. As it was in the early hours of the morning, I assumed people might still be sitting by the fireside.

Peeking through the tent door, I was startled to see the campsite in brisk activity. A few Papuan children from the nearby village had grabbed the bat and ball we had abandoned the day before and had begun to play a game. Some of the older kids from our campsite already had got up to join them. It was such a friendly game that I had to be in it. The next thing I knew was that they had recruited me, a French woman for whom cricket remained a mystery, into fielding for one of the teams, although I wasn't sure which one was mine.

Les langues et la politique
Language and politics

All regions produced remarkable artefacts but acquiring great Sepik river carvings was always very popular with expatriates. Some of those were fine wooden-crafted items, including imposing Sepik hooks and totems representing the spirits that guided their folk through their life.

In the Sepik region, there were extraordinary examples of traditional architecture in the form of the Haus Tambaran. A communal worship centre, it had tall decorated hardwood pillars supporting a massive house structure. A prominent ridge pole formed its frontage, with large carved storyboards which outlined some local legends. The roof was designed as a sloping structure that decreased in height all the way down to the ground. This feature was used as inspiration for the facade of the PNG's modern-day house of parliament, a striking architectural landmark in Port Moresby.

Another area which had a major cultural impact for PNG was on the southern coast around Port Moresby, where Motu was the dominant language. A contact version of this language developed into Hiri Motu, which with Tok Pisin, English and PNG sign language then became one of the four official languages of Papua New Guinea. The influence of the Motuan people who lived around the capital had always been strong socially but it also had an economic impact. They were famous for designing *lakatois* as sea vessels. These were double-outrigger canoes made of bamboo. Their sails were made of handwoven reeds. The Motuan people had a long history of using *lakatois* to trade along the coast. Because they lived in houses on stilts over the sea, they fished, crafted items and exchanged goods with the people along the coast who derived their staple from sago palms. On the Papuan coast, carvings related to seafaring. Along the southern coast, Trobriand Islanders carved designs on thick tree bark which they displayed on the prow of ships. These mainly figured spiralling shapes often described as symbols of eternity. Although similar in style, they have a quite different texture to a similar bark material called *tapa* cloth, which is Fijian.

Standing on the Papuan coast near Port Moresby was the striking village of Hanuabada with all its houses on stilts over the sea. It was a lively centre with lots of people fishing from canoes and with children running along the boardwalks between the houses and diving in and out of the water. Another popular and famous meeting spot in Port Moresby was the Koki market, where people flocked to buy fresh seafood, fish and crabs for their families. and where they enjoyed a yarn with friends.

In the far western border with West Papua, the men from Telefomin and Ok Tedi in western New Guinea wore as a cover for their penis a long curved gourd, which Europeans thought to be designed as a phallic artefact. They became perceived as a symbol of erotic male art in the Western world. When considering Western views of voluptuous women, however, no one could construe eroticism from the sight of women with their swinging breasts as they walked uphill while balancing large *bilums*. Hanging over their backs with their handles secured over their foreheads, those *bilums* were a symbol of the women's multiple roles and of their hard work and skills. In them, they lay a baby and its bedding precariously placed above their load of firewood. The use of *bilums* diversified very fast. Among expatriates, the signature gesture to say that you embraced your new culture was to hang a *bilum* over your shoulder on the way to the market. There, the ubiquitous *bilum* symbolised expatriates and Papua New Guineans alike. With *bilums*, heavy with books or tinned food, trailing over their shoulders, the search for *buai* or *kava* to chew or drink for an evening of fun seemed to be made easy. In fact, walking about in the cities of

Australia, I've sometimes spotted people who've lived in PNG by the way they carry a *bilum* either as a dress item or as a shopping bag.

When we arrived in PNG, Peter and I both undertook to develop our professional potential through the university. Peter being an educationist, started researching the history of education in PNG from the colonial days of missions and early government intervention. He published a history of PNG education and later obtained his doctorate in the same field.

At first, I started teaching but also wanted to top up my qualifications from France with a practical teaching certificate appropriate to the English-speaking world. I obtained a postgraduate diploma of English as a second language at UPNG. I also tutored and lectured there. The highlight for me was the co-production of a *Teach Yourself English Grammar* workbook with the Professor of Languages John Lynch.

I also spent time on a research project collating the sociolinguistics features of English in Papua New Guinea. Part of my research technique involved socialising with people, and I found it stimulating because I spent time talking and mixing with many PNG students, scholars and citizens outside of the classroom. Many of the students and staff voluntarily contributed more and more of the idiomatic phrases I was collecting and we had fun discussing them. I also found the newspapers' letters to the editor and other informal sources of language like noticeboards to be great sources of information.

After a while, I signed up to do a master's programme in PNG English, or the English spoken in PNG. I worked well into the night after the children went to bed. Most days I went to bed in the early hours of the morning for a short sleep until the gecko on our back wall started chirping at the hint of incoming dawn. When I submitted my project, I was advised to widen the research topic and it was suggested I should update it from a master's degree to a doctoral thesis. I couldn't resist the challenge and after taking two years' leave, I managed to finish it as a doctorate.

This is how I delivered a third superhuman creation that was in a way my third child. The outcome of all that hard labour was entitled Papua New Guinea English, a Doctoral Thesis. It weighed five pounds twelve ounces, was heavier than either of my children at birth, and its gestation period was much longer.

Those who speak several languages benefit from the advantage of a greater awareness about the people around them and their world. I recall with embarrassment how my absolute lack of know-how during my first year as a tutor put my students at risk during a class. One morning I was standing in an upstairs teaching room when I noticed that the back-row students all looking out of the window and whispering to each other. I wondered what I'd said that brought such distraction to the lesson. Then I became aware of the whole class staring at me, but I didn't understand the word someone repeated to me until a translation came through.

'*Guria*,' one of the students called out. 'Earthquake!'

I looked up to the students and called out, 'Don't panic!' and then made for the door ahead of them. I think I even dragged the tablet arm of a chair into the doorway with me.

By then, all of the upstairs classes had emptied into the corridor and the students were running down the stone staircase, which started to shake furiously under us. It went from left to right and there was a groaning sound, although no one, not even me, made any noise. By the time we reached the open space in the quadrangle below, it was over.

People were milling about, so I said to a student who was near me, 'We might go back to class then!'

'No,' he replied, looking sideways.

I learnt that day of the danger of aftershocks and of the safety regulations in times of earthquake. During my next class with the students, I asked how they knew an earthquake was coming that morning.

The answer came as a uniform explanation. 'The trees were shaking in the distance.'

Had I been aware of it or known of the meaning of the Tok Pisin word *guria*, I might have cleared the class first. Instead I'd blocked the way out of the door from my students with a student chair! I felt foolish and inexperienced and the class kindly accepted my apologies.

Although Papua New Guinean teachers were able to staff secondary schools, the university lecturing positions when we first arrived were still allocated mainly to expatriates. Papua New Guinean staff, besides the vice-chancellor, were administrators, tutors and technicians. By the time we left UPNG, the staff allocation had started to change and Papua New Guineans were recruited in the professional positions.

In my last year in PNG, in order to complete my language doctorate I had the interesting experience of auditing the class of a linguistic lecturer from the highlands who'd completed her master's degree in Canberra. I was pleased to attend Julie's class as she'd been one of my students in my first year of arrival.

I learnt how Melanesian languages used features that were rare in European languages. For example, there are pronouns like 'we' *mitupela* (he and I) that excludes the person you are addressing while another 'we' can include the listener *yumitupela* (you and I) from that group. I also came to understand that categories could differ in naming colours or describing feelings.

Over many years, I found that diverse protocols had distinctive significance to different people. Greetings in particular differed widely around the world. In PNG, the way to start a conversation was by asking each other, 'Where have you come from?' and follow that through with 'Did you travel well?' Tok Pisin, '*Yu go we nau yu kom?*' merges into one the two questions 'Where did you come from' and 'How come you are here?' Then people would check on each other's relatives. A while later, a very different informal conversation might follow these sets of very traditional greetings. The initial formalities were always present at the start of any occasion and were often elaborate.

Graduations at the university campus were colourful events. Some of the graduands chose to wear traditional costumes under their gowns, and to bear face paint and display birds of paradise feathers in their hair. Many opted with pride to have the full string of their names read out to confirm their home identity.

Some differences in meaning across languages may often have derived from environmental factors. Differences between cultures were reflected in the languages of coastal people and highlanders from inland. A significant cultural item of the highlander culture was the 'axe' needed to cut wood while a seafaring 'canoe' represented the islander lifestyle. Later and to fill modern cultural needs as technical and transport necessities arose, highlander or islander languages borrowed words for these items from each other. They did this the same way that French and English borrow from each other as in '*le weekend*' or 'a *coup (d'état)*' respectively.

People around the world use a range of parts of the body to express varying feelings. In French, '*J'ai mal à l'estomac*' refers to bad digestion, possibly bile, whereas in PNG English 'My stomach is on fire' shows direct anger. Later I heard that in Aboriginal Australia an angry person might say, 'I'm feeling wild', while Australian English speakers might simply 'chuck a wobbly'.

Language idioms helped convey the speakers' mood with people using the specific phrases relevant to the circumstances of their social groups. For Tok Pisin, for example, people like to quote the phrase '*karim lek*', translated as 'to get a leg over'. The phrase comes from traditional courting ceremonies. However, some English speakers just tried to say they wanted to get together with someone and get a leg over, which in English has more of a sexual context. Speaking in Papua New Guinea English, if you wished to meet a partner, you might be 'trying luck', perhaps from 'trying my luck' in English and '*traim tasol*', just trying, in Tok Pisin. The English spoken in PNG was for me a wonderland of creative idioms where language thrived.

Being generally gregarious and because I was also from a second-language background myself, I often felt comfortable approaching people to make conversation. I found it quite easy to adjust my vocabulary to different occasions. To show enthusiastic approval, in PNG English, I might say 'That's *feiva*', whereas in Australia, I could say, 'This is solid' or 'It's cool'. In French, I might say, '*C'est chouette.*' PNG English was a topic popular enough for the *Times of PNG* to publish a string of articles I wrote over several weeks.

The use of the English language to express one's thought became a chance for the writers to play around with and exploit the full potential of the official language, as it applied to the Papua New Guinean context. Within a few years, a New English was born. This was the era when a long line of New Englishes was emerging around the world. PNG English is a literary language on a par with African, Singaporean, and Northern American Englishes, and separate from its other official languages Tok Pisin or Hiri Motu.

Besides choosing the English language, PNG people often chose to express themselves in Motu or Tok Pisin. The latter had a wide following orally and in writing. At that time, there was a regular cartoon that was developed as a series in the media. Entitled 'Izuzu Lu', it owed its name in jest to a character called Lu who drove the famous type of utility vehicle which was commonly used as a taxi service on PNG roads. Nicknamed 'ute' both in Australia and PNG, this popular vehicle had a back tray that could sit families, their valuable pigs and their faithful dogs. In the towns of PNG, Izuzu Lu became a popular satirical character. He was driving a distinctive Izuzu ute and perpetuating jokes about life at the market and other trendy venues.

The cartoon, complete with Tok Pisin captions, covered the Papua New Guinea lifestyle in Port Moresby, called *Mosbi*. Printed in the national newspaper, it eventually extended to the rest of the country. It mocked the manner in which both expatriates and the PNG elites tended to use Tok Pisin mixed with a lot of English jargon to impress others and eventually became a publication well sought out by PNG and expatriate readers alike.

The early years of PNG independence reflected the prowess of its artists and authors. They produced works in all forms and from all provinces. From artisan to playwright, they formed a plethora of new voices. The musicians from the first national band, Sanguma, resided at the National Art School. From them I first heard the surprising sounds that thongs could make when slapped against tubes. They also demonstrated during the Pacific Festival of Arts at an Ella Beach gathering in Port Moresby the capacity of the two main types of drums we'd hear in PNG. The colourfully carved drums called *garamut* were hollow or slit logs, often used by people from the coast and the islands. They were rarely small because they were often carved directly from tree trunks. The sticks used to draw sound off the drums' concave area were carved from branches that matched the trunks' size. Coastal people as well as Sepik River people preferred to strike the stand-up *kundu* drums we'd heard in Tapini and Goroka. With a stretched snake skin at the top, and a handle on the side, those drums accompanied traditional *singsings*.

Any festival featured the latest play by Nora Vagi Brash. John Waiko and Kumalau Tawali were prolific in all genres. Works of poetry like 'Reluctant Flame' by John Kasaipwolova flourished in booklets and leaflets. The short story 'Manki Masta' preceded Russel Soaba's many works of fiction. The abstract art of Akis and Kauage came to signify the modern Papua New Guinea art style, with two-dimensional drawings of the spirits, as they saw whitefellas.

There were high-profile people from Manus and Milne Bay who championed the philosophy of diversity in Melanesia. This was the catch cry of the then Father John Momis, an islander and ex-priest who was later to form a political party. For a philosopher, he was practical enough to make key alliances with various parties, amending his political platform as needed. He was in great demand at the university for his speeches and ideas. Like John Momis, many literary figures went into politics.

I once joined in with Nora Vagi Brash, the playwright who was also active socially for the betterment of women's status, on a protest march to speak to Father Momis. It was an impressive group of hundreds of women that set off, and we were also pleased to involve a few men. Women and men left the university amphitheatre where we'd held weekly meetings. Our group was protesting against the lack of fair treatment that was afforded to the women who fell victims to men's random harassment and rape in the streets of the capital. I felt happy that we made a lot of noise and that the issue was given full exposure. Although our protest didn't result in direct protection of women, I felt that with Nora we raised public awareness of the feminist views of women's harsh social conditions of the time. As it turned out, we'd misjudged Father Momis's expertise. He specialised in decentralisation of governments, which he followed through to negotiate for the state of Bougainville.

We once went on a holiday outside Papua New Guinea. Our Port Moresby friends Andy and John recommended that we should stay in some chalets on the island of Tanna, which they knew well. We travelled to Port Vila, the capital of Vanuatu, and spent three weeks on Tanna, a small Melanesian island in the south of Vanuatu. From Port Vila to Tanna's capital Lenakel, we travelled in a three-engine aircraft that looked, sounded and acted like a helicopter. The flight was memorable. The aircraft was slow and didn't fly very high. The first small island we stopped at, the pilot made us hop out while he went to collect the mail. He walked to a tiny cabin on the other side of the open field where we had landed. People stood to the side of the strip smoking cigarettes while waiting for the aircraft to take off again. When it did, I looked ahead at the pilot, who was sitting cross-legged examining his trousers and socks. He had picked up some burrs on his clothes in the field so he spent the next leg of the journey all the way to Tanna busily removing the burrs. Because we wore shorts, we'd been spared this ordeal.

Lenakel is the name for both the capital and the language of the island. The small bush resort where we stayed had very pleasant beaches with shady coconut trees, woven-roofed chalets and beach shelters close to the sea on its western side. This setting was so peaceful that I remember listening to the gentle lap of the sea while relaxing in the shade of the coconut tree with the children playing in the sand and Peter reading a book. This image has remained the vision of ideal bliss which I use as instant recall of peacefulness whenever I practise meditation in yoga.

On the eastern side of the island, however, all the sand was black due to the effects of lava from a nearby volcano. With the help of guides, we climbed the entire slope to this active volcano and looked into its crater to hear and watch rocks being constantly catapulted upwards while the volcano rumbled and made growling noises. That trip was a special experience which the whole family still talks about, and yet we missed out on seeing the night lights of the seething fire from within the volcano because we couldn't get a babysitter for our young children were too young.

For that visit we were, however, able to select the guide by the language they spoke. Because of the split cultures that colonial powers had imposed on Vanuatu, the guides who were available on the island were either French or English speaking, a reflection of the immediate past of Vanuatu before independence. As my children rarely heard French spoken outside the home, I was pleased with that option that allowed them to talk to the guides in French all the way up the volcano and around the island. Vanuatu, the following year, gained its independence from England and France and was able to include Bislama as the official Melanesian language in its constitution. Bislama, like Tok Pisin, is the language developed from an English and Melanesian-based contact Pidgin.

During my years living in PNG, something momentous happened that widened my understanding of the Pacific. To start with, I learnt that France wasn't prepared to offer independence to the indigenous people of New Caledonia, who named themselves Kanaks. My chance to find out more about the Kanak people came with the arrival at UPNG of three young students whose study language wasn't English, but French. They had enrolled in the university courses but couldn't speak fluent English. I was asked if I could be of help to them. I was able to give them the social interaction that allowed them to increase their English language skills. We had a few parties and they met many Papua New Guineans. At about the same time, a group of new Vanuatu citizens, or Ni-Vanuatu, were reading law at UPNG. This meant the Kanak students could have access to bilingual students. In fact, some married into PNG families, while they also acted as contacts for some of the visits by some of their country's leaders.

Around 1980, Jean-Marie Tjibaou, the Kanaky leader, came to PNG in an official capacity, and I spent many sessions in Port Moresby translating for him. With Yann Uregei, Tjibaou worked to raise support on a basic issue – his Independence Party wished to register New Caledonia for independence at the United Nations. They'd decided to rename the country Kanaky. I've rarely met anyone so convincing of the cause he pursued. For me, he was in the same class as world heroes like Nelson Mandela and Xanano Gusmao. Once in Port Moresby I was able to hear his line of argument when he held his own with a journalist from *Le Monde*. They had what we now call in Australia a robust debate. He predicted the socialist Mitterand's coming to power as president of France, but he was mistaken in his belief that Mitterand would champion the Kanak cause internationally.

I remember one night Jean-Marie Tjibaou emerging from our study, where he was staying with us as a guest. The Kanak students had arrived and it was time to serve dinner. Jean-Marie Tjibaou came through with a charming smile of defiance proudly waving a coloured-in piece of paper. He had put the final changes to a design that was to become the symbol for independence – the Kanaky flag. The food had to wait as he commented on the significance of the colours. Green was for the land of the ancestors. Red stood for the united blood of the Kanak people. Blue symbolised the sky and the Pacific Ocean, while yellow represented the sun. This was a man of conviction. Soon the case for Kanaky independence was officially lodged with the United Nations.

He was later asked to Port Moresby again as a guest for a conference on the south-west Pacific. 'PacificMyNuHom' is the title he gave his talk. Translating his speeches wasn't difficult. He was a logical, well-schooled person in the French tradition, who used classical language. I heard later he had started his studies in a seminary. His arguments were linked and sequential. He imparted luminary words to his arguments. He reflected his broad vision of the Pacific as a united entity and his passion for his people and his advocacy of independent Kanaky.

There were then, as there are now, obvious parallels between the plea for independence for the peoples of West Papua and the Kanaky peoples, yet neither issue has been resolved. Tjibaou's speech was broadcast on PNG's national radio. I knew that the French Embassy staff could track me down. I didn't realise then that the PNG government and probably the Australian one were watching. Mitterand, once he became president, unfortunately didn't meet the expectations Jean-Marie Tjibaou had of him. He allowed delays for the independence timetable, which wasn't considered under his presidency.

By then, I had moved to Kalgoorlie in Western Australia. My new location made it hard for me to keep in contact with issues in the Pacific. I was shocked one afternoon to hear an ABC broadcast announcing that Jean-Marie Tjibaou had been assassinated in New Caledonia. Some of his compatriots didn't have the patience to wait for the great diplomat to lead them to the negotiated resolution he'd carefully mapped out. They may have thought that they could jump phases to get further and faster. 'Divide and rule' is sadly a motto of colonial powers. From over near the Indian Ocean, I sat down and cried for this remarkable champion of the Pacific.

Thirty years after painstaking negotiations, independence for Kanaky has yet to become a reality. Although his name is celebrated in present-day New Caledonia through the creation of the Tjibaou Cultural Centre, his spirit must be hankering after Kanaky. I'm still committed to the cause and have declared to my Kanaky friends that I won't visit New Caledonia until it becomes independent. Wielding hope for the Pacific, there have been signs that Tahiti might get there first. Still waiting.

A few years after we arrived, we became conscious of the increase of homeless youths in the city. Young people from the rural areas were attracted by the bright lights of Port Moresby. Unable to find work, some seized the chance to break in and grab some food from houses. They were called rascals in Tok Pisin. The city gradually became more security conscious, although on the university compound we were quite safe.

As crime grew more dramatically, some rascals, small pockets of tough youth, adopted more offensive behaviour. Individuals and companies started to erect fences in order to isolate the rich from the poor. A mix of access to weapons and criminal behaviour led to many assaults on both expatriate and Papua New Guineans. We were lucky at number 13 on Tenth Street and didn't experience any of this first hand, except for the day the kids left their bicycles in the driveway while we went to the beach and we returned to find them gone. We figured it was our responsibility to put them indoors.

Camping and outings at night became restricted. At that time, in the 1980s, there was no television in Port Moresby, so we occasionally went to the drive-in cinema. It was our favourite outing and the kids spread out their sleeping bags in the back of our station wagon and watched such cult movies as *The Pink Panther*.

Peter and I tended to sit on canvas chairs at the front of the car. One night, one young man tripped over our loudspeaker and, presto, my purse disappeared out of my picnic basket. The following Saturday morning, I went shopping and a young man greeted me outside the car. Although I couldn't place where I had seen him, I returned his greeting. As he walked off, he asked, 'You going to drive-in tonait, Misiz?' It wasn't until then that I realised how visible we were in our expatriate bubble.

Leaving Papua New Guinea after ten happy years there was the toughest yet the gentlest of experiences.

'We've come to see you out. It's for good luck.' Our Melanesian neighbours stood at the door. 'It's our custom,' they said. 'We like to safeguard our friends as they leave their house.'

Their presence also took the fuss out of locking up and dulled the ache of glancing at the house for one last time. Arriving at the airport, I sensed a sweet smell. The scent got stronger, reminding me of the frangipani tree I had left in bloom in the front garden of our house.

'We made these leis for you to wear,' a group of waiting friends called out. 'Look, there's one for each of you! Try them for size!' Someone said 'size-o' and giggling resounded throughout the group, a Papua New Guinea English in-joke, no doubt.

After I hugged a couple more friends who had come to see us off, I noticed my flowers were wet with tears. Ten years of seeing people come and go and it was my turn to be *going pinis* – I was leaving for good. The circle around my family and me was getting larger yet more blurry. Melanesian people were familiar to farewelling expatriates, a regular post-colonial mission.

'On behalf of your Ni-Vanuatu, Kanaky and Papua New Guinean friends and colleagues, we want to say we indeed had good times together and *yumi olgeta*, all of us, wish you and your family well.'

By that time, letting go was becoming a real dilemma. Embracing one another felt good, but in the end, I'd have to let everyone of those hands slip out of mine. The lei around my neck was getting bruised, wetter, and the inebriating smells made me reel with emotions.

'I can't find it.' I was fumbling through my *bilum*, muttering to myself. 'I wonder what I did with it,' I said, rummaging through the bag. 'It isn't there!'

Unable to find my camera when I wanted to keep a record of this significant moment made me even more emotional.

'Do we really have to go?' my daughter asked.

'We've been here many years, you know it's time we left.'

Not the answer the poor little girl in ponytails was hoping for. 'Why can't we stay a bit longer?' she went on.

I turned to take my son's hand and, with my daughter still tugging at my neck, I started to address the farewell party with what I meant to be a long formal speech. '*Yumi*, we…' After that, talking was no longer an option. I was left with a tight smile and tears interfering with my vision. The scene became one happy heartbreaking blur. Moving on and away from the group, with my family around me, I started to wave at the crowd of Melanesian companions cheering us on, in various languages.

'Don't worry! *Maski!* You'll like Australia. *Oi-be*, you'll see!'

The group was still shuffling while guiding us towards the tarmac where the aircraft awaiting us stood bearing the colourful Air Niugini plumed insignia.

Our Melanesian friends stopped there, forming a semicircle either side of the hostess at the departure gate. The sound of the last Tok Pisin words I was going to hear for a long time echoed. '*Lukim yu gen!* We'll see you again. *Lukim yu behain!* Goodbye.'

Of all the break-ups in personal friendships and relationships, that day meant the greatest loss for me and for my family. We were leaving behind a ready-made extended family on the Waigani housing campus. I was to find that even extensive networking in Australia could never replace the close ties I had experienced in Papua New Guinea.

Still waving goodbye to the outside world, we entered the Boeing bound for Australia, and settled into our seats.

The passenger near the window next to my husband leaned over, and in a jarring brash American tone called out, 'Can you keep these flowers away from me. I'm allergic to the smell.'

Those words, from a person I thought to be a tourist, resounded along our small row of seats. Their immediate effect sparked off a new emotion in me – some kind of rage. My eyes darted towards the window seat and I performed what some call a Gallic shrug, using French as an escape valve. '*J'ai pas compris ce qu'elle a dit!* I didn't get what she said!' I exclaimed, turning to see my kids by then well ensconced in their seats.

That person couldn't possibly be asking us to remove our precious frangipani, the symbol of our lives and friendships in the tropics, woven together into personalised leis and ceremoniously placed around our necks as a farewell gift by our Melanesian friends. Somehow that remark epitomised the change in our cultural lifestyle that was to come.

Peter sat down and politely removed his lei. Taking a deep breath, I sat across the aisle from him and fastened my seat belt. The children had already secured theirs. The three of us wore our leis all the way to Brisbane, or was it Sydney, I now wonder – our first port of call after leaving Port Moresby Airport. Such a potent moment that I couldn't recall anything about the rest of the flight or even where we landed.

My children said they had to force me to surrender my lei at one of the quarantine booths. When landing at all airports in Australia, passengers will spot multiple green and gold fruit and vegetable quarantine receptacles which double up as Welcome signs. These stand so tall that they render everything else invisible as you take your first step on Australian soil. I however insisted on keeping the PX trademark labels of Air Niugini Airlines as a keepsake from this heart-rending trip. My son's initials were also PX, as in Patrick Xavier. It was indeed hard for me to let go.

The only thing clear in my mind now was finding my camera when I emptied my bag at the hotel. There it was, where I had packed it, brooding and snug in the side pocket of my backpack, too late for farewell snaps.

Australia

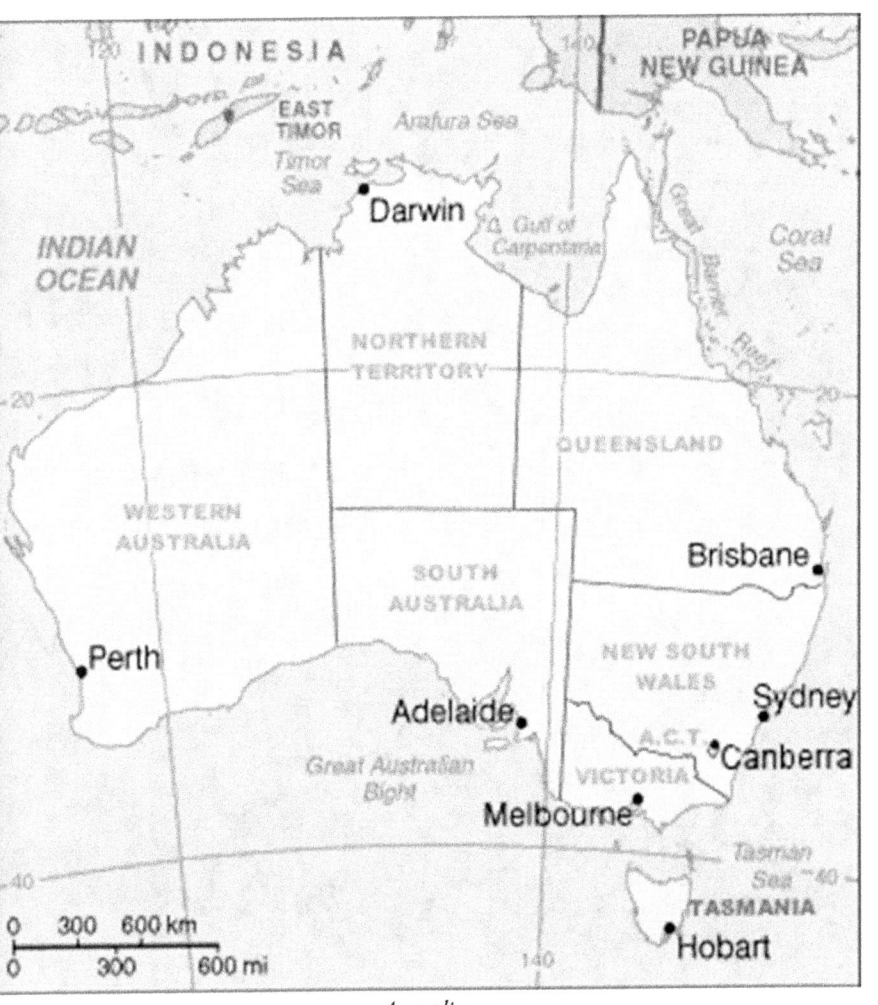

Australia.
(https://en.wikipedia.org/wiki/Australia)

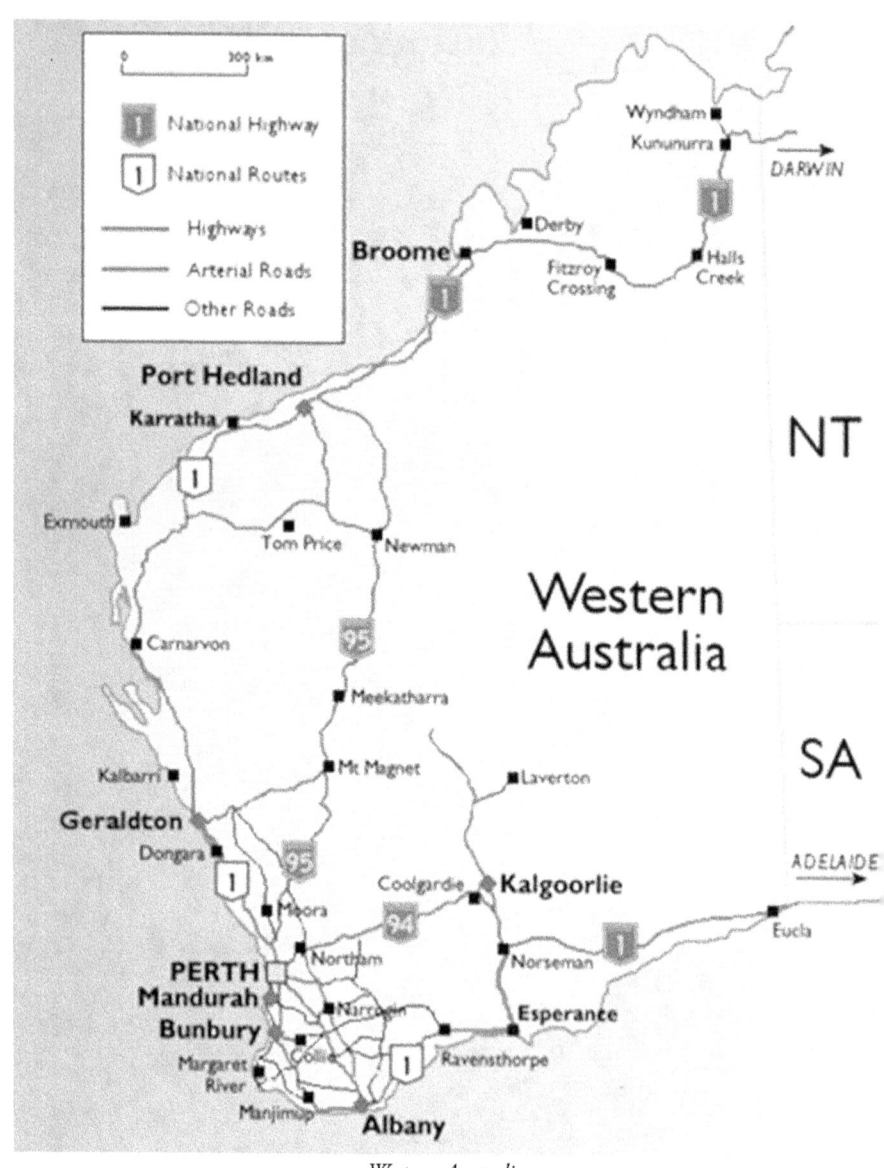

Western Australia.
(https://en.wikipedia.org/wiki/Western_Australia)

Chocs culturels
Cultural shocks

'Will they think I'm a migrant?' I had puzzled over the question before I came into the country. But I focused instead on Australia's wide open spaces, '*Le grand espace Australien*', and its exciting opportunities. The distances were huge and the population was sparse. First the beaches spread for kilometres on end then there was the interminable number of hours between Canberra and Perth and finally the long drawn-out streets of Kalgoorlie stretching across each other to form geometrical grid patterns.

A little house on a quarter-acre block of virgin bush awaited us. We pulled out every weed and planted a lawn. School started and some kids asked our daughter where she was from, saying she looked a bit dark. Was it because she wore a yellow T-shirt with a Papua New Guinea design for her team sport event, I wondered? That one comment set the scene for me. I made sure I bought the plain yellow sport uniform shirt she needed. Although we had come from Europe originally, we didn't seem to fit the European mould any more.

Australia was a continent of its own, where English seemed the wrong language to use. Everywhere you went people looked and sounded different.

I had started to think I was fitting in until one day at the newsagent's a pimply shop attendant had difficulty in responding to my request, 'Can I have three boxes of matches?' I felt taken aback by the slow service. I wanted the local paper and three boxes of matches. 'No, not two, thrrrree boxes of matches.'

On the way home, I noticed I'd been short-changed. Years later, I realised that the youth behind the counter probably didn't try to cheat me on purpose or because I had a 'funny' accent but that he probably lacked basic maths skills. Sometime later, I started teaching English as a second language and needed a map of the town. I pretended to be a tourist. What of the spelling of 'enterance' over the door of the tourist bureau?

'No worries, mate.'

Nobody seemed to worry about it but me.

Going back to my English language students, I used this as a teaching tool for spelling awareness. And for the following week's homework the students spotted errors such as 'dinning room' in the local paper, *The Kalgoorlie Miner*.

On the first occasion I went to the shops in Kalgoorlie, I couldn't help but notice that people were buying brand-new household equipment in massive supermarkets. I'd heard that every other year when people moved for a new mining post they simply left everything on the verge for council pick-ups and then went shopping for the same goods wherever they started their new jobs.

Once I finished shopping, I could no longer find my car in the hypermarket style car park. It was before the days of electronic clicks on car keys. A pleasant couple came to help and we started a conversation outside in the open car park.

'No, I'm not from Perth, or Melbourne. The only family I have in Australia consists of a husband and two children. We're making our own life,' I wanted to say.

I realised later the open car park was the place where people socialised as they would when in a market place in southern France.

Back at the house, I was trying to settle in but the look of those long streets worried me a lot. I felt I should meet someone so I knocked on my neighbour's door. As she asked me in, there on the hall wall, I spotted a clock in the shape of Zambia. It was exactly like the copper clock we used to own in Zambia. Although my neighbour hailed from India, she had also lived in Zambia. It might be a small world I lived in but where I was it had very long streets!

In this world of long and wide streets with large open spaces, we planted a lawn, added some trees and kept watering for many long years. I quite liked setting up the garden but of course in my new surroundings I had to fit in on many levels. The main issue that came up for me was always my French accent.

'I can't quite get you, you'll have to speak more slowly,' someone said.

'Simply change the word, and start again, they'll get it in the end!' I said to myself.

I found it strange that, wherever I lived before, everyone seemed to follow what I said, but then their first language wasn't always English. Neither was it here judging by the names in shops, notices and telephone books, Boganovic, Aroyo or Demeis. And it seemed there was an Australian way of saying them. The same was true of Aboriginal names or Wongi words. I found it strange how Australian people are always experts on Aboriginal names. I expected names that had Indigenous provenance to be pronounced phonetically and instead they were always anglicised names with an Australianised emphasis on vowels. For example, as in the place name Kuringgai, I thought of it phonetically as *guringai* but the Anglicised version people recognised was more likely to be Kur-ring-gai. The place name in WA I had most difficulty with was the country town of Carnarvon which I emphasised as 'Car-nar-von instead of the accepted Car'narvon.

While calling overseas the night before, I had said, 'Yes, we live near the desert, and yes there are Aboriginal people in town.' It was tempting to add, 'Yet few people seem to be aware of this.'

My mother was asking me about Aboriginal people.

'Yes, there's an Aboriginal family in the street next to us... Of course their children go to school.' To get my message across, I used an example that the French could relate to – people's eating habits. 'They're just people like us who like to sit outdoors and eat outside even if they aren't having a barbecue.'

Life in Australia was hard to explain when writing back home to my relatives in France. When I next wrote to them, I might send them a photo of the empty space around the ghost town of Kanowna or perhaps of our long shadows over the deserted beach at Cape le Grand National Park.

Landing in Perth when we first arrived, we had to spend a few hours in the city centre until we could fly to Kalgoorlie.

Our taxi driver, hearing we were a new family migrating to Australia, had offered to give us a rundown on some West Australian history. 'Alan Bond, just because he's famous, managed to have the only high-rise hotel erected on the seafront in Perth,' she said, 'and Observation City, as he called it, is a deeply resented building.'

Although we didn't pass Observation City in Scarborough Beach Road or the port of Fremantle, we also learnt that Alan Bond had just won the America's Cup.

'And in Fremantle,' she added, 'tourism has taken over, just like that. They've spoilt Fremantle with all sorts of fast food and fish and chip cafés. It all happened overnight. And they've distorted the idyllic character of the port. Businessmen are so greedy they even reclaimed part of the sea.'

Peter and the two children sat up in their seats listening with interest but I was quiet. Our move to Western Australia saw us all uprooted from Papua New Guinea, the most multilingual tropical island country in the world, to one of the largest developed countries that claimed to be monolingual. I was shell-shocked by this major upheaval and it wasn't just due to jet lag. I had a pang of internal turmoil, a feeling of unease. For the first time, we were to live in a country we could call our own having been born in various countries where English wasn't the first language (except for England of course!). Behind my short-lived silence was a single-minded resolve to hang on to any prop that allowed me to mix and merge and to do so as early as I could. I was anxious to make a start to my new life in Kalgoorlie.

Scanning either side of the road from the back of the taxi, I started to feel better. Lined by acacia and low-growth sea-swept tamarind, a scenery which for me exuded warmth, sunshine and reminiscences of long-forgotten personal experiences in Mediterranean climes. I relished this new environment. It, however, meant a total change for our children. It was a concern for us that both had left all their friends behind and they'd have to adapt to a different school system. But they seemed cheerful and interested in their new country. I wondered if after ten years of tropical humidity they might welcome their first taste of winter.

Nathalie was eleven years old and showed she had retained some of her study topics. Instead of asking, 'Are we there yet?' she broke the silence with, 'We're going to live in a semi-arid desert.' Then she asked, 'Why couldn't we live in a nice place like Canberra? Do we really have to wear winter clothes?'

In the meantime, Patrick, who was in his teens, spotted the prominent ovals and soccer grounds in the hope of finding activities he could relate to and eventually join. 'Look, an Italian Club here! Italians are great footballers!'

I regained my voice. 'Yes, they were also some of the early gold diggers. And the school might teach Italian,' I said.

'But Italian isn't the same as French,' he argued. 'I've done two years of French and you can't expect me to switch to Italian.'

For his part, Peter was his usual reassuring and rational self. 'Don't worry, you'll soon make new friends. You might even go on school camps and get to see more of Western Australia,' he said.

Most of their statements turned out to be right over time.

As visitors to Perth city centre, we felt that the one and only Hay Street Mall at the time exuded a small town 1980s mood. After a walk up and down twice and two checks of the animated London clock on the quiet mall on that Sunday in Perth, it was a relief to head for the small Sky West air terminal that was to take us to our destination, the town we'd heard so many contradictory rumours about, Kalgoorlie. We couldn't wait to see our new home. It turned out that a rather run-down hotel, the Sandalwood Motel, was to be it for a few days. Its redeeming feature wasn't the small cold swimming pool or its location at a respectable distance from the brothel activities, but the heavily scented and fruit-laden lemon trees outside our room window.

Soon after our arrival, someone took us on a tour of the poorly lit-up tin structures that formed the renowned red light district – a total of four of them! We emerged from this experience feeling let down after the many yarns we had heard about Kalgoorlie's brothels. We had expected the venue to be a mini-version of the famed Amsterdam precinct. It had obviously been 'sexed up' by our overseas Aussie friends. As soon as they had heard of Peter's impeding position at Kalgoorlie College, they had gone to all the trouble of procuring us a couple of taped documentaries of ABC television coverage. They wanted us to have a preview of the titillating night life in remote Western Australia.

The real surprise for me was the layout of a town with long wide streets, right-angle grids and the laid-back, veranda-covered main street. It was reminiscent of many of the early Wild West films I watched during my youth in France.

On the day we arrived, there was some action at the Hannan Street traffic lights, with a pub on each corner. Heaps of Boulder City Footy Club supporters were flaunting their souls as well as their bodies. 'You bloody beauty!' they chanted. Parading their black and yellow team's colours and waving scarves, beanies and banners, they jigged on top of a bus. The celebration of a long-awaited victory consisted mainly of shouting at anyone around and we were it.

We soon learnt of the petrol-head lifestyle and of the revving of cars, a common mining country town habit, it seems, in the proximity of traffic lights. Because they were located at the main intersection, they tended to house a uniformity of landmarks – a pub, a liquor outlet, another hotel and pub, and, in the case of Kalgoorlie, a chemist. It took these car drivers sporting P plates with pride no more than three minutes to reappear at the traffic light opposite the one they had just left in a haze of fumes.

A few years later, on a chance visit, we stopped at a depressed-looking Broken Hill only to watch what seemed an action replay of those scenes – three-minute going around the block by bored P-platers.

A few weeks later, I was sitting at a cafe in Hannan Street one morning reading the paper in search of the town's cultural life. In the century-old and respectable local rag, *The Kalgoorlie Miner*, I spotted an advertisement: 'Happy Hour Topless Bar –The pub with the family atmosphere'. Puzzled at the thought of the strange family set-up they must have in Kalgoorlie, I decided to buy a copy and cut the notice out. It was my turn to send media snippets of Kalgoorlie to my Australian friends.

Just as dominant as the public houses in Kalgoorlie were the bleak motels you could find along any of the highways. They sat in the old mining towns within a two-hundred-kilometre radius off Kalgoorlie and were a reminder of the former hotels of the gold rush. Less than half an hour north-east of Kalgoorlie was the hotel at Ora Banda, Spanish for 'Band of Gold'. It reminded me of the setting in the cult film *Bagdad Café*, which featured spinifex haphazardly rolling across the road as trucks went swishing by. Yet it exuded a harsher impression than the mellow romanticism portrayed in that film.

This establishment became famous for being the scene of the fatal shooting allegedly by the owner, a retired senior police detective, of one of the leaders of a bikie group which patronised the hotel. Then it was the centre of a killing spree and complex court cases for a few more years. I realised later that motels were also prominent icons along the Nullarbor where they doubled up as roadhouses, complete with Australian-style microwaved burgers and chips and Coke fridges. They formed roadside experiences that were duplicated all the way across the northern regions of Australia – the Pilbara, the Kimberleys and the Top End.

After a week, we eventually got the keys to our house.

'I bag this room,' Patrick called out.

Nathalie ran past us racing to the room at the end of the passage. 'This is mine and that'll be my own shower!' she claimed, pointing to the bathroom.

We soon decided the kitchen could take a table and the dining room would work better as a study. Looking out to the veranda, I thought that the narrow strip of cement on the edge of the red earth could make a great outdoor meal room. Yet something was missing, it seemed.

'Can we have a dog? Nathalie asked. 'See, it's a huge yard.'

It was big and soulless. We were still missing Hot Dog, our Port Moresby pet we had handed over to a good home.

'I've already told you,' I said, 'we'll have a dog but only if it's trained and not too big.'

'Are we going to buy a car too!' Patrick was cheering up.

'Definitely an Australian one!' Peter said.

Not as exciting as choosing a pet dog or a car by the looks on everyone's face, our first task was to look for suitable home furnishings. Having left Europe in 1968, we were in 1986 moving permanently to Australia and the only furniture we had to our name were a cow-skin stool from Zambia and some Kwila shelving from Papua New Guinea.

So our first family expedition in Kalgoorlie was to explore the shopping potential of the town. Having spotted the fish and chip shop for that first evening dinner, we saw there was a tourist bureau and a square named after Saint Barbara, the patron saint of miners. It took us a while to realise that the entrance to the major supermarket was through the back street car park, a common feature of many large stores in Australia. We walked around to find a massive car park facing a walled-in K-Mart. This vision was strange and so was the sharp penetrating taste of nickel in our mouths emanating from the nearby smelter. What a contrast with the open-air Koki market in Port Moresby, where we would stroll around looking for fresh crabs and mangoes.

As we entered the shop, the shock of trolley consumerism affected me, probably because I'd spent many years away from urban communities. People must do a lot of cleaning in mining towns, as there seemed to be a broom and a mop sticking out of everyone's trolley. I also noticed they held rubbish bins and a battery of saucepans wrapped in cardboard, dutifully enclosed in plastic bags standing upright as if supported by the inevitable new toilet brush.

The way we all bumped across the aisles into each other was a hazard. And our obvious consumerism made me feel I was joining the consumer society that I'd tried to avoid in my earlier years. I didn't realise that in the days before companies introduced fly-in fly-out employment, in the eyes of the Kalgoorlie mining community we were mere blow-ins.

Before coming to Australia, I didn't expect I'd stroll down long streets that were so wide you couldn't see the house numbers on the other side. I'd never walked along invisible kerbs covered with red dust and in full sun at thirty-five-degree heat. I didn't imagine I would walk from my house to a fuel station just to buy a loaf of sliced white bread at a 'ginormous' price and pick up a Carnarvon banana off the counter for more than a dollar. That's when I heard my mother's voice. She used to complain about me always leaving everything to the last minute. I thought that must be true of my shopping habits too! In my youth roaming around in the vineyards of Southern France I couldn't have guessed that I, a French girl from the wine country, would switch to being Australian, drive a four-wheel drive into the bush (literally), attend barbecues or eat Italian pasta or a Chinese takeaway after a film while drinking, of all things, a beer!

Late one Sunday night in Kalgoorlie, I was standing by the back veranda with my left foot resting on my right thigh – like a heron. I had just opened the sliding door to warm up my limbs that were numb from the constant airflow of the air conditioning. I was leaning against the wall gesticulating with my right hand towards the veranda. In my left hand I was holding the telephone handset. I was in the middle of a phone call to France.

'Of course it's hot outside…ide.' I'm pointing towards the folding chairs while registering that there's an echo on the line again.

'*Ah bon, alors vous ne mangez pas dehors*? So you don't eat outdoors then?'

'Oh yes, we have barbecues…yuz.' I spotted the barbecue plate that still needed cleaning.

'Surely you don't sit down for a meal out, not in the heat!'

'Not really...we just stand around and drink white wine...ain, as an aperitif...iif, if you like...aik. Some drink it all the time...aim.' I've started looking for my words in French.

'So it's not like England.'

'Oh no, it isn't the same, at all...all.' I'm laughing now.

'The Australians, do they drink tea?'

'We do have afternoon tea here too...oo.' I'm conjuring a typical Aussie day.

'*Alors vous ne buvez pas de café?* So you don't drink coffee?'

'*Oui il y a des cafés...éé*, but if you want a good cup...up...' I know I'll have to hang up soon. It's such a bad line.

'So they make good coffee?'

'If you want a good café, you make it yourself...elf.'

After a few more sweeping statements, I say goodbye, hang up and close the sliding door.

How can you talk about your feelings and your frustrations with an echo that doubles and bounces your phrases to linger in your subconscious? Hearing those repeated word endings, I thought 'That was the wrong word I used there' or 'They'll think we only drink white wine in Australia.' As I put the receiver down, I knew that I wasn't really speaking with my mother. Once again, I'd fudged my feelings behind trivial talk.

A pattern developed over time for long-distance communications. Whichever country, town or village I ever left, I'd write back to family or friends. However, the pleasure of writing letters overseas after a while slipped away. So when I noticed after a few months that my regular letter writing routine was phasing out, I guessed that to be a sign that I'd started to let go of my previous home and possibly was feeling some ties with my new surrounds.

Because I'd moved to a developed country where English was the first language, I wondered after a while what I was learning besides new English idioms in my new environment. Maybe trying to keep a low profile? Not easy, as I've always talked too loud, too fast and at the wrong time. This trait of mine had nothing to do with language, however. I was the same when I was a child back home and liked to make people laugh to get out of awkward moments. I was also the funny one in my family, the one who always broke everything, the one who got away with kicking a flowerpot off the balcony. 'It wasn't me who broke it, it was my foot.' As a child of a large family, I always feared I wasn't heard, and I felt my views were mostly ignored, hence my efforts to be funny to at least be noticed.

These survival tactics re-emerged after a few years of embracing the Anglo-Saxon world through my married and working life. I had then and still have a wealth of strategies at my disposal, aside from the ability to amuse others. English not being my native language, I was able to develop a way to pick out the strings of discourse and meaningful conversation that I wanted to take on board and to push the rest aside, as if I hadn't heard it. Linguists call this selective listening. It made my life much easier in my daily Australian ventures and it gave me the option to switch swiftly to a neutral mode and to act as if I was saying, 'Sorry, I didn't quite get that.'

This became very handy when being exposed to sexist or racist jokes. It was rare, I found, that people repeated a bad joke or a comment once they realised it could be offensive. I once questioned someone talking about 'the gin in the ditch' saying, 'I thought around here everyone drank beer.' Nobody spoke up to enlighten me with the red-neck alternative and colloquial use of 'gin' when referring to an Aboriginal woman. The 'I didn't quite get that' tactic was also useful at other odd times like when being stopped by traffic cops. In the rare cases people attempted to mimic my accent to my face, I could always respond with 'I can do it better than you!'

Anyone in my now nuclear Australian family could tell you how they jostled with one another in the futile attempt not to have to sit next to me at the cinema so they could avoid answering my eternal question, 'What's so funny?' I had the habit of speaking out just as the audience had regained their composure and it was sure to embarrass my children. My excuse afterwards was 'I'd never remember what the joke was to ask you later!'

One of my harshest experiences was the day my two children started to look like everybody else in the schoolyard. One day, I went to attend an assembly. A sense of dismay overcame me when I realised I couldn't recognise them in the crowd. The children told me later they had expected me to spot them right away and I hadn't imagined otherwise. There I was, trying to remember the colour and style of their hair. But they had had a haircut in keeping with the latest fashion and the sun had neutralised their hair colour. There was only one criterion I could use – height. After all, I thought, they weren't tall. 'Look for the small one, not that short, the ones on the edge perhaps?' Working my way through to the middle, I found their friends first. Then I caught a glimpse… 'Was that really them? Oh yes, of course that's the uniform, no wonder they all looked the same…' And they'd been waving to me all that time, wondering why I was so reserved and didn't smile back.

When the children started to use Australian English, I wasn't worried. After all, they were already using English at home anyway. One English was as good as another as far as I was concerned. I remembered there were times I didn't catch what people said or what was meant by the turn of phrase they used. When I heard Nathalie's friend was too 'crook' to go to school, I wondered how she could develop the 'croup' overnight. It was the cryptic Australian rhythm and speech forms that threw me. Although I didn't know many of the idioms, I guessed some of them. When one of Patrick's friends said, 'We gave it the flick', I gathered the meaning. I'm not sure, however, that I fathomed the full connotations of a remark like 'Don't worry about this guy. He isn't the full bottle!'

Sometimes I'd catch on to the meaning of a word like 'cool' years after it was out of fashion and then I'd start using it myself. But my children laughed at me for being out of date or for using it in the wrong context. I was in luck after a decade because 'cool' came back in and soon even the French borrowed it. The children's type of language didn't worry me nearly as much as their newly acquired Australian behaviour because at least they heard their mother tongue in the home even if they'd stopped using it in conversations. So in my mind, language was a secure bond that I had with my children and that we would never lose.

Behaviour, lifestyle, manners, greetings, eating patterns and associated social skills – these were the real bugbears which used to haunt me even as far back as in the Australian expatriate community in Papua New Guinea. I didn't know if what rattled me most was seeing my children 'disappear' into other peoples' house for sleepovers or hosting birthday parties at my own home. There I'd have to watch them act differently to the way I'd brought them up – the running around, the games they played such as Pin the Tail on the 'stupid' Donkey – that was a lot for me to accept at once.

There was also the new version of Musical Chairs – 'Let's do it with cushions' – and that after I'd just shifted all the chairs in the house for it. Pass the Parcel was always the easiest. I could understand the sense in that. I always knew how to arbitrate if two of them grabbed a present at once or when the game was due to end, because I'd prepared the parcel. I felt more involved in that game than in any other ones. I even got to like it! We'd planned it together and that gave me control.

I still had difficulty, however, accepting the 'going out to people's houses' for no special reason. My mind was racing. 'Whose house is it? How long will they stay there, what will they do, what time should I collect them, what will I talk about to the parents when collecting them?' These were troublesome questions for me. There were a lot of complex skills involved, including finding their friends' places.

'What do you mean house 675?' I asked.

'Oh, I meant to explain. They use lot numbers, not street numbers where she lives,' Nathalie replied.

Not knowing what was correct or the norm was the worst and I never got used to it. While I took my kids back home in the car, my first words always were 'Why did the parents not come out to greet me when I arrived?' I'm pleased to say that my children cooperated to help me out. They explained the party games to me, prepared the parcel with me and told me how they'd wait outside for me at their friends' house. They even gave me the phone number so I could announce that I was on my way. Together we worked out a compromise that appeased me and minimised the various levels of cross-cultural gaps. This must have lasted for about sixteen years…a lot of years not to feel comfortable in a parent role.

My early days in Australia weren't always easy-going. Like many migrants do, I was probably trying too hard to become Australian. My efforts centred on a need to feel accepted. Yet I only wanted to be included up to a point. I wanted to fit in but I didn't want to integrate. Obviously like my Gascony ancestors I was rebelling against the idea of losing my particularly *têtu* (hard-headed) identity. While fighting imaginary barriers that were invisible to all but me, I was presenting a front to show how much I could fit in.

'Yes, two hundred kilometres, of course, I'll drive down,' like most people do…yet I'd never done more than a few small town errands by car before. 'Can you travel for work?' a job interviewer asked me. 'Not a problem,' I said. 'I've been on dirt roads before.'

Well, that was true, but that was in Africa, twenty years back and it was just to get my licence. Of course before the interview I had had a go at driving a four-wheel drive, for practice, the whole of fifty kilometres on a dirt road. In the end, not only did I get that job, but I managed to go solo on all types of the rough roads in north-western Australia.

Was I becoming Australianised? I didn't think so, because I took stopovers for breaks, coffee and a smoke every one hundred or two hundred kilometres. That wasn't done when Aussies cover seven hundred kilometres in six hours – 'No time to stop. It's all about getting there.'

As an adult, there were other challenges I had to face, such as inviting people for drinks or for a barbecue. I agonised over what types of food to serve and importantly in my mind at what time. When I asked around, they said, 'Whatever!'

Once, we had invited lots of people. It was still early in the evening and some guests were still arriving. As I went to change the music, I saw out of the window a couple carrying their own chairs and folding table but they were leaving. I asked Peter about them later. He explained they'd brought their own picnic equipment and had asked if he minded that they cooked their own fish on the barbecue. I had caught a glance of them earlier on and soon they'd gone home without another word. I suggested to Peter they might have run out of gas at home. But according to him they were real guests! He said they had asked him to apologise because they hadn't managed to catch up with me. That puzzled me.

For me, the Australian socials have always been a problem. In my early years in Kalgoorlie, I declared my attempt to widen our circles of friends somewhat of a failure. In fact, I called this passing phase, 'Waiting for BYO'. I felt that the strangest of patterns had developed. I invited people for dinner. Guests came and went. We organised barbecues galore. We went on picnics and pub drinks. I seized every chance of lunches and morning teas I could fit onto my calendar. I had spare drinks in the fridge, ready for action in case of a bring-your-own last-minute invitation. After undergoing a few massive municipal pool parties and regular functions held in hotel foyers, I started wondering what to do next.

Early on, I'd joined local clubs and women's associations and held eclectic conversations with people I never remembered. I'd attended community meetings, fund-raisers and the theatre. Enough, I felt. Yet I still awaited that elusive invitation to someone's home, one that said BYO at the top.

My shock in the booming mining town of Kalgoorlie came on the day when I popped in to the District Education Office. Anxious to meet Aboriginal people, I thought I'd make contact with some Aboriginal teachers. They'd point me in the right direction, I figured.

'Where have you come from?' The liaison officer was staring at me. 'We don't have any Aboriginal teachers in the district.' He was still busy filing.

'I guess they all work in the city then,' I said.

He looked up again, explaining, 'There is a handful in Perth.'

I don't know who was more surprised, the person in charge of Aboriginal studies or me. I'd come from a developing country where there were Papua New Guinean teachers in all the high schools.

I must have looked puzzled.

'Well,' he went on, 'one of the universities in Perth plans to offer Aboriginal teacher training to some regions of Western Australia.' Trying to reassure me, he added, 'They plan to hurry the process by targeting some of the teacher aides.'

It turned out that each school in the area employed about two Aboriginal teacher aides. The ones I was lucky to meet were ten-year long-standing staff. They had to wait another ten years or so to further their career path and some are still out there waiting.

Later, in the north-western region of the Pilbara, I was to meet a few of the teacher aides. Many formed part of a *mooditj* ('strong' in the southern Nyunga language of WA) women's group who were active in the community. One of them called Allery often fronted up for face to face meetings with any government official, like health or police, to discuss local decisions that affected the community. Allery didn't live far from the school. People called on her for all kinds of emergencies.

Sometimes she brought home a child left stranded after school. While she was busy inside, there might be a voice at the door calling out a reminder of her next duties.

'Don't forget! Community meeting at school tonight!'

She waved, smiled and said, 'Oh no, another *wadjella* (white people) meeting!'

During the day in school, she wrote and transcribed songs for language teaching. The children learnt how to sing, 'She'll be coming down the mountain when you come,' along with a hymn, all in the Yindjibarndi language. She took her class to sing to dignitaries, including Prince Charles when he once visited.

In the classroom while she was about to instruct, there'd be interruptions.

'Excuse me, but can you give a talk at Friday's assembly?' The principal was in the doorway.

'Again, and what about this time?' she asked.

The reply came, 'The no school, no pool policy,' she said.

'Oh! All right then!' came the response, followed by a reserved nod.

In school, she would also explain, to teachers who hadn't yet attended cultural awareness workshops, protocols like the cultural renaming of some people after a death in the community.

The extent of some elders' knowledge and skills became clear to me through one of the desert women, an art and language instructor, the well-known artist Mary Pantjiti McLean. She lived in the goldfields and taught a way of carving artefacts, called the hot poker method. She took the TAFE adult Aboriginal students through all the learning steps. They were taking this unit for their Advanced Certificate of General Studies. She taught them how to name the appropriate tree and cut the right part of the tree branch out in the bush. Then in the subsequent weeks they had to carve and decorate the stick they obtained over the open fire. In the last session, they had to polish it to a finish. In one of the sessions, I saw two Aboriginal youths who were sharing an innocent joke during her demonstration suddenly freeze into silence. She was yelling at them, 'This is learning, you know! You aren't supposed to laugh, not for this.'

She was an elder in the traditional sense of the term. One afternoon I found her waiting outside my office.

'I knew you wouldn't be long,' she said. She explained the imprint of my foot on the ground showed I was running to the administration block. She had figured I'd rush back.

Most of the mature-age students studying in the community college had started their early schooling at the Aboriginal Tjitjiku preschool. When I met them, they were running the centre that their own children (*tjitji* in Wongi) attended. The Kalgoorlie Wongi families and teacher aides showed the same determination as those in the more distant Pilbara. Aboriginal parent groups strove to ensure that their children could obtain elusive jobs.

In spite of the lack of teacher training, many Aboriginal workers held health certificates from Marr Mooditj, the Aboriginal health workers training centre in Perth. Combining health and education expertise, they coordinated a healthy food project at the school canteen. Funding, however, wasn't consistent. These trained staff had to switch from health to education and apply for either state or federal grants in order to keep their projects alive.

In the meantime, it was the Aboriginal leaders who moved the issues on the ground. For them, politicians and public servants, however well-meaning they might be, were of the 'come and go' persuasion. They either came for a transitory visit into a remote community for an hour or so, or for a one or two-year contract. Sooner or later, they left.

The words of an Aboriginal leader in the community stayed with me. 'It's like the cowboys and the Indians', he said. 'Cowboys come and go, but the Indians are here to stay.'

Once in Australia, I continued to enjoy my career in adult education wherever I lived, teaching English as a second language. Mining towns in Australia always had a wide array of migrant families who came from many parts of the world I knew little about, like former Yugoslavia, China and the Philippines among others. Through my students, I was able to learn of people's earlier lives and varied customs.

And then one day my life changed when I started to teach English communications to a new group of students. That morning, to find my class, I first had to locate where the Aboriginal Enclave classroom was. Wedged on the edge of the campus and facing a back road, there was an older white-painted transportable building. Walking up the steps, I saw a group of mature Aboriginal women sitting up waiting patiently for their new lecturer. During class time, the students were friendly and contributed a great deal to the discussion of the text we studied that day. It was about earthquakes, so the lesson soon expanded into several students conjuring up memories of the 1968 Meckering earthquake for whoever among us hadn't heard of it yet. I realised later that was probably only me.

At the end of the class, I joined the smokers' group outside, where everyone was chatting. Two of the Aboriginal women from the group took me to one side.

The one named Barbara said, 'From the things you said, we reckon you're new in Australia. Is that right?' Her eyes were smiling.

'Oh! Yes. Very new, and I'm trying to learn,' I replied.

'Well,' said the one called Carol, 'there's nothing to it, you'll see.' Then she nudged me, adding, 'Don't worry, Anne-Marie, we'll show you what to do and say,' flicking her cigarette butt onto the open road, out of sight.

Barbara was standing the other side of me. She looked around with the confident eye of someone who owned the place then nodded as if to cheer me up. 'Yes, that's right,' she said, 'we'll teach you everything you need to know about Australia!'

And they did, I am pleased to report.

I learnt how Aboriginal people liked to approach a newly arrived person in the community and talk to them before they were exposed to the many stories and myths about Aboriginal students always turning up late for class or taking off on 'walkabouts' all the time, which wasn't true. Women and men often referred to the early personal contact and conversation they had with newly arrived non-Aboriginal persons as a good time to try 'to turn newcomers around to our ways of thinking'. I guess it was a built-in mechanism that imparted a sense of cultural awareness at a time when such training courses didn't exist for the non-Aboriginal people on their arrival in community groups. As a result, some newcomers understood the need to listen to Aboriginal people from the start and to wait patiently to be consulted before they contributed their views or alternatives.

I learnt that people were very keen to be self-sufficient and start small family businesses. For example, emu farming was a successful business in Coolgardie, as were its oil and by-products. It was interesting to see how well cross-generational family businesses worked. An example of this was screen printing, where a younger adult dealing with the finances teamed up with an older artist with design skills or vice versa.

At public open day events such as NAIDOC (National Aboriginal and Islander Day of Commemoration), cooking recipes extended to mincing fresh kangaroo meat, and a popular dish on offer to visiting children was kangaroo mince with spaghetti. The organisational talent of the women to meet the needs of large groups was phenomenal. Watching them, I was placed in the advantageous position of being guided to see Australia from their point of view, that of insiders.

Over the years, I watched Barbara, Carol and many more women and men balance their duties of family life, committee attendance and studies. At times, it became too much and they'd need to take a break. They could be soft and gentle one moment talking to their kids and in the next breath they could callously call out to put into place any guy that dared to hassle them for anything as much as a twenty-cent coin, a cigarette or to make a smart alec remark at them. And in the following breath, their laughter came. These outbursts of belly laughter took me by surprise. Loud as they were, they stemmed from a sophisticated sense of humour often called black humour. That, the Wongi women told me, meant making fun of themselves. By caricaturing their own personalities and those of their peer group, they seemed to say, 'You see, that's how we are. You can take us or leave us.' Of course that genre of humour was catching. You wanted to stay with it just for the laughter and the company. A great survival tactic, I felt.

I studied the desert language of Kalgoorlie, Wangkata, also called Wongi. I learnt some of its sounds and vocabulary, like *ngurra* to mean place or camp, which I'd hear again on some television documentaries whenever central Australian languages were spoken. Many languages, from Western Australia to South Australia and part of the Northern Territory, are thought to have had a common ancestor language. The desert languages have complex verbs in their grammar. In Wongi, the same verb *pitja* (take, carry) can indicate the direction of your move as in *ma-pitja* (go away) or in *ngaliya-pitja* (come here). I've always had great difficulty getting my head around long verbs formations.

Weeks, or was it months later, a new lecturer, Heather Nimmo, who became my friend, said, 'Have you heard of that great café in town? Why don't we try it for lunch?'

I asked her about her family and when speaking of mine I realised it was time to talk to my relatives in France. I'd written to my mother and sent some photos. A few days later, I was on the phone to France boasting about my new life, telling them about the house, the one-day apparitions of hibiscus flowers and the frangipani trees whose name in French sounded like a French gourmet *gâteau*, the *frangipane*. Then I explained my job and the children's school system. Giggling down the phone, I challenged my youngest brother, François, to come and see us in Australia.

As I put the phone down, a feeling of emptiness grabbed me as if my whole world, which I had talked to them about, didn't really matter. Although I'd been busy making friends, it seemed I hadn't adapted as well as I thought. It occurred to me again that the lack of closeness with the people around me was having a negative effect on me. It was time for our family to go on a Christmas holiday to Europe. An extra bonus came when François decided to travel back with us for that summer.

After François' return to France, my phone conversations with my relatives were never the same again. Because he'd filmed a lot of his stay, he'd organised a family viewing session at my parents' house soon after he got back home. As a result, for the first time members of my family understood some of our circumstances. On several occasions I'd shown them a few home movies of us in the garden or at the beach. These hadn't had any impact on them. But François' home movies seemed to open a window to Australia for them. He, being a French resident, was one of them and they related to us through his eyes.

Besides meeting with Heather for coffee, I joined her in her book club. That opened opportunities for me as I met other professional women in that group with whom I could also discuss Australian issues. Eventually, I found out socialising on a more amicable basis did happen in Australia – often for families like mine who had migrated recently. I found there the sense of community that I'd been looking for. You could pop in to people's houses or they called you in if you hadn't done so. It felt different from the contrived 'welcome associations' that had sprouted in some towns to give newcomers their first cup of tea on Australian soil and you didn't have to bring a plate! The experience was impromptu and felt genuine. This wasn't like an intrusion on each other's home. It didn't have to be formal. You could have a drink, or not, and sample someone's food or walk around with them in their garden, talking.

That's what I felt was the hospitality I'd been longing for. This wasn't in keeping with my own childhood, as I remembered my mother saying, 'You aren't to go to people's houses.'

But this closeness worked for people from other Australian cultural groups, women from Chile, the Philippines, Former Yugoslavia, Thailand, Scotland, China, Mauritius or East Timor. I believed it was all to do with the sense of extended family that they were missing. We had experiences in common and we needed to share them. That was the 'mix and merge' that helped me find a sense of belonging.

Le claquement du portail
The clanging of the gate

'And there are daily flights from Perth there and back!' said Peter. 'Karratha has a college, a large theatre and hospital facilities. And guess what, there's also a covered shopping mall!' For Peter and me, it meant that it was a relatively luxurious place to live. A new posting at Karratha Community College, after a few years of life in Kalgoorlie only a half-day from Perth, meant we'd move away to the West Pilbara, 1,500 kilometres north, past the Tropic of Capricorn. Once again, we had to accept we were to live at more than a thousand kilometres from a city centre.

Some called this area 'up north'. I admit that there it was hot and it was dry. It was in a region of Western Australia that mined iron ore and gas. It also qualified as a remote regional area and ticked all the criteria for isolation in Australia. So the existence of a full-scale shopping centre, which prided itself on being the largest between Perth and Darwin, was significant for our family. There wasn't going to be a lack of basic supplies as there had been in places we'd lived in before.

Karratha was a recently established coastal town, which together with nearby Dampier serviced the West Pilbara inland iron ore mines of Tom Price and Paraburdoo, as well as the offshore natural gas fields exporting liquefied gas through the massive facility on the Burrup Peninsula. It also catered for the mining towns of Wickham, Roebourne and Point Samson.

Starting from the late 1960s, it had attracted equally unusual and intriguing sets of people. Arriving after them were teachers and newcomers. In Karratha, this group became more accepted by the time the next wave of workers arrived. Called fly-in fly-out, FIFO, the new workers who commuted between shifts were rarely seen in town. The FIFO structure was a threat to the community by its lack of social or economic participation.

The town of Roebourne became the place to accommodate Aboriginal people from different cultural and language groups who were no longer employed on the old sheep and cattle stations in the early 1930s. The merging of families from different cultural groups made life difficult for them at the time.

In Roebourne, Aboriginal residents made up the majority of the population. There, I learnt more of the complexities of Aboriginal languages and of Australian historical events. In contrast to the Kalgoorlie region, the top end of Western Australia had a wider range of languages. Geographical features and local differences gave groups their separate identities. Neighbouring languages could differ greatly from each other even if the number of speakers was small.

When the settlers arrived, they took over the prime coastal land. Missions soon followed them. European settlement resulted in damage to the language and lore of many Indigenous groups. Some of the people adapted their traditional customs to fit in with the imposed changes that affected their food, clothing and routine.

Although sugar and flour were introduced, native methods to collect honey were maintained, and kangaroo in the ashes with damper were still served as a treat and as a healthy diet. Some or even the same people also managed to retain enough tradition based on culture to be able to revive their knowledge and language later. Most families were able to identify and find the plants that brought down fevers and eased skin ailments and remembered their language names. This information was to become valuable and helped the people who started ecological business ventures.

By the time I worked there, a range of Aboriginal community groups had forged a strong sense of identity. There, like in many places in Australia, by the mid-1990s there were community groups that ran language and tour events of the Burrup or Murujuga, around the Ngurin River and the magnificent Millstream National Park, often called an oasis. They were also qualified to offer cultural awareness training all based on the Ngarluma and Yindjibarndi cultural organisations and multiple art groups in Roebourne.

I was amazed to be able to walk to petroglyphs that anyone who knew their way along the ridges parallel to mining crops could find. In fact, the Woodside gas exploration company when it first set up the plant had removed a very large group of painted stones from the area they needed to build on and piled them up together on the hillside in an enclosure out of their way in order to build the gas mining plant. They were neither secured nor carefully enclosed and they still weren't fully itemised. Some are still being dated but must go back to at least 40,000 years, which means they are twice as old as Lascaux's world-famous cave paintings.

At the time, I saw an old illegible piece of semi-official signage lying face down. These relics weren't listed anywhere as ancient treasures and the only recognition of these remarkable remains was the slumping remnant of a piece of barbed wire so trodden that its barb had hardly survived the wear and tear of casual passing scavengers and their four-wheel drives. The rocks were piled up together on the ground, either resting against others or wedged against more unwieldy ones.

These ancient painted stones displayed a range of drawings of the early fauna, such as a whale or a porcupine. On the Burrup peninsula, there also was a quiet, eerie area which was the site of a dreadful event. A narrow stretch of water, called the Flying Foam Passage by the Europeans, lay just between the northern promontory and some nearby islands. Aboriginal people had died in an ambush in 1868. One soldier had raped a Yaburara woman. The Yaburara men had come to avenge her and killed a white policeman and two other men. There was armed retaliation by police and settlers over eight days.

Between one hundred and one hundred and fifty men, women and children were struck down in what is now called the Flying Foam

Massacre. There were only ten survivors of the Yaburara people, all male. This genocidal act murdered the Yaburara people on the Burrup peninsula. The Ngarluma Yindjibarndi, Wong-goo-tt-oo and Yaburara Mardudhunera peoples have been the custodians of this sacred site ever since.

We spent a ten-year spell in the dry heat of the Pilbara. During that time there was no rain to speak of outside the seasonal cyclones. The first year there, I planted some pawpaw trees and within a year a cyclone brought them down across the back garden. I persevered and planted new trees and was able to pick my own pawpaws off the trees every day in the later years. There were cyclones every other year, cyclone parties and people going troppo, or mad, in their houses. The cyclones built up at the time of the tropical monsoon season, which was the hotter season in Australia between October and March. The humidity of that season made people more tired mainly because they had to spend time outdoors securing their yard to avoid the chances of flying equipment and debris. The change in everyone's routine when a cyclone warning was announced was noticeable, as people tended to gravitate towards the stores to stockpile on candles, tinned food and liquid beverages of all kinds. There were queues at fuel stations, which soon ran out of batteries, candles and fuel. A circle of panic ensued, with people's word of mouth rumours sending one another for the missing goods to various parts of the rest of town.

Vegetation suffered too from these wild climactic events. A bougainvillea plant in the path of the cyclone could lose every one of its leaves in a few hours. The winds and rain devastated gardens. Interestingly, this then allowed the bushes a later burst of rejuvenation – whereas people who had gone troppo didn't recover so well from their few cyclone vigils.

Arriving in Karratha, I'd decided that since Peter had full responsibility for the college I couldn't apply for a job directly from him. It was the first time since we'd left Europe that Peter and I no longer worked in the same institution. It was unusual but we had both been careful to remain independent of each other at work although it sometimes required measured judgement. I was getting close to fifty years of age. Both my children were studying at university away from home. It was to be a turning point in my life.

This is how soon after our arrival I came to travel the forty kilometres out of Karratha to the regional prison education centre and to walk into the longish dark main room of the open-plan minimum-security prison education premises. There in a far corner propped up near the door blocking the window was a rickety old metallic shelf, strewn with what appeared to be second-hand children's books and a few copies of religious texts. There was an unlit cubicle with a computer in it and a see-through door into an eerie grey-bricked L-shape area. That was the art room. Flanked parallel was a library which only opened a few hours a week.

I turned to the superintendent and said, 'Yes, I feel I could do something about education in here.'

As he walked back to the offices, with the long-handled key dangling off his side pocket, the superintendent said to me, 'I notice you didn't jump when the gate clanged.'

I looked back. Behind us, a large sturdy grey iron gate separated the heavily fenced prison yard from the administration area.

'Oh, yes, the clattering sound,' I said.

'It often makes visitors shudder,' he added.

'Oh!' I laughed, 'I was brought up in a police barracks. My father was a policeman and every day, just to go to school and back, I used to hear the jangling of gates and the rattling of keys.'

By the time we returned to his office, he offered me the position of prison education officer.

That day, I became a self-manager. Being in charge of setting up an education centre provided me with independence in my career. As education manager of a remote centre, I took decisions locally via the superintendent before I received formal confirmation from the head office of the Department of Justice in Perth. That could take a long time to come. Adjustments would take place later and if I had to make changes I could always say, 'Head office has asked us to make changes.'

From then on, all the positions I took up for the rest of my career had a built-in degree of autonomy and a comfortable distance from a Perth-based administration. In such conditions, I felt, the workplace flourished and so did I.

After the allocation of a few desks, bookshelves and a whiteboard, the room looked more inviting and the students helped brighten the bare walls with noticeboards, posters and maps. Once we opened for classes, the education students felt they had ownership of the centre and the place took on a life of its own. The prison population at the time was about 90% Aboriginal people who were in and out for short periods for alcohol-related minor offences. Alcohol was also referred to as grog, and most drug issues at the time came from marijuana, which Aboriginal people called *gunja*. For some, incarceration became repetitive because there were no jobs and little chance of rehabilitation for outgoing offenders.

Many of the Aboriginal students I taught in the prison centre had missed out on regular education. But some had retained the refined skills of calligraphy from their early days. I was embarrassed to show the scribbled snippets of my handwriting. I had students who started an exercise book by ruling lines off the side and the top of the page with a ruler and a red pen when they were able to get hold of such rare items in prison. Others had vivid and detailed knowledge of their traditions, both visual and oral. Many possessed a range of practical hands-on skills that spanned trades and the arts. Most could speak about three languages besides English. All professed a handy mathematical skill. They knew multiples of six – a common influence from Aussie rules football, I realised.

They soon explained to me the blue, white and yellow remnants they stitched together weren't for the foreign flag of Sweden or Ukraine. They were making a West Coast Eagles banner, at the time the only West Australian footie team. 'You'd better get that right!,' they said, deploring my ignorance.

One of the highlights was field trips with the minimum-security group, which took a while to arrange because the trips were integrated with the curriculum. The aim was for the students to acquire new skills that they could contribute in the community.

We first asked an Indigenous park officer to do a short course about local flora and fauna, and the students had fun listing the properties of the flora and learning their Latin names. Many of the students had knowledge of their names either in Yidjibarndi or in Banjima, a language from a neighbouring area which had many speakers living in Roebourne, and we found that sometimes the names were similar. Then we prepared to have an outing for the project.

Getting permission for the outing wasn't as hard as organising bookings for prison transport, a bus driver and some prison guards. There always was a last-minute check to ascertain whether the selected students weren't barred from the trip for reasons of logistics, which could emerge at any time in prison administration. By going just after breakfast, we could go on day trips and have a work party at the Millstream visitor centre where work involved some of the skills of a ranger, an occupation many students aspired to.

The native Millstream palm was gradually disappearing. The trees had fanned leaves and were identified from other green palms by their different greyish tone and large woody fruit. It was badly threatened by an introduced type of date palm that choked much of the native vegetation by its dominating height and roots. This major drawback surfaced when wildfire affected the area, so restoration work had been started. The work was never complete, however, and there was need for a regular uprooting of the invasive green date palms to promote the regeneration of the native vegetation.

At Jirndawurrunha pool near the Millstream visitor centre, it was hard work and the students had to stand on the edge of the river to pull out the intrusive vegetation. Of course they had the advantage of being near a very cool water steam, which was a welcome relief from their regular walled-in environment.

There, we were able to spot some unusual species of dragonfly and several common rocky country grey kangaroos, the euro, but only spotted some flying foxes taking off as we arrived. The area was of great significance and Deep Reach or Nhanggangunha pool is a well-known water pool to the Yindjibarndi people due to the presence of *warlu*, the rainbow serpent. For this environmental study unit of their program, the students then went on to write up about the flora, fauna and significance of the area as part of their writing project, which also including their illustrations. The students' write-up showed a high level of knowledge retention and a thorough understanding of land and water care.

A few years later, there were regular horticultural work camps that the prison ran at the Millstream National Park for minimum-security prisoners for a few weeks, as a rehabilitation phase before their release.

Aboriginal people weren't able to obtain jobs, although a resource mining company was at the time setting up a permanent mining camp on their land. People from all over Australia, including newly arrived migrants, were recruited for all positions. Very little effort was made to involve the local Aboriginal people in these developments. The video *Exile and the Kingdom* portrayed the difficult dilemma of survival for the Ngarluma and Yindjibarndi people. Before he passed away from mesothelioma, Roger Solomon observed in the documentary that the only thing the people in Roebourne got out of the development was a new prison and a pub.

'Can we watch that film again?' Someone was at the door. About once a week on Friday afternoons, small groups of students who had finished their duties for the day came to ask if they could access the resources. They liked documentaries. By far the most popular was the *Bush Tucker Man* series. Bush and tucker together made for riveting viewing. The Aussie swagger of the hero was a style that captivated the majority of men students in the class.

There was also a strong sense of place among most students. Many hailed from the Pilbara and knew about each other's languages and customs. They always made space for those who were from the nearby region like the Gascoyne who were Yamatji speakers.

'That word *yamatji*, it means your friend, you know,' someone said to me.

I watched different groups, making sure we made space for the one or two whitefellas who shared incarceration times with them.

They liked to tease me. 'Time for your fix?' they said when I went out for a coffee break and a cigarette.

On my return, I heard someone say, 'Here comes *Jarda* (Old Woman)!'

I didn't know the local language but it was a good move to make a start, I thought, and decided to join the Yindjibarndi language class with the students. Like many Indigenous languages, it has a complex structure and as with all languages practice makes perfect. I haven't practised, although I remember the greeting, *Wanthiwa*!

Going to work was a pleasure and students gained a sense of pride and purpose within the education precinct. That was the only time of the day when the prison officers – or screws, as they called them – weren't watching over their shoulders at what they were doing.

Although many prison systems have used correspondence studies as their main educational medium, I found that short courses taught face-to-face had a positive impact on the students' outlook. The students started to gain enough confidence to join TAFE colleges once they completed their prison time.

A great feeling of achievement for me came when one Aboriginal student gained a traineeship with the giant Hamersley Iron Company after his release.

Through steady progress, we expanded the education centre to take in several small groups at a time, relocated the art room to a brighter spot, and upgraded the library and computer rooms.

The resources were minimal. When I was there, no one had so much as a desk and chair in their cell. Through their opened louvres in lieu of air conditioning, they looked on the windswept and heat-hardened terrain outdoors. I found it strange that people outside decried the comfort of prison life while I could see there was no such a thing. I still hear the sound of Scrap Metal's and the Pigrim Brothers' music in my head, along with country and western songs. Among the sad songs, there was one that caught everyone's attention. It started with the very sad exclamation, '*Ee-yow-wee, Ee-yow-we*'. Bob Randall was singing. 'My brown-skinned baby, they take him away!'

A few years later, I felt the need to make my own escape from prison and rejoin the outside world. By the time I left, the library had relocated next to the new education centre and it started to open daily. Hearing the heavy gate's last clang, I thought life on the inside had been but a microcosm of the wider world. The discrepancy between those worlds was the massive over-representation of Aboriginal people behind bars.

My decision to leave the prison education system and start working as a community worker was not a random one. The change of direction in my life was connected with my father. I took the decision to resign soon after I emerged from a difficult phase which centred on his death from cancer.

Nanou has always had the terrible responsibility of making the difficult phone calls. She rang to tell me how doctors had diagnosed him as suffering from an advanced lung cancer and predicted he wouldn't live for much more than two years. Confounded by my initial shock, my feelings of anxiety started to compound with the frustration of not knowing what to say or do. The messages I received were quite contradictory. What my siblings told me about my father clashed with my mother's words on the phone when she didn't even talk of him suffering from a terminal illness. I couldn't make sense of this until one of my sisters-in-law, possibly because she could apply a less subjective view to the situation, provided me with an interpretation that I thought rational. She said that short of using the words 'terminal cancer', which for their generation was taboo, my parents were covering all the crucial final steps associated with terminal illness. She said they'd started visiting family members and the villages of their youth and told me it was probably best not to speak too much about it!

What! Keep quiet! Me? That'd be a first! But then who was I to rock the boat? I was so far away while they were dealing with the day-to-day issues. How was I to insist, using my newly acquired Anglo-Saxon world view and from distant Australia, that we sit down in a circle to inform my father he was dying and that it was his right to be told.

I thought Peter and I were clever to use the excuse of wishing to enjoy a European summer holiday that year to visit my father before he got worse. His first words as we arrived were 'So you've come to see if I've got a foot in the grave.'

That made me decide not to travel again all the way across the world, in case he assumed it meant he was close to death. We drove with him to places like Ribérac in the Dordogne, where he'd grown up. We also stopped at a couple of fields where he'd love picking mushrooms. He wanted to visit the town of Blaye, built as a defensive fortress for the Gironde estuary, which was bombarded in 1940 by the German army and set on fire in 1944 by the allies five days after I was born in Libourne. On those trips, he talked for the first time of his experiences during the Second World War, or so Peter told me. He wouldn't have discussed it with me of course, as I was a girl.

It was about six months later one morning when I woke up in my bedroom in Karratha from a short dream where he had spoken to me in the Périgord version of Occitan. '*Soi fotut*. I'm done for,' he said.

At the time, I guessed the logical explanation of the dream was that I was preoccupied about my father's health. The dream itself during which my father told me in his own voice of his self-assessment was unexpected of course.

I hadn't heard anyone speaking Occitan for about thirty years. But it was strange to hear it because my father only ever spoke to his close friends from the region or his elders in Occitan, but certainly not to his children, and not to me. I remember my mother telling us the story of being shamed and laughed at in her first week at school because she used a phrase of Occitan to her teacher in class.

She was asked, 'What's your mother doing today?'

'*Penchena ta s'enane a la feirat.* She's combing her hair to go to the fair.' Her reply in Occitan was looked down upon as a patois or a poor local dialect in the way local languages have often been belittled in many parts of the world. She told me how the children had made fun of her that week and that she'd decided not to use that language in school again.

Later that week, I woke up with a headache and, unusual as it was, I took a sickie. During the day, a phone call came through from my sister in France to say that my father had died. I packed my bags so fast that I managed to secure a flight to France and get to Libourne in time for his funeral. As predicted by the doctors, my father had lived two years from the first diagnosis, and it was my belief that he'd known he was dying. I assumed my dream to have been a case of science and spirituality merging into a harsh reality. After the funeral, I spent some time, although not long enough, with my mother and my relatives. It wasn't till well after my return that I could start my own grieving for him.

The next summer, we took a holiday and Peter and I drove to the east coast of Australia to see our friends again. On our return trip, we were crossing the Nullarbor one morning, having left Ceduna on the way to Yalata. It couldn't have been more than an hour after setting off when we made out the shape of a car in the distance on that long hazy highway ahead of us. It was standing still by the side of the road with its bonnet opened. As we approached, we could see a long-bearded Aboriginal man waving us down.

He reminded me of some of the Aboriginal elders I'd met in the places I had lived. There in the Kalgoorlie goldfields and in the Pilbara town of Roebourne, a friendly wave and exchange of greetings was the natural way to acknowledge each other when walking around town. This was a contrast to pacing your way about in artificial arcades or plazas at nearby Karratha. I also remembered one weekend drive on the remote unsealed road of the Pilbara, not far from Roebourne, where our car once had a puncture just on the last stretch home and before dusk. Two cars of Aboriginal families had stopped to help us, providing us with help and reassuring us they knew that road and its hazards.

That morning as we approached the stranded car, we pulled up to see how we could assist. The driver asked whether we carried a spare hose as he was short of fuel. We said we didn't but we asked him if he wanted a lift to the next community. The soft-spoken man reasoned that he could certainly come and get some spare fuel from Yalata and could easily catch a lift back to the car.

'Yalata, you see,' he said, looking what I thought was intently westward, 'is my country,' adding, 'That place over there down the road, just about an hour or two, that's home to me, that's where I belong.'

At that point, his passenger who, it seemed, had only just woken up, became quite keen and restless. He liked the thought of going to Yalata. 'They've got good food there, you know,' he said, making towards the car as if he would join in with his mate.

We started to point out that we only had the one space in the car but the driver appeared to have stopped listening to any of us.

He took my husband to one side and said, 'You go. Don't you worry about us two! We'll be right! You go ahead!'

I felt sad for him because all along I was sure he kept on looking wistfully west towards Yalata.

He then surprised us further when he took us aside to explain. 'You see, you can't take that one there.' He was pointing in the direction of his co-driver. 'He's the one who's in trouble in the first place. This car he borrowed is no good anyhow! We should have got to Yalata before dawn.' He resumed looking west towards Yalata then turned to us. 'Yes,' he said, 'you go, off you go, we'll be all right. Thanks all the same, but you see it's Monday today and the Justice van will be coming along soon and will give us a lift back into Ceduna.'

We must've looked puzzled as he explained to us as if it should have been obvious. 'You see, Monday is court day.' He explained he was the man's relative as well as his parole officer and that he had been trying to get him back to his place in Yalata at the weekend. Then he said,

'The Justice van will take us into Ceduna. I'm supposed to be on court duty today anyway.'

I now think that the driver may have started west for practical rather than emotional reasons and have looked in the distance hoping to see the usual Monday Correctional Services vehicle. As a responsible officer, he had tried to accompany his relative back to the village that he wasn't supposed to have left.

As we neared Yalata, our car crossed paths with a white van with a government logo, the sort of prison people's transport vehicle we call in French *le panier à salade* (the salad shaker), and I think I've heard a few nicknames for it in Australia, the most popular being the 'paddy wagon', which has a definite anti-Irish tone. I was familiar with people telling the time from looking up at the position of the sun but I realised that the movement of government vehicles also provided a good guide for people to identify place and time on isolated desert roads of Australia.

It wasn't long till we reached Yalata. While refuelling there, I saw a shop with artefacts and cards from the nearby community. I picked one of the lengthy pop-down postcards you can never fold back into shape, and I still have it wedged in my old road map. It has photos of people weaving baskets, men spearing kangaroos, people sitting down around a fire, women collecting bush food, vegetable food or *mayi* and families sitting down sharing the kangaroo tails cooked under ashes.

I remember the store didn't serve coffee. I sat there and drank a cup of tea for a change. It was the strongest mug of tea, my first real taste of billy tea. I thought the damper took the strong bush tang off it. I was still thinking about meeting the two men we had encountered earlier. They must have been people from the Western Desert, I figured. On one occasion I thought I had heard them use the Western Desert word for 'yes'. I recalled very few words I had learnt but I had memorised that one. I can't remember now whether they pronounced it as *yuwa* or *uwa*! I've heard there's a difference in how it's pronounced depending which part of the desert you live in.

Still, for me it was altogether a positive and memorable interaction. I learned a lot from the encounter. It seemed as if in the Australian settlers' mind the concept of desert has little sense of value attributed to it. People often think of it as a place either to explode bombs in or to dump people in. For the Aboriginal man I spoke to on that long stretch of tar surrounded by scrub, this was clearly home and he was comfortable with his environment and in control of his and other people's lives.

Prison education suited me fine but was becoming demanding. By my third year there, each day when I got home I felt run down and exhausted. Suddenly I felt a need to go back to work with migrants. An option came up at the time in community work instead of in the field of education. It meant letting go of adult education. At the time I didn't know why the decision appealed to me. I found out later from my mother, after my father's death, that he hadn't liked me working in a prison although I was there as an educator and not as a law enforcer. But for me what had changed? I always tended to resist the authority of my father, the policeman in uniform, before. Did I no longer need to do so? This could well mark the time when I started to understand how I had been tilting at imaginary windmills for most of my life. As a new citizen of Australia, I must have started to accept that my heritage was in Europe and that I was part of a community of migrants like many of the people I lived among.

On a personal level, I often used to be wary of people who presumed to know who I was and what I might think or do. I always feared people would stereotype me as French. I overheard conversations at times when people made throwaway remarks about how much they loved Paris, how beautiful the French language was and how much they liked the idea of life in rural France. That used to puzzle me. Not every French person came from Paris, all languages were equal, and although some thought it romantic to live in rural France, my childhood experience had taught me that there were also the muddy realities of life.

In the meantime, while I was using up my energies, fooling myself that I wasn't really very French, my mannerisms betrayed that I was. Could I possibly deep down have wished to be the French girl that my family used to know, the girl who had a natural disposition to act on impulse and to make others laugh? I'd kept a French attitude to humour, although I still haven't worked out what it consists of. Catching on to the Australian humour was fun, but it wasn't easy to plan the timing of my repartee in conversations. At times, I have hassled my own children to decode the dreadful automated knock knock jokes that I didn't understand.

In group conversations, my exuberance, loud gesturing and the enthusiasm I showed towards the people around me seemed to amuse not only my English-speaking friends and colleagues, but my French acquaintances and family too. An outgoing style worked well for me both socially and professionally and I'd been wise to keep to that open attitude to life. But I'd faced taxing challenges because I tried too hard to bypass my nationality of origin to ensure I fitted in as Australian. Perhaps not unlike the Aboriginal women that I had met, I needed to feel that people accepted me as I was and for whom I was.

One of the most relaxing experiences in all my travels is sitting down with some Aboriginal friends just watching the world go by and listening to Wongi or Yindjibarndi stories. To me, these are the sounds of Australia.

So that was it. From then on, there would be no more soul-searching and no cultural cringe. At last I'd found what I felt to be my Aussie way.

Au Nord du Tropique
North of the Tropic

I started as a community worker on time for a celebration of International Women's Day and later Harmony Day. There was a lot of multicultural activity in the West Pilbara. I was involved in organising festivals that brought together up to thirty groups from about forty countries of origin. Maori and Indigenous families linked in with Yamatji and Nyunga visitors or performers from further south, while the bands often travelled down from the Kimberleys.

Over the years, I met many of the migrants and Aboriginal residents in the community. One migrant woman from the Philippines arrived to join her family. She had no idea of the distance from Perth to the Pilbara. She told the story of how she assumed she'd take a taxi from Perth airport to Wickham till she realised it was a two-day trip by road. Another woman who had arrived from Croatia, on hearing of the long travel ahead in kilometres, got into a car presuming that driving out of Perth she would start seeing some forests as she would over such distances in her own country.

My community work and casework revolved around the West Pilbara population who had recently settled from overseas and who, with their families, needed support to gain an understanding of services like health and education. Initially, people needed interpreters. As a community worker, I took newly settled people to sign up for English courses or other relevant studies.

Another role was to help people get their overseas qualifications recognised. This was always harder for people whose first language wasn't English. I knew of this first hand. When I first arrived, having completed overseas degrees and a doctorate and lectured at the university of PNG, the first question asked of me was why I didn't have a Western Australian teacher training certificate.

In the mid-1990s, restrictions on immigration into Australia were a problem, particularly for people from Former Yugoslavia. I met a professional Bosnian woman who had lived in Australia before the conflict erupted. She was applying to sponsor her father but at the time she didn't elaborate about her family's trauma. His age seemed the main difficulty. To obtain a health certificate, he'd travelled across unsafe regions via several countries around Belgrade. The health certificate had been lost because of the complex mail consignments. So he was a year older when he had to obtain a new certificate that again had to be issued in a friendly country by a doctor whom Australia accredited. At the time, she didn't speak of her relatives but only of their immediate situations at the time she was filling in the forms. I would only hear of the harrowing story of her surviving family and her niece after they had arrived to safety.

When, after about three years, her mother and father arrived, they were accompanied by their widowed daughter-in-law. The child's father had died from an enemy bullet. When he was hit, he had been carrying Mari, his child, who had survived and had come with him to Australia. The first thing Mari did was to show everyone she met the scar she had incurred when her father had been shot dead and her arm had been grazed. This young child had clearly become the focus for that family. Soon she started school in English.

A few years later, I saw them on the day of their citizenship ceremony. They had made a few friends whom they invited to the event. They treated the day with joy, as if it was the child's birthday party. That was one example of a situation in my career when I felt I could let go of my clients. That family had achieved its own dynamics in its new country.

There were occasions, however, when problems for some women developed after their arrival in Australia. Domestic violence was often common in the male-dominated mining region, and often linked with isolation. People, I felt, were unlikely to have a family member visit them at weekends to provide the checks and balances that most social groups provide. I came across a woman from the Philippines who had married an Australian man after he had visited her and her family on several occasions in her home country. On arrival in Australia, he started to treat her in a cruel and brutal fashion. He kept her in an isolated compound with gates locked from inside. She was to talk to no one, and had no money. When he had had a few drinks, the husband abused his wife and even on one occasion forced her hand into the barbecue fire.

It was only after she attended Sunday church once that people realised she lived there. Someone contacted me for a rescue action. I managed to get her out of the house but she was so distressed she forgot to take her passport with her. Once she reached a refuge, the Immigration Department asked her to prove his ill-treatment of her in a court of law. His character wasn't under review, hers was. In the meantime, she received a bridging visa and started to work. It took another two years for her to obtain her own resident visa. She felt that the world she lived in had gradually changed from menacing to accepting.

'My father was sitting in this room last night,' said Darby.

I stared at her.

'Don't you believe me?' She glanced at me.

I'd managed to get a reaction from her. 'I do,' I said. 'It's even happened to me. Only last year my own father spoke to me in my sleep in his home language,' I said. There was a pause, then I asked her where her father had been in the room.

'In the same chair you're in.' She was staring intently.

'Did he speak to you?' I asked.

'No,' she said, 'he just sat there looking at me.' Darby had switched from looking vague to looking more focused already. 'I didn't tell the nurses,' she added. 'I think they wouldn't understand.'

I knew very little about Darby. On the previous day, I'd received a call from the tiny township hospital at Wickham. Darby apparently was from Papua New Guinea. I was thinking while driving across to Wickham that the few years I myself had spent in Port Moresby could be of help in my initial contact with her. A newcomer to Wickham in the Pilbara and to Australia, Darby was suffering from extreme prenatal morning sickness and she had become dehydrated on several occasions.

The nurse who rang had said she worried Darby had reacted badly to this first pregnancy of hers but seemed to be suffering from culture shock too. 'She isn't feeling well at all,' she said, 'but she's agreed to see a visitor.'

Darby had only been in Australia for six months. Born in one of the islands of Papua New Guinea, she'd trained as a schoolteacher. In her first year teaching, she'd met an Australian engineer who worked with a company contracted to Port Moresby and they'd got married. Soon after she'd arrived in Wickham, she'd become pregnant and suffered from nausea. She explained she'd received a letter from home, and her mother sounded unwell and hassled. There was unrest due to the closure of a large mine in their area, which disrupted local services. Darby was worried about her. 'That's probably why my father came to visit me last night,' she said. 'He was smiling as if to tell me she was better now.'

She told me how some 'freedom fighters' were creating havoc in many villages, but that radio reports on the situation in Australia were scarce. We discussed how long mail took to reach her, as Wickham was about two thousand kilometres away from Perth on the western coast of Australia.

'And how do you feel now?' I asked.

'I don't like being in hospital but at home I get worse. I think there's a bad smell in the unit where they housed me. I don't know if it comes from the paint or the carpet,' she said.

We discussed the options of having the carpet changed, in case she had an allergy.

She grimaced. 'I worry the nurses will get fed up with me coming to stay every other week.'

I couldn't tell if she was concerned for the nurses or about what the nurses thought of her, but Darby looked troubled indeed.

'My husband's worried,' she said. 'He wants me to get better but I don't know how to right now!'

I was thinking of cultural isolation. We discussed the standard activities available in the town. We had to agree that in this small town there were only two options – shopping and church.

Church, she said, was a disaster. 'Last week I forced myself to attend,' she said, 'but I was so distressed I went to church with my hairdo half-finished.'

She said that as she'd walked in, a child had called out, 'Look at that black lady with the funny hair!'

'Everybody went quiet,' she added. 'I couldn't look at anyone after that.' Vulnerable as she seemed, her exposure in church must've hit her hard.

'I wonder if that child regrets speaking up in church!' I said. 'As a kid, I used to get into trouble at home.'

I'd managed to make her smile. By the time I finished telling Darby about what a socially awkward child I used to be, we were both having a good giggle. It was mid-afternoon and a nurse brought the tea trolley down the corridor. As I left Darby that day, she was busying herself sipping water from a straw. We hadn't made a bad start, I thought.

Within a week, I heard Darby was due to go home again. On my last visit just before her discharge, we drove across to her unit to reassess the smell.

As we arrived, she pointed to another unit nearby. 'The lady there is nice. She brought me some homemade soup. She only comes from Perth but she's lonely here,' she said. 'I guess she's miles away from home too!'

Darby was deeply despondent as we came close to the front door of her unit. 'There isn't any tree or shade outside,' she said, 'and worst of all, the neighbour on the other side is my husband's manager.' Her face tightened.

When we got to her door, she retrieved the key from the bathroom window ledge pointing out that the toilet was near the front door. 'We can't possibly invite anyone over, not with the toilet by the front door!' she said.

The carpet was definitely old, but I didn't pick up the pervasive smell she had experienced but then if it was a cigarette smell I wouldn't have noticed as I was a regular smoker. She showed me through a nice, neat unit which hardly looked lived in. All the furniture was standard company provision. It looked bare and functional. In contrast, the spare room she was preparing as a nursery was furnished with all the latest modern baby equipment, a bright carry cot, a baby bath, a cot and a dangling mobile with birds that chimed.

'Not a bad place really,' she said, 'but no other children in the neighbourhood.'

Coming back, we drove past the main area of the town with pretty houses, neat lawns and trim hedges.

'That's better than the bosses' row where I live,' she said. 'I wonder why they housed me in a unit over there, where the people are old with no small children.'

We had a chat and decided to ask about the option of Darby living in a three-bedroomed house. We went to the town office – the name given by mining companies to the mine administration offices. The staff were pleasant and said they'd put her name on the larger-home list. She seemed to come to life at the thought of moving in a house closer to more people for her to meet.

Darby struck me as a very grounded person. My view was that social isolation compounded with homesickness and a new pregnancy had sparked off her illness. Soon she relocated to a house with an umbrella tree and a lawn with hedges of hibiscus bushes. After giving birth, she didn't stay in the hospital very long. She was keen to nurse the baby in a home surrounded by other families with children.

When I first met her, Darby had mentioned she wanted to upgrade from her teaching diploma to a university degree so she could teach in Australia. The baby did well and the following year a cheerful Darby went shopping with the baby in a sling and soon started her studies by correspondence. Two years later, she put her child in day care during the teaching placements she had to do at the Roebourne primary school. By the time I left the area, she'd become a teacher and attended the new gym in town regularly.

Our arrival in Australia coincided with the children's teenage years. Peter's mother first had visited us in the Zambian copper belt. Patrick was then only two years old. Initially, she'd waited for him to come to her, which he soon did with a book. He asked her to read him a story. Over the years, our children grew fond of the adventurous grandmother who came from afar to visit, read stories and make gingerbread men.

Peter's mother visited us on two later occasions after we moved to Western Australia. Her first trip was to Kalgoorlie. The second visit, years later, was to Karratha in the Pilbara region. Before she left the United Kingdom, she informed us she'd decided to bring her own folding wheelchair.

A few hours before, the airline transferred her from the Singapore leg at Perth airport to a Pilbara-bound smaller jet. The aircraft was just about to land on the hot Karratha tarmac when we arrived at the airport that sunny afternoon. The Ansett Airlines manager knew Peter and suggested he go onto the aircraft to help his mother down. Peter said later how self-conscious he was when the Ansett staff started to hoist them both down from the plane on a forklift platform.

Unaware of the technical manoeuvring, I was waiting in the arrival lounge, standing just inside the double glass door. I watched the faces of the regular trickle of business travellers, mine employees and government workers. Their first steps on the tarmac were slow as if, before even the flies descended on their faces and backs, the heat had already claimed their energy. As the passengers approached the airport building, I noticed they consisted of the two groups typical of remote Australian residents – the board shorts casuals and the long socks formals. Karratha had a small population and every other passenger, even the ones I didn't know, seemed to tell me with a smile that my husband and mother-in-law were on their way.

Before she left England, Peter's mother had to have a minor operation to clear her eye duct. The operation was successful but she was to wear a patch on one eye for the length of her stay. She chose not to tell us about the eye patch, as she felt there was 'plenty of time to make jokes about pirates'. She'd survived the last two-hour ordeal of her flight from Perth to Karratha. In the end, I had to meet her near the outdoor luggage belt where Ansett offloaded her from the forklift with Peter carrying her hand luggage. With a glint, she started smiling. She was in her wheelchair, one eye covered by a black patch. If she was tired, she didn't let on.

We'd planned some sightseeing but the inaccessibility of some venues became a problem. Most of the picturesque spots – the Karajini National Park, the Burrup peninsula and its petroglyphs – were gorges and rock formations which weren't easily accessible. The wheelchair ruled those out. We discarded the idea of driving inland to the asbestos-ridden town of Wittenoom, although some people raved on about its sunsets. So that left two choices – travel nine hundred kilometres north to Broome or five hundred south to Exmouth.

Peter's mother had turned eighty-two just before this second visit. Last time she was in Australia, in Kalgoorlie, there'd been the saga of the flat tyre, while driving around deserted goldfield towns. We were about a hundred kilometres away from Kalgoorlie, near the small town of Menzies. While we changed the tyre, she had to sit in the shade of the mulga, with a bottle of warm water. She sat enigmatically by the roadside until we decided to drive straight back home and she started to chat again. So I wasn't surprised that, after a brief discussion, she wisely opted for the shorter trip to Exmouth with its less humid climate. We booked a chalet downstairs at a motel, and set out a few days later.

To get to Exmouth, which is the most western point in Western Australia, you first drove three hundred kilometres south through a slalom of dead kangaroos, or roos, littering the highway. Then after a bridge over a dry riverbed, you encountered a stretch of the highway transformed into a landing site. Someone had drawn aircraft designs on the tarmac so both the Flying Doctor and the road user would know where an oncoming airplane was to land. This section of road, the A1, is the main artery that goes around Australia. It'd just been set up as an emergency landing near accident spots and just a short distance from a much-frequented fuel stop, the Nanutarra Roadhouse.

The main feature of the roadhouse was a veranda where you could sit not far from your car. We brought the wheelchair over. A couple of multilingual parrots greeted us in the language of the last passing tourists. By the time I left, they could say '*Bonjour*, Cocky.' Their cage was conveniently placed above the only telephone box for three hundred kilometres. The open phone booth was located on the edge of a ramp, the constant thoroughfare to an enclosed room that looked more like a glasshouse than a café. Attached to it, sounding as if it was about expire at any moment in the forty-degree heat, was a wheezy contraption, aspiring to the status of an air conditioning system. It spewed hot recycled fuel smells that whirled back into the dust by the café door.

This roadhouse was patronised by regular bus travellers, backpackers and overseas visitors bound for the tourist spots of a round Australia trip. It served what was listed as 'Meals' so long as you liked chips with everything. The pie was at a premium, though not homemade, however, and came with chips and free sauce. On the counter stood red, brown and yellow plastic bottles of sauce with oozing stains down their sides. They also sold souvenir spoons for the tourists, the type you wouldn't have given to any aunt, even if she were twice removed, and certainly not to your mother-in-law.

Further back from the veranda was the on-site caravan park that even the grey nomads didn't stay in because they had to pay. A row of double articulated trucks and coaches seemed to block its access permanently, providing a photo opportunity for tourists. Presumably to maintain their internal air conditioning, their engines were always left running, adding to the noise and pollution.

While we ordered the food, a willy-willy had come sweeping across the road, spraying red dust over the car park. I saw Peter's mother wiping off her good eye with a tissue. We decided to have the toasted sandwiches inside and braced ourselves to wheel her chair up the ramp. It wasn't much cooler there, despite the noisy air conditioning and the large tall fan trying to compensate for the door banging wide open whenever customers carried their hamburger, chips and Coke outside. As we sat down, we heard the regular sound of frying flies, which drew our attention to the bluish electric fly zapper over the kitchen hatch.

Peter and his mother stayed indoors waiting for their Anglo-Saxon tea with milk while I went to buy fuel. The office was a sort of shack, leaning against the toilet block. Numerous dog-eared notices told you how management refused to take standard credit cards for fuel and didn't fix punctures. There was even a cryptic notice that said, 'Don't ask me about the weather because I don't know.' I took that to be in jest.

The attendant was a gruff, unshaven man with a singlet bearing the word 'redneck' across his chest, a superfluous descriptor. Near the road, there was a wooden sign indicating not distances but whether the adjoining roads were open, closed or passable by four-wheel drives only.

As we got back into the car, I made a point of telling Peter's mother that it was good she hadn't come during the cyclone season, because when cyclones crossed the coast, all roads leading in and out of the roadhouse were flooded. Over a few decades, the Nanutarra Roadhouse had become famous for housing stranded voyagers, mostly on its roof.

As I finished the cyclone story, Peter told his mother that we were halfway to Exmouth. 'Only about three hours to go,' he said.

As we set off again, she gave us her cheeky glinty smile and said it made a sunny change from her annual dreary trips to the shores of Skegness.

In Australia, fighting the outdoor elements is sometimes not as harsh as all the stories about the dangers of the bush may lead you to believe. You might have driven through the night and following sets of double articulated trucks you may have just successfully completed in excess of a thousand kilometres manoeuvring your way past the dead kangaroo carcasses, not hitting the live ones. At that point, you have a good excuse to decide to call in at a roadhouse for a bite of breakfast assuming you will have a peaceful rest.

However, handling a simple indoor transaction like ordering a meal and eating it there can be a worse ordeal, in my experience, than surviving the outdoors. Getting hold of the 'free coffee for driver' isn't a simple matter. You have to find the truckies' mugs and inferior coffee powder on the trolley with the wooden spatulas and help yourself swiftly before the milk runs out. Sometimes you might decide to sit in the wrong part of the restaurant where tablecloths and cutlery are displayed on the tables and attendants stare at you. It seemed imperative to have to get up again, rejoin the queue behind the bus load of tourists that just arrived and order your meal there. Alternately, you could buy a banana and perhaps a slice of soggy cake off the counter. I know people who have failed in their attempts to obtain any food at all because of mixed-up orders. Getting a hamburger without onions is hard, but with onions yet no tomato can be very tricky. As for my personal issue with having my coffee served after food, rather than before, I think I've given up hope on that.

There are also toilet key sagas involving massive keys – this mainly applies to towns where some roadhouses owners worry that the Indigenous population from town may wish to use the bathrooms. This is often the case in red-neck towns with Aboriginal communities around them. The issuing of toilet rolls at a Pilbara roadhouse I consider somewhat of an aberration as I only ever saw that once. I found no toilet roll in the cubicle and went back to the counter to ask for one. When the attendant passed it to me, she used the desk stamp saying 'Fortescue Roadhouse' and pressed it on several places on the rolled-up leaves side as librarians do on the soft side of pages for their books.

I don't intend to give a bad name to the remote roadhouses of the round Australia A1 highway. But I have seen some rather bizarre examples of customer service.

In one of the Kimberley roadhouses, the person behind the counter chose to serve the non-Aboriginal customers in the shop first. Then he turned to the Aboriginal client who was waiting patiently. 'You know you can't afford these flash (smart) sandals,' he said. 'Here's a pair of thongs. There you go.'

I shouldn't have been surprised because I had seen the same in one of the stores in Roebourne and was aware that some shopkeepers and taxi drivers held accounts and key card numbers for many of the Aboriginal town residents. That's why they were in the position to control what people could or not buy at any given time.

Our next stop was at a country town with the main street dissecting the bush in half, with food for thought on one side – a deli and a newsagent; and on the opposite corners the refuelling stops – a roadhouse and a pub. Keeping a low profile in case I met another aggressive male shopkeeper wasn't an option. As we walked into the deli-cum-newsagent, I noticed it was empty, and that's always a bad sign. One after the other we set off the ongoing continuing ring of a doorbell. I wandered around in a daze to check what they sold. Gradually I started to sidle my way to the man at the counter, who had stared at us since we walked in.

'Do you have any antiseptic lozenges? And do you sell stamps?' I asked.

'Chemist, post office? Are you having a go?' he said. Once he started to volunteer his views, there was no holding him back any more. 'And if it's cash you want try your luck across the road. They take EFTPOS over there,' he added with a worrying grin.

I handed over a couple of sausage rolls.

'Did you want some sauce with those?' he asked.

We were about to leave when he raised his voice in the direction of the quiet shelf where Peter was fingering the previous day's *West Australian*. 'Are you going to pay for the paper or are you just reading it?'

Isolation can have strange side effects. That shopkeeper was only rude but I remembered that, after life in remote locations, sudden social interaction can lead to disorientation in people.

Once, after a year of living in remote Mwinilunga in Zambia, we left the bush to go into town for the first time with some colleagues who had offered us a lift to the copper belt, where we could buy a car. Halfway down, we reached our first stop. Solwezi was only a small remote centre with sparse population. Because it was a bush road intersection, it had a fuel station and a handful of shops, yet was still three hundred kilometres away from the populated towns.

I recall how my mind was numb when I stepped out of our friend's car. I stood there on an empty and isolated section of pavement that went nowhere. I felt baffled by the movements around me. I was staring in shock at the incessant movement of vehicles in and out of the fuel station. I didn't know where they were going or even where they could've come from. I think I was dazed to realise that I didn't know any of the people around me or in the passing vehicles or anything about them.

The next time this happened, the confusion that seized my mind was more logical. I then had children with me to worry about. One morning in late December, I'd just landed in London from Papua New Guinea. As a family group, we attempted to take the tube and exit at a station at Oxford Street for a spot of shopping. We were horrified by the claustrophobic oppressiveness of the crowded streets of London at Christmas time. Gradually and step by step, a steady, close-knit crowd carried us in the direction opposite to that in which we wished to go. We ended up marching across the street alongside hundreds of people to the sound of the bobbies' whistles, guided along by a horse-powered police force. Hidden by the dense movements of the crowds, all traffic lights had become invisible.

In the end, the throng pushed us into the unbearable heat of Harrods floor grates, whose plush carpets obscured the entry gateway. At that point, I'm proud to say my children resisted the crowd movement and regained some sense of independent personality. Patrick sat down to take a stone out of his shoes and Nathalie pulled her socks and shoes off, saying, 'Ah, it's warm here at last!'

Both then opted to walk barefoot at ambient warmth into the shop. Dissuading them from walking barefoot into Harrods was my next dilemma.

It was a relief to be able to plan great holidays every other year to visit our relatives in Europe. We flew out of Papua New Guinea via different routes, which meant we went home via Hawaii and Disneyland, via Japan, via Manila and Singapore or Hong Kong. It was great fun and provided for all of us opportunities to see new places. Overall, the trips made a great contribution to the education of our children, who also loved their Christmas and New Year holidays with their extended family, as our main destination was mainly France. Because Peter's family was smaller, we always seemed to spend more time in France than in England. It was lucky that Peter's mother could visit us overseas on occasions.

Apart from the great benefits it gave us, it provided the added advantage to see a different side of our children. As soon as we reached a crowded venue, usually an airport, they discovered that there existed white people who were older than their parents. We discovered that the few photographs of family groups we had shown them when talking of their grandparents were insufficient. Patrick stared at any of the more mature tourists in airports. He'd turn and say, 'I think I saw my grandfather.'

It was heartbreaking. He even chose to sit near the people he felt were his grandparents. The lack of an extended family contact at the time formed a wider gap than I had estimated. I always worried that they missed getting to know their family in Europe. I sometimes feared it would affect them. I am pleased to say they have tried very hard to involve their own children with Peter and me and we have benefited from that pleasure since their children were born.

Our children have, as children do, made two major criticisms of our parenting. Nathalie, for example, protested that I was over-committed to my work. One year, I made a binding commitment to be home from work at a given time. I was able to keep that promise mainly because the education centre closed early afternoon.

As for Patrick, he was critical of his father, who took him to his football matches on weekends but quite blithely read his newspaper inside the car and didn't even know even know his position on the field.

Patrick always was the one who criticised me about my smoking and never let up on it. I know he'll have noticed that on the photo of me dancing on the night before he was born I was holding a lit cigarette.

Of course, having become addicted to cigarettes in my early days at university, I had no qualms in smoking throughout my adult life or when pregnant. I argued that it was Dr Spock's fault. I had read that he felt that having a beer while breast feeding could help the mother relax. I always preferred cigarettes to beer. Social norms had changed by the time my children's generation were having babies. They'd neither drink nor smoke. It made sense but it surprised me to hear of pregnant women avoiding cold meats or soft cheeses from the deli.

The first time I gave up smoking, I had to go down to zero from forty a day. I suffered from serious withdrawal symptoms. It was a New Year decision in Papua New Guinea. Peter supported me and gave up too. It worked, although it was hard. Seven years later, I was in Australia and went back to smoking and it didn't involve Peter. After several attempts, I gave up for good when my first grandchild was born. I could go back to it any day now if I didn't watch myself. A very badly written but well-motivated book by Allen Carr called *The Easy Way to Give up Smoking* had the greatest impact on me for my final attempt. It was certainly harder than giving up on the Valium tablets doctors had given me in my mid-twenties. It's hard for me to describe how much I have been dependent on medicated antidepressants at various times in my life. One reason, I'm sure, doctors prescribed them is that I used to be very worried about my gushing personality. People, I thought, were always wishing to bring me down to becoming calm and moderate. This was true in my Franco-world and in my Anglo-world. I have hated that all my life and wasted a lot of time kicking against the perception of me as overactive.

My new country had dealt my family a fair hand. Through our travels and my studies in English, I was able to have a challenging career and work with people from whom I learnt many variants of the English spoken around the world. In spite of our isolated places of work, our children managed to be bilingual and receive a decent education.

Then one day approaching my fifties, just as I thought I had acclimatised to my new life at last, human rights issues flared up again across an election year. Due to the detention of asylum seekers, displaced children were also in custody. Although the dilemma of asylum seekers had reignited internationally, in Australia the issue built up due to the actions of consecutive governments of both parties. Onshore refugee camps and later offshore detention centres didn't prevent deaths at sea, deaths behind bars or protect people from being sent back to their countries to face danger. All these added to Australia's already shameful high count of deaths in custody of Indigenous people.

It alarmed me to hear the term 'sedition' as the topic of discussion that morning as I tuned in on the radio. It was a sharp reminder of the sound of the Gaullist France of my youth. More than three people gathered at a street corner meant, my father used to argue, that the police had to interrogate them as they could be plotting sedition. And I thought I had got away from conservative French governments, only to find myself haunted by similar laws in my twenty-first century life in Australia. The sound of the word 'sedition' had a strange effect on me. I knew that, contrary to what I thought, my activist days weren't really over. I'd started my life as an anti-militarist rebel during my upbringing in France and there I was, as an Australian citizen, ready to take on the authorities again. I was pleased to take up a position with a human rights organisation. It was Amnesty International Australia.

Our focus, as a non-government organisation or NGO, was to diminish political injustices and the persecution of minorities around the world. My work kept me busy and fully engaged. On one occasion, the Turkish authorities had just arrested a Kurdish Iranian woman and were going to send her back to Iran. Her brother in Australia contacted us saying he knew that she would be 'killed' if she re-entered

Iran. Working from within Australia, our team used the well-oiled mechanism of an international organisation and combined efforts and resources to speak to staff in Ankara. Thanks in part to our activism, the Turkish authorities agreed to let her go if a third country offered her refuge. In the event, it was Sweden rather than Australia which offered the young woman a visa. Some of us in the Perth office were disappointed that Australia hadn't taken up her case.

Many of the Australian volunteers and workers on the team had their origins in a wide range of countries and some were well aware of repressive issues first-hand. We called results like that 'good luck stories' and they made a difference for us too. The team members gave up their time and expertise. I gave up smoking and embraced my new challenging job.

As a team or in small groups, we discussed any concerns with other activists. One day, I chose my favourite example of modern cultural revival. It was the work of the Maori community. The people there have been able to reinstate their languages and ceremonial values by teaching in the Maori language in day care centres, where at least two generations caught up with their language and customs at once.

At the end of a group discussion one afternoon, a young woman uttered a comment that I had already heard some people from multicultural backgrounds in Australia make.

'Me, I'm nothing,' she said, 'just a big mix of everything. First, my family came from Africa, others were from Asia and some from Europe as well.'

I looked up and she wasn't speaking in the controlled terms that some Aussie friends used in case people thought they were boasting. I was astounded that this young, efficient professional was putting herself down. I'd noticed earlier that she'd sneered at her own language, calling it 'that funny dialect'.

I didn't feel on those two occasions that she was talking in jest, so I challenged her. 'What do you mean nothing? Are all these multiple origins of yours not good enough?' I asked.

We had a long chat and as it was the last day of the week we moved on to have a coffee together to keep on chatting. We ended up debating many aspects of multiculturalism and all that it could do to empower individuals and groups. And then as, we exchanged our experiences, our talk changed to giggling and happy laughter. What a treat to let go of inhibitions and share a chuckle together, speaking freely to each other!

Exhausted by the time I went home, I sat down and felt quite restless. I didn't know what was different about our discussion. But on that day I had turned the tables on myself. I spent the weekend puzzling things out. I realised that my inner voice was very similar to the way that young migrant woman had spoken about herself. Could I possibly over the years, like her, have been putting myself down? Wasn't that in truth why I'd laughed so much with her? While everyone, including me, assumed I was happy in my skin and that I had a firm belief in sharing cultural values, I began to feel that it had been a shaky illusion. In fact, I acted as if I should play down my own worth in front of others. This was very disruptive for me personally because the more I went about showing other people the way to feel accepted, the more I repressed self-acceptance.

Like that young volunteer, I'd been blind, unable to accept my own worth. Following the boost of my stirring talk with that young person, I saw through some of my past negativity. It was as if I'd lifted a mask and lightened my outlook towards my life. Two things were to drive me from then on. One was that I wanted to accept what was left of my culture of origin, the other was that I wished to be proud of it. The problem hadn't been with my cultural background, it had been with me. I think I had forgotten how to be myself.

I was well on my way to reclaim my inner life, and with a flourish, when we again had to face the upheaval of moving. This time we were to leave Western Australia, where we'd forged twenty years' worth of genuine friendships and of lively and cordial social contacts.

Peter had found a position and we both liked the location. We transferred to Adelaide in the not too distant state of South Australia, about three thousand kilometres away. Something had changed in me. When the time came to say goodbye to my friends and colleagues, we had a fun farewell party. On my way out, I gave a swift glance back and a last wave to my many friends and colleagues. There was no need to look back. It was all with me, and I could move on.

On this occasion, I felt I no longer had to check over my shoulder to make sure that no one was judging me or about to make a casual remark like, 'We don't do things like that in Australia!'

Instead, I heard the warmth of welcoming alternative statements, 'Of course, you'll find South Australia different from the other states.'

Résistance
Resistance

What a major change of scene city life was for me. It could be very taxing at times, especially on the way to work in the morning. Sometimes it was a battle obtaining a cup of coffee at all. Someone told me which latest funky hip café to go to because the waiter was the best coffee-making expert in town.

So there I was, in a queue that went out of the front door into the street, when someone in front of me ordered a croissant with their coffee. At half-past eight in the morning there were muffins galore but no pastries left. I heard the muffled order and it didn't take the cashier too long to remove her pinafore, walk past the queue of customers, out of the door, across the street, to the bakery to buy a couple of croissants and return with a bulky paper bag. By that time, the barista had, against all regulations, offered to take the next lot of coffee orders. I watch him lining up five cups in an uneven pattern then placing a spoon through one of the cup's hook to indicate the non-decaf cappuccino, or was it the other way round? I'll never know.

Waiting time was over and the original cashier with her pinafore back on was asking me if I wanted something to eat with that. I dared not ask for a raisin toast in case they had run out of fruit loaf as well, so I pointed at the paper bag behind her on the shelf and said, 'Do you have a croissant left in there?'

It was the best customer service moment I experienced since arriving in Australia. She was happy to accommodate my needs and I managed to leave the counter with coffee and food, all paid for. The problem was that there were no tables inside. I had no luck outdoors either.

I came back in weaving my way in and out of the queue. 'Excuse me, pardon, *scusi*, oh sorry!'

I briefly considered whether to share a table with the guy with bacon and eggs. Instead I opted for the newspaper reader, who seemed to expect no one. He left. I got to savour my well-deserved breakfast.

Only once did we ever attempt to thin down our bookshelves. It was just before leaving Western Australia. We had made the major decision, the children having moved on to their own lives, to relocate from a four-bedroom house in Perth to a city centre apartment in Adelaide. We had to have a family conference about parting with our books. This was as painful as having to put the dog to sleep, which we'd done the year before.

Some time after we had moved to Adelaide, I started wandering into the online second-hand book mart. All of a sudden, a picture caught my eye. I was on eBay and there was a familiar title. It was a children's compendium of folk tales. On closer inspection, the book was available from a bookseller in Western Australia. There was an entry about its good condition, and a reference to a handwritten inscription. I immediately logged out. I couldn't look at 'More details…' about that book or any other on eBay. I couldn't bear to witness my children's personalised birthday inscriptions floating in limbo on the net. I haven't dared go back on eBay for books after that. Letting go of our books had been a lot more traumatic than I thought. That episode still holds a heavy sinking feeling for me.

I was adjusting well to Adelaide as a city. I'd been to a meeting that had gone well and felt on top of the world. I was looking forward to whatever Peter had cooked that night. It was dusk and life was good. Yet on my way home from the city one evening, the lone figure of a man walking towards me gave me a sense of cultural disquiet. There he was, walking down Frome Road, carrying a stick, a sort of crooked branch taken off a tree. Besides the stick, I couldn't tell what he was carrying or wearing. I never seemed to notice any details like that. I couldn't even remember anything about my own clothes either but I knew that I was carrying a backpack. That wasn't so much to project an image as it was a necessity for me. Suffering from carpal tunnel syndrome, I got around the issue by not carrying heavy handbags or sling bags any more. I preferred to leave my hands free.

Adelaide is a good place to walk across the Parklands, and I always carried a bottle of water and a book wherever I went. And he was carrying a stick. There are no loose dogs in town as people are very environmentally aware and the only dogs you see attend the obedience school sessions on the oval or are always on a leash with their owner at peak walking time. We were likely to cross paths outside the zoo but then again I doubted if a stick could do anything should any animals escape over the walls, fences and past the moats. But it was after seven by then and there was just him and me. I could see he was a young man. There are a lot of students who live in North Adelaide about fifteen minutes from the university buildings. He must be from overseas, I thought, as I got closer. I wondered if he was from Asia, yes, India perhaps. I had met Indian families in Zambia and he looked Indian, although I could have been wrong.

We were just about level and, as you do in Adelaide, a small town by most people's standards, I looked to make eye contact as we met. He averted his eyes with a side glance towards the giant mural on the zoo wall. What was that look in his eyes I caught sight of? Shame – yes, he was looking sort of ashamed. He certainly wasn't proud enough to sustain my look. I thought it strange and kept on walking and so did he.

What was that unusual emotion I felt? I didn't turn round to look at him again. But something troubled me about that young man. I recapped. A young Indian student walking with a stick who wasn't comfortable in himself. Then I realised what he was doing – carrying a stick as a deterrent against attacks. My smile left me. Forget the feel-good meeting or the appetising dinner. I recalled reading the *Advertiser*'s article on the previous Saturday: 'Indian community leaders protest to minister about slow government response'.

There'd been several attacks in the beautiful culture-conscious city of Adelaide. It started with a small group assault on one overseas student who had just arrived from India. Then there had been more. Indian students for some unknown reason had been bashed. And it didn't take place on Hindley Street or anywhere near nightclubs or trouble spots. It was in the suburbs; Prospect, I thought. The heads of universities had made a joint statement, something about it jeopardising future student intake. No action had been taken. These attacks had reminded me of the ones in Russia where I had heard of racist bashings against African students. I remembered the Amnesty International campaign encouraging people in Australia and around the world to write letters of protest to the authorities.

By the time I got to the Albert Bridge, I crossed paths with yet another overseas student. Before I registered that he also looked to be from India, I made automatic eye contact. He smiled back and he wasn't carrying a stick. My mind went into overdrive. Did he make contact because we had something in common? After all, was he not a vulnerable student from Asia and me a vulnerable woman walking at dusk?

Next, as I crossed the bridge, I caught sight of a burly fellow coming up behind me in the distance; he was still under the plane trees making his way up towards the bridge. After I got my water bottle out of my backpack and took a sip from it, I kept on holding on to it. It was an insidious feeling. Did I really think if ever someone came for me, I'd chuck the bottle in their direction? Then I came to my senses and it was my turn to feel ashamed and I wasn't comfortable with the feeling at all. As I replaced the drink bottle into my bag, I glanced to my left only to see the burly man walking west while I kept going north. He was probably on the way to watch the cricket.

'Where are you from then?'

'Western Australia,' I said. And people thought I was making fun of them. My French accent always betrayed me, but I now used it to my advantage. 'But I arrived in Western Australia, way back, about twenty years ago!'

Adelaide was kinder than Kalgoorlie had been. It took me only a handful of years to get a sense of belonging. I think I really became a South Australian when I eventually learned how to stand in a queue parallel to the kerb on Grenfell Street waiting for a bus. But at first I lived in North Adelaide and loved walking to community venues in the city. Joining the Writers' Centre as a volunteer helped me, and not just as a writer. With the Multicultural Writers' Association, we started to work on an anthology of multicultural writing to bring our work to a wider audience. It was a treat to make contact with such a wide array of ethnicities represented in Australia. I was proud that we could include the work of some of the new migrants from regions of Africa and the Middle East and to be able to promote Aboriginal voices in an anthology we called *Culture is…*

This phase of my life allowed me to revive a sense of community and of the extended family I craved. I was still homesick for my family in France and for my Western Australian contacts. Also, editing the anthology took me back to English language and literature. Through this community-based project, I felt that I found my self again. It fed my spirit and my social needs. It also opened the door to new horizons for me. That is when I switched to writing full time.

We took up citizenship within three years of arriving because we were keen to participate in Australian customs. Everyone took their citizenship vows very seriously. If you had a perceived foreign accent, it wasn't easy to pass for a local. I knew acceptance of people's differences to be true in France, where many French people are of North African descent. You could be a black Australian if you came from overseas, just like a black person in France could be French. Every country carries clusters of racism. However, I puzzled what made some Australians misunderstand Aboriginal Australians so badly. Possibly many just didn't know anyone of Indigenous heritage and were unaware of the issues affecting them.

The best I could be was a migrant citizen. Being French was an advantage because there was no large group of Francophones in remote

Western Australia, so I could preserve a sense of uniqueness. However, most English-speaking countries have a love-hate relationship with the French. If I had to try to change an image of myself as acceptable French, I didn't know what to do. In professional circles, I found being myself was easy.

There are times I have felt uncomfortable. It always is related with the political climate. Recently, a young shop teller asked if I had a pension card for discounts.

'I only have a senior's card,' I said.

The lady behind me asked how long I had been in Australia.

'Oh, about thirty years,' I said.

The shop teller handing me my change asked, 'How have you managed to stay here then?'

'I'm a citizen,' I said, wondering what she thought that meant.

I have heard negative jibes or watched people being put down and have sometimes made remarks to attempt to rectify a bias. Yet if the remark is about you and when it concerns you, it is much harder to deal with.

Many of the migrant and Indigenous families I have met have to juggle the pros and cons of extended families. The same applies to me. I have acted as an independent person and have managed soundly living away from family. Yet I have felt the family links never dissolve even if we rarely see one another. In contrast, the small nuclear unit of only two children meant that my family in Australia felt too narrow at times when, for example, our children first left home. We couldn't talk to other relatives in the country about it.

It reminded me of the ordeal of my best friend back in France, Dominique, the most independent peer of my generation. I knew she also understood large extended families. I had on many opportunities discussed with her the leverage a southern European family could exercise on daughters. Dominique knew me well enough to be there the year I went to visit my father when he was ailing with lung cancer. Then she watched my mother's ups and downs after her minor stroke and kept in touch with me and my sister. She herself had lost a very close female member of her family in tragic circumstance when she was younger, and for a second time during her later life. I was grateful for her friendship when a few years later my own mother went without warning just three weeks before I was due to visit her. I wasn't totally unprepared for the event.

My mother was the most vigorous and lucid of the residents in the nursing home she had moved into after a stroke left her partially paralysed on the left side. Because she had kept on walking with the help of her trusty walking stick, we all encouraged her to go and see a film about Edith Piaf, which she did in the film room downstairs before her heart gave overnight. I had talked about the film with her on the phone. I couldn't wait until I spoke to her next to tell her how lucky I was that the film *Ballon Rouge* (*Red Balloon*) had screened that same week in Adelaide. *Ballon Rouge* was the only film that she had ever made time to come and see with me and she had enjoyed it! It was revived not long ago and I had such pleasure watching it again but was unable to tell her as she died the following week. I was going to ask her why she had taken me to see the film in the 1950s. I was also toying with the choices of presents I could take to her. I had planned with my sister and brothers to get together for Mother's Day at the end of May at a nearby family restaurant. And I who had never baked a cake or known how to order a theme cake even for my children's birthdays, started to dream of a cake. I'd order four small cakes merged in the shape of two interlocking eights as she was about to turn eighty-eight.

The only way I understood the second stroke that suddenly took her overnight three weeks before I was due to visit her there, was that perhaps she didn't want to go out for lunch on that Mother's Day, and probably feared that her birthday celebration would be more of an ordeal than a pleasure. I, on the other hand, had been childishly plotting all sorts of surprises during my visit. But my Maman wasn't keen on surprises. She had led a very orderly life – some of us would say overly orderly. The thought of her *vive*, lively, daughter organising a fancy outing for her may have been more than she could bear.

I made it back to Libourne for the funeral and my friend Dominique was there once again. She ensured that I spent a few days in our hometown. Although none of my family lives there any more, I felt comfortable being in a place I belonged to. It's all about identity, the dogs taking over the pavements, the rickety overpass people still used to the railway station. Walking in my home town typified a slice of life and of self that is quite intense. In the end, I realised that the doctor was right. My family, Dominique and I all knew it: my mother's heart had just stopped beating.

Gulping my coffee, I hopped across the step through the back gate, where I caught sight of a snake in the couch grass. I ran, through the relentless cold sleet and rain, for the study across the backyard. I had come for a short respite to the Varuna writers' centre in the Blue Mountains and although it was summer it was a wintry weather day.

I reached the door but couldn't find my keys. Scanning the yard in the vain hope of a sheltered way back, I spotted the reddish hue of a budding rose in the *roseraie*, as I called the rose garden. Pointing at it, I said, 'I'll have that one.' I smiled. That should inspire my writing. I raced back to the kitchen door, spilling my coffee on the ground to add to the damp of my sneakers.

Dripping with rain on the kitchen floor, I grabbed the best scissors. The coffee from my cup added brown stains to the wet floor. I stepped over the spot to avoid the mess and make for the door again but remembered it was the keys I needed. Oops! I slid over the wet patch and nearly lost my balance as I reached for the keys off the kitchen bench. My mother always said I was no good with my hands. Perhaps she had meant my feet? Coordination – lack of – was a problem with me, I'll admit to that.

Wary at the thought of lurking snakes, I jumped over the cement step and landed in a puddle. I got to the flower bed and cut the rose. I unlocked the study door. Away from the rain at last, I felt ready to make a start. I dropped keys and scissors and switched the radiator on full, still holding my cup. But there was nothing left in it. I heard my mother's voice '…spilt coffee…' but I didn't remember how that went. I wasn't going to cry over some instant coffee that was already cold and watered down by rain. So I bravely leaned over the desk to switch on the computer. Ouch! What was that? It hurt! I forgot I was holding the rose in my left hand.

I glanced at the shelves but there was no vase and there was no water either in this shed that I used as a study. 'I'm not going back out there in the rain again!' The red petals were still soaked and dripping wet.

'A vase? Of course, I remember! On the ledge, there always was… there it is!'

It was the type of green ceramic hot water bottle people often used in cold nights. A red flower? But the bottle was green. In spite of my coordination problems, I could, I suppose, mix red and green. I was sure it wouldn't clash; it simply wouldn't match. I twisted the top off the bottle. There was no water in it. Still, I inserted the rose. Bending to smell it, I got a wet nose.

My first achievement of the day – snake encounter, soaked feet, spilt coffee, sore finger, wet nose – but flower in vase! I wasn't going to give up. I sat down in front of the computer ready to start writing. As I looked up through the windowpane, I saw a weakened sun trying to peer through. The rain had stopped. A good time to go and get another coffee. I heard my mother's voice again: 'Don't forget your keys!' That's when the tears came. I had not been able to write for a year. That day was the first anniversary of her death. It was time for me to start my new life. Could I have matured into an adult Australian?

Le cycle de vie
The cycle of life

Peter and I married in the late 1960s and at the time of writing we had two more years to celebrate a union of fifty years. Not that rare any more, but special, I feel. I have had a very up and down life full of fun, sometimes sadness and sometimes excitement.

So I have had no major hurdle except for… Well, I turned seventy. That meant that the three wristwatches I ever owned, and rotated wearing in turn over several decades as the batteries needed replacing, had reached exhaustion, and I could no longer either get them cleaned or repaired. A few months ago, I bought one that looked very much like the first one I ever wore. It was a small simple two-tone silver and gold watch which had only one new practical feature: its luminous hands. It matched my silver name-bracelet, a type of wrist bangle called a *gourmette*, which people in France tended to wear a lot.

I have had a *gourmette* for fifty-five years now. It was an important gift from my sister and she paid for it with her very first earnings. I remember a year after she had left home for her first job in Paris she came back by train for her first annual holiday. She had purchased the most simple yet classy silver *gourmette* with my name engraved in the handwriting style of the Lucida font. It has needed no repair. Whenever I wanted to adorn my style with jewellery, the simplest way was always to wear my watch and my *gourmette* to make me feel good. For me, happiness is wearing a *gourmette*!

I always found that leaving a place after about six years was hard. Then I learnt that parting from people after ten years from a community I felt I belonged to was heart-rending. In the end, after I went through multiple farewell get-togethers with promises to meet again and visit each other soon, I started to realise that I probably might not keep my promise. That was heart-breaking too.

The intensity of my farewell to our friends at Port Moresby airport when we were leaving for Kalgoorlie had shown me that, although it reflected my mood, an outpouring of emotions affected children most of all. The extreme farewelling scene at Port Moresby airport could have explained a lot about the reluctance that we all had initially when arriving in Kalgoorlie. From then on, although it was probably too late for my children, I developed two sets of safeguarding skills.

First I attempted to keep my emotion in check. Then I decided to rein in my hopes of keeping contact with my past friends. In subsequent farewell sessions, I changed my demeanour and embraced my friends saying, 'There's no need to say goodbye. It's a small world, you know. We're sure to meet again!' But I think that was a mistake. I wished I hadn't held my tears or hopes so well and that I hadn't used such clichés either.

Farewelling, it seemed to me, had become a booming business in Australia and I didn't gauge this only by the size and frequency of the removalist trucks on the roads. I had in mind the new farewell wishing-card shelves that many newsagents had to add in their shops. Some of the genuine words of friendship I received were so heart-warming I wanted to treasure and frame them by my bedside. Had I done so, the regret I felt on leaving all those friends and places wouldn't have diminished.

Although I always missed the kindness of my previous acquaintances and colleagues around me, there was neither time nor place to say so, except perhaps when I left the West Pilbara. I published an acrostic poem in the local paper. It unravelled, with words of farewell, my mobile number for all to keep. Two months later, I received a call from the Ngarluma Yindjibarndi elder of the Roebourne (Ieramagadu) community on Christmas Eve. He was wishing me friendly Christmas greetings and it was a good feeling to hear from him in my new house. Sadly, he passed away soon after but his warm wishes have stayed with me.

After I moved, however, I concentrated my energies on fitting into the new place as soon as I could. 'I have no problem adjusting to any place,' I said.

Next I started to act as if I believed my own words, boasting to the people I met or to anyone who asked me how I was how well I fitted in. However, after several sets of separation over three decades, I have found that finding my bearings in the new environment seemed to take longer each time. To survive total changes of environment, I felt the necessity to put extra space between the friends that I had made and myself. This might reduce any regret at losing friends but it also encouraged me to absorb the feel of my new community, including any sense of isolation and loss. In the end, I started to feel guilty that I had let people down. It was mind-spinning.

It took me many years to realise that it was me that I let down and that the problems I experienced were also mine and not the fault of 'others' like the 'red-necks' or 'blinkered settlers' I always liked to blame. I couldn't say it, but in some ways, I had felt ashamed of my 'foreign' French accent. It was time to start explaining that I spoke with the same accent as my first English teacher, as teaching then was from textbooks and with no audiovisual aids. We only had the teacher's words as a model. Whether people believed it or not, that was my truth.

When I had first arrived in Australia, I resented the issues like nuclear testing in the Pacific that had given my country of origin a bad name. Later, I realised that France seemed significant enough to hold definite meanings for Australians. On the one hand, some people looked up to France as a country of fashion, and French clothes and songs were appreciated for their perceived sophistication, while on the other hand, others stereotyped the French as arrogant. I guess a thousand years of Anglo-French rivalry is hard to overcome.

Others never had much of a problem with identifying me. People assumed I was from France or from Europe somewhere. Trying to become Australian in my mannerisms was an unrealistic, self-imposed target. Over years, I set myself a lot of impractical goals. Looking back, I know I was trying too hard.

I was a person who didn't like to divide allegiances. So when I lived in Adelaide, I had to push aside the West Australia I used to be familiar with. At first, I felt separated from the one and only Australian background I knew well. Around Adelaide, for example, I didn't know place names or family names. My only point of connection was with the Aboriginal language, the Western desert language I had studied in Kalgoorlie. Although it was a different desert language and not the main Indigenous language for southern South Australia, which was the Kaurna language, the desert connection allowed me an in to the South Australian community.

At a National Aborigines and Islanders Day Observance Committee or NAIDOC event, I met with one of the Aboriginal elders who used to teach Pitjantjatjara at the University of South Australia and to translate the Western Desert language at the hospital. She invited me to her home for a cup of tea and made me feel welcome in Adelaide. The only friend we had so far in Adelaide we had first met in Western Australia.

Within about two years, someone asked me to join her social media group. A new pattern developed as soon as I embraced electronic and social mailing. What I liked most about this medium were the photo attachments. I saved them in a folder, and that wasn't very different from the part of my brain where some of my memories were hidden. I found sending email messages instead of letters or phone calls easier. If ever an email bounced, that wasn't as bad as the bothersome and depressing echo of international phone calls. You could forward emails after they have been truncated by an internet server. And on social media, people can talk to one other without too much emotional involvement. However, I have always been a face-to-face person and the initial excitement of being able to talk to family and friends over the web, and of Skyping them, became one of my pleasures in life.

Recently, I've admitted that my perception of the people around me could be wrong and that leaving valued personal friendships behind was foolish. Lately, reopening some of those memories has helped me regain my strong sense of resolve. It's been an uplifting experience, a welcome change from feeling uprooted and lost, and has helped to keep me grounded.

I graduated to becoming a grandmother of four grandchildren all within a handful of years. In Aboriginal English, many grandparents refer to their grandkids as 'grannies' and this is how I think of them as a group. Altogether four years apart, a girl Zara from Patrick and Amy's family, and another girl Maija from Nathalie and Pete's within the same year. Soon Samuel was born as a brother for Zara and Erik for Maija. For them, I wrote some picture story books. I also hope they read this memoir in the future. Over a spell of four years, Patrick's two children lived in the eastern states in Canberra, and Nathalie's in Western Australia in Perth. I was lucky enough to go and stay with them frequently and get to know them when they were small.

Soon after my four grandchildren were born, we moved into a small courtyard home close to the beach near Adelaide. There, the two families were able to visit and stay with us over the Christmas holidays and it has been great fun for Peter and me to entertain the children with storytelling and activities. Peter decided to provide an extra children's touch to the yard, so we placed a large wooden doll's house on the veranda.

Not long ago, I went back to Perth to farewell my daughter and her family, who were leaving Australia and moving to Finland, where her husband came from. It was hard to let them go and for the first time I realised what my mother must have felt when I left France. It might not have been the English she resented but the fact that I was espousing such a different culture, and was away from home. Could she have worried that her son-in-law took her daughter out of her reach?

After they had left, Patrick pointed out to me that they were doing just what I had done, leaving their home country to live in a different culture. That helped me put in perspective my family visits within Australia that I had assumed would go on for ever. And he was right. Despite my initial anxiety about losing closer contact with them as a couple, as well as with their children who were both below four years of age, I began to accept their move.

Now when I visit Patrick in Canberra, I find a family for which my son has provided a French legacy. A few years back, he asked me to check with my mother and the rest of the family in France and changed his name by deed poll to my maiden name. It's like having my namesakes as relatives in Australia. And they are. I also have the opportunity to visit my own family of origin in France on the way to my daughter's in Finland.

In the meantime, it is great to follow Voltaire's suggestion, '*Il faut cultiver notre jardin.*' So I do cultivate my garden, even if it is only a courtyard.

www.ingramcontent.com/pod-product-compliance
Lightning Source LLC
Chambersburg PA
CBHW071812080526
44589CB00012B/761